GENETIC NUTRITIONEERING

Genetic Nutritioneering

Jeffrey S. Bland, Ph.D.

with Sara Benum

KEATS PUBLISHING

LOS ANGELES

NTC/Contemporary Publishing Group

Library of Congress Cataloging-in-Publication Data

Bland, Jeffrey, 1946–
    Genetic nutritioneering / Jeffrey S. Bland, with
    Sara Benum
            p.   cm.
    Includes bibliographical references and index.
    ISBN 0-87983-921-X
    1. Medical genetics.   2. Nutrition.   3. Genetic
    disorders—Nutritional aspects.   4. Chronic diseases—
    Risk factors.   5. Chronic diseases—Prevention.
    I. Benum, Sara H.   II. Title.
    RB155.B59   1998
    616'.042—dc21   98-33642
                                                  CIP

Genetic Nutritioneering is not intended as medical advice. Its intent is solely informational and educational. Please consult a medical or health professional should the need for one be indicated.

Published by Keats, a division of NTC/Contemporary Publishing Group, Inc.
4255 West Touhy Avenue, Lincolnwood, Illinois 60646-1975 U.S.A.

Printed and bound in the United States of America
International Standard Book Number: 0-87983-921-X
10 9 8 7 6 5 4 3 2 1

ACKNOWLEDGMENTS

IN THIS BOOK WE ARE bringing to nonscientist healthcare consumers exciting information my HealthComm colleagues and I have been providing to healthcare professionals for the past two years. We have discussed the impact of nutrition on genetic expression and subsequent human function in a series of professional seminars titled "Nutritional Modulation of Genetic Expression and the Promotion of Healthy Aging." Nearly 6,000 health professionals have attended those seminars.

Doctors in many specialties have given the material favorable reception. At a time when doctors are often viewed as distant, resistant to new ideas and not interested in patient care, I am encouraged by these doctors' extraordinary commitment to improving their skills and the care of their patients. I dedicate this book to the practitioners and researchers who bring this level of dedication to improving the health and well-being of us all.

I am deeply indebted to my associates at the Functional Medicine Research Center, our clinical research facility in Gig Harbor, Washington, for their personal dedication to the patients and their pursuit of knowledge that helps improve health outcomes. I owe special thanks to Dan Lukaczer, Barbara Schiltz, Kim Jordan, Nancy Stewart, David Jones, Constance Brown, Scott Rigden,

Linda Costarella, DeAnn Liska, Gary Darland, Eleanor Barrager, Darrell Medcalf, Margaret King and Jane Soudah for clinical contributions and research pursuits that have kept the information in this book alive and current.

I also acknowledge the contributions made by Stephen Barrie, president of Great Smokies Diagnostic Laboratory, for the collaboration in the development of functional laboratory diagnostic tests for the application of the concepts presented in this book.

I would have been limited in my ability to describe the concepts in this book had it not been for the activities over the past seven years of the Institute for Functional Medicine and its five Symposia developed by Susan Bland, its executive director and my loving and patient wife.

I want to acknowledge Sara Benum, my dear colleague at HealthComm, the "demythologizer" who translates my thoughts to more understandable English. Sara was able to make sense of my first draft, while Stephanie Roberts provided invaluable library support, working in HealthComm's library, to find the hundreds of citations I used in the book. Thanks, too, to HealthComm graphic artist Margot Boling for her creativity in rendering my hasty sketches into understandable figures.

I want to thank Phyllis Herman, the remarkable editor at Keats Publishing, who is not only superb at her craft as an editor, but has the added advantage for the development of this book of being a nutritional professional.

At HealthComm International, Inc., we define functional medicine as the field of health care that employs assessment and early intervention to improve physiological, cognitive/emotional and physical function. In a sense, this book represents the best of functional medicine. The many people who contributed to its development worked effectively as a unit to provide information that can help promote healthy aging. I feel very fortunate to be a part of this group of dedicated health professionals.

JEFFREY S. BLAND, Ph.D.
Gig Harbor, Washington

CONTENTS

INTRODUCTION

A SCIENTIFIC REVOLUTION IS TAKING place in university and industrial molecular biology laboratories around the world. The results of this revolution will irreversibly change the way medicine is practiced and may result in the extension of both life expectancy and health span, or disease-free years of life. Many scientists have compared this scientific revolution to Darwin's articulation of the theory of evolution, or the quantum theory. This revolution is the Human Genome Project.

Events that are occurring every day in laboratories involved with the Human Genome Project would have been considered science fiction two decades ago. The Human Genome Sequencing Project is the attempt to analyze the nearly six billion pieces of DNA that comprise human inheritance factors. As of 1998 only approximately 2 percent of the human genome has been analyzed, but the amount of information about health and disease patterns is already staggering.

Many people have expressed concern that we might be better off not hearing about the messages locked within our genes. Those messages might tell us how and when we are going to die. Critics of this research project fear that a deterministic and fatalistic view of an individual's future might result. The results achieved by this research to date, however, have led us to the opposite conclusion. Genetic inheritance is merely the template upon which we build our unique life experience. That experience of life, in turn, gives rise to the expression of who we are and how we function.

Genetic Nutritioneering synthesizes the amazing scientific information that describes how diet, lifestyle and environment influence genetic expression and health as we age. Scientists involved with the Human Genome Project and affiliated research are learning that such age-related diseases as heart disease, adult-onset diabetes, arthritis, digestive disorders, loss of mental acuity and certain forms of cancer are not inevitable consequences of aging. They are being recognized, instead, as the results of a poor match between the genetic needs of the individual and the choices he or she makes regarding overall diet, specific nutrient intake, lifestyle and environment.

In reading *Genetic Nutritioneering*, you will learn not only about breakthroughs in molecular nutrition and genetics, but also about applying this information to your life. The goal of this book is to give you tools you can use every day to reduce your long-range disease risk and increase your energy, vitality and well-being. You can unlock the tremendous potential for good health that is stored within your genes. That potential may not be optimally realized at the present time due to a mismatch between what your genes need and what they are being given.

The work of thousands of scientists and health professionals has contributed to the information in this book. Knowledge and paradigm shifts occur not by the work or insight of a single individual but through the accumulated contributions of many people exploring similar questions from different perspectives. At a certain point in history, the implications of this evolving body of knowledge become self-evident, and a cultural transformation occurs with its acceptance (i.e., the paradigm shift). The information contained in *Genetic Nutritioneering* will positively impact the evolution of our healthcare system.

For years we have been exposed to public health recommendations to reduce our risk factors for heart disease and cancer. Suggestions such as lowering our blood cholesterol, quitting smoking, managing blood pressure, and reducing dietary fat and cholesterol have aimed at preventing heart disease. Unfortunately, though, we all know of people with none of these "risk factors" who have still died of a heart attack. Similarly, to prevent cancer we are advised to eat more fiber, stop smoking, stay out of the sun, reduce our dietary fat intake, eat more fruits and vegetables and avoid smoked, cured meats. Yet we know of people who followed these recommendations and got cancer anyway.

Does this mean all disease is inherited and we can do nothing about it? As we explain in *Genetic Nutritioneering*, our genetic inheritance does play an important role in defining our risks to most age-related diseases, but healthy aging is even more controlled by how we communicate with our genes through our diet and lifestyle. Improving health as we age depends not just on the better delivery of general health messages, but also on the application of these recommendations for the needs of specific individuals as determined by the strengths and weaknesses of their own genetic inheritance.

Genetic Nutritioneering puts you in charge of your own health program. It accesses the medical and nutrition information emerging from the Human Genome Project to enable you to communicate with your healthcare providers to encourage the delivery of services tailored to your particular needs.

We are witnessing a renaissance in thinking about health and disease that is comparable to the great periods of cultural evolution in human history, and we can apply this information to our health needs today. It is a time of amazing paradox. On the one hand, we have developed a managed care medical system that delivers less and less care and contributes to the existence of an increasing group of medically disadvantaged patients. On the other hand, a new medical paradigm built upon the discoveries of molecular biology is opening up remarkable new ways to keep people healthy all through their lives. This opportunity, which is shared by healthcare consumers and doctors alike, is the focus of this book.

GENETIC NUTRITIONEERING

1

Your Health—
Genes or Environment?

YOU HAVE NO DOUBT GROWN accustomed to thinking about certain aspects of your physical body, its function and your health as immutable, given or cast in stone. For example, if you have brown eyes, you know you will never have blue ones. If you wear size 13 shoes, you will never wear size 6. By the same token, until now you probably have thought that if your father, your uncles and your grandfather all died prematurely of heart disease, you will be likely to suffer the same fate.

We have a name for the given characteristics we know we can't change. It is *heredity*. You *inherited* your brown eyes, the size of your feet, your predisposition to disease. They are your fate, your destiny, the hand you were dealt.

This mental image of a genetic destiny we all carry with us is very strong. It is built upon long history and well-accepted evidence. An example of that evidence is the sea captain from England who, with his brother, settled in Martha's Vineyard in Massachusetts in the 1690s.[1] Both brothers carried the recessive gene for deafness. Through intermarriage, by the middle of the 19th century, nearly 25 percent of the individuals living in some isolated up-island villages were born deaf. Hand signing became a standard method of communication. This example demonstrates the power of genetic inheritance.

In his book, *The Island of the Colorblind and Cycad Island*,[2] Oliver Sacks, M.D. describes people born with achromatopsia, a genetic condition in which the eyes do not develop properly so that affected individuals can see only black and white. In describing his visit to an island in Micronesia where this genetic defect is very common, Dr. Sacks explains how genetic defects can be accommodated and how limitations in one sensation can result in extraordinary development of others. Because their eyes are very sensitive to light, individuals with achromatopsia modify their environment to lower the light to which their eyes are exposed. They also develop the ability to see shades of gray and texture that individuals with normal color vision cannot perceive. In this example, the combination of genetic uniqueness and environment defines the function of the individual.

However, if genes alone determine the size, shape and function of our bodies, how can we explain the fact that the average height of adult Japanese men and women has increased nearly six inches since World War II? The genes have not changed. What has changed is the nutrition of Japanese children and adolescents. Nutritional environment combined with genetic inheritance yields what is called the "phenotype" of the individual, his or her observable size, shape and function.

PHENOTYPE: The entire physical, biochemical and physiological makeup of an individual, as determined both genetically and environmentally, as opposed to genotype.

In their recent book, *The Bell Curve: Intelligence and Class Structure in American Life*,[3] Richard Herrnstein and Charles Murray suggested that intelligence is strictly genetically controlled. If genes alone were responsible for intellectual performance, it would be hard to explain the accomplishments achieved by Down syndrome (trisomy 21) children at the Institutes for the Achievement of Human Potential in Philadelphia, Pennsylvania. Staff members at the Institutes employ a comprehensive training program of learning and motor skill development, physical training and conditioning and nutrition intervention to help parents assist their initially brain-injured children in improving their intellectual and physical skills. Institutes director Glenn Doman has described these programs in several excellent books.* Seeing the progress that can be made by one brain-injured child who was initially unable to speak or walk would convince anyone that the phenotypes of intelligence and function are a combination of genes and stimulation from the environment. Thousands of such children have gone through the programs at the Institutes and, over several years, developed skills in gymnastics, playing musical instruments and memorizing their lines for roles in Shakespearean plays.

THE GENETIC REVOLUTION

Events that would have sounded like genetic science fiction a few years ago are now daily news. We have not only seen the cloning of a sheep named Dolly from a fully mature cell taken from the udder of an adult female sheep, but some scientists are working to set up a lab to clone human beings. Until 1997 geneticists believed that once a cell had differentiated from its embryonic stage to become an adult cell it could not go back and become an embryo again. The cloning of Dolly in Scotland by Dr. Ian Wilmut and his research group has resulted in a questioning of that belief. In Wilmut's landmark scientific paper in 1997, he shook the time-honored concept of genetics and developmental biology when he stated, "The fact that a lamb was

---

* Institutes for the Achievement of Human Potential, 8801 Stenton Ave., Wyndmoor PA 19038-8397. Telephone: (215) 233-2050. Fax: (215) 233-3940.

derived from an adult cell confirms that differentiation of the cell did not involve irreversible modification of genetic material required for development to term."[4] What this development suggests is that, under the right conditions, *all* the genetic information encoded as your inheritance—from every stage of your development from an embryo to an elderly adult and for every cell type in your body—is potentially accessible to *any* cell in your body. Although the cloning of a sheep using Wilmut's procedure has not been duplicated by others, it does raise significant questions about our past belief that genetically controlled development is a one-way street.

This concept is so profound that it is hard to accept. It opens the door to the discovery that at any chronological age you might access messages locked in your inheritance that describe a younger, healthier you. Aging may not be a one-way street. You may have the biological capability to "engineer" a younger you by awakening sleeping genetic messages. The term "genetic nutritioneering" does not mean changing your genes. It does mean engineering a lifestyle, diet and environment that will enable you to get the most from your genes. To this end, the pages that follow outline a program which will enable you to improve the way your genes function in the control of your health and vitality.

In her book *21st-Century Miracle Medicine,*[5] Alexandra Wyke describes this genetic revolution. She points out that between 1960 and 1990 the United States witnessed an increase in healthcare expenditures from $200 million to $1 trillion annually, yet members of the public "are manifestly no less sick today than they were three decades ago." Wyke, who is managing editor of *The Economist* in charge of its healthcare publications, predicts that the first major breakthroughs in health will occur in the next few years as a result of accessing the incredible new genetic information. When properly applied, according to Wyke, this information will allow us to express our phenotype as the best of our inheritance factors while suppressing those messages that result in reduced function, premature aging and disease.

In the past, the central focus of medicine has been the diagnosis and treatment of disease. The result has been major advances in health with the reduction of infant mortality, treatment of bacterial infections and communicable illnesses and use of surgery and medications to treat specific diseases. The attempt to know more and more about specific diseases has led to the era of specialty medicine, each medical specialty having its own language and technologies. The result often has been the treatment of individuals as collections of organs, each ministered to independently by a specialist, without taking into account the entire organism.

David Deutsch, Ph.D., a world-renowned mathematician at Oxford University, recently stated in his book, *The Fabric of Reality*,[6]

> The science of medicine is perhaps the most frequently cited case of increasing specialization seeming to follow inevitably from increasing knowledge, as new cures and better treatments for more diseases are discovered. But as medical and biochemical research comes up with deeper explanations of disease processes (and healthy processes) in the body, understanding is also on the increase. More general concepts are replacing more specific ones as common, underlying molecular mechanisms are found for dissimilar diseases in different parts of the body. Once a disease can be understood as fitting into a general framework, the role of the specialist diminishes. Physicians . . . may be able to apply a general theory to work out the required treatment, and expect it to be effective even if it has never been used before.

GENETIC NUTRITIONEERING AND THE HUMAN GENOME

In *Genetic Nutritioneering* we are developing a general theory to explain the occurrence of a number of health problems associated with aging and to understand how to unlock sleeping messages in our genes for both the prevention of and recovery from those health problems. This concept has its foundation in the extraordinary discoveries of the Human Genome Project over the past decade. This ongoing international collaborative project among scientists around the world is focused upon "decoding" the genetic information locked within the 23 pairs of chromosomes called our genome.

GENOME: The full set of genes in an individual.

HUMAN GENOME PROJECT: A large international effort to elucidate the genetic architecture of the genomes of man and several model organisms.

Most scientists originally believed the Human Genome Project would simply uncover information related to the diseases an individual might get as he or she grew older. It opened discussions of ethical questions regarding whether individuals would want to know about diseases they would get if nothing could be done to treat those diseases. In her book, *Does It Run In The Family?*,[7] Doris Teichler Zallen describes this concern.

> We are now in a period of rapidly deepening knowledge of human genetics. This knowledge permits an unprecedented understanding of the relationship between our genes and our health. . . . But genetic information often includes an element of uncertainty. And genetic information is laden with baggage. This baggage is historical, ethical, emotional, social. In some instances the information can be useful and important, and in some, it can be harmful.

Jerry Bishop and Michael Waldholz, in their widely heralded book, *Genome*,[8] describe the breakthrough concept that emerges from the Human Genome Project. This concept, which is already revolutionizing the way medicine is practiced, is that our genes do not in and of themselves give rise to disease. Rather, in most cases, disease results when the individual elects a lifestyle or diet that alters the expression of the genes in such a way that the weakness or uniqueness of inheritance factors results in a phenotype we call a disease.

> The ability to reach into the human genome and pluck out the single gene that renders its possessor retarded, crippled or destined for an early death is of immeasurable importance to tens of thousands of humans who suffer genetic disorders. . . . But unmasking the identity of genes that render people *susceptible* to any of a host of chronic and crippling diseases is an entirely different matter. These aberrant genes do not, in and of themselves, cause disease. By and large, their impact on an individual's health is minimal until the person is plunged into a harmful environment.

DISEASE—INHERITED RISK, NOT INEVITABLE OUTCOME

Most people assume that diseases like diabetes, heart disease, high blood pressure, stroke, arthritis and cancer are results of genetic inheritance factors. The Human Genome Project is proving that genes are only a part of the story. More important than genetic inheritance is the phenotype—the result of gene expression and function. In terms of your health or disease state as an adult, your phenotype is determined by the way you have treated your genes throughout your life. What you have eaten or drunk, inhaled, surrounded yourself with in your environment, endured as stresses, participated in as activities or suffered as injury, infection or inflammation—all of these factors alter the expression of your genes and contribute in a major way to your state of health or disease.

When we use the term "expression" in this book, we are

referring to the way messages that are locked into your genetic inheritance factors are translated and ultimately influence your function. These changes in function result from two important influences that modify how your genes are expressed. The first is how the messages in your genes are transcribed, and the second is what happens to the cells of your body after the genes are translated. (Cell biologists call these "post-translation" effects of gene expression.) Although molecular biologists and geneticists like to differentiate these two factors, they will be combined under the term "expression" in this book. We have done this because it has been found that many of both the transcriptional and post-translation influences on genetic expression can be modified by the way you eat and the choices you make in your life.

NUTRITIONAL MODIFICATION OF GENETIC EXPRESSION

This powerful new, integrated view of the mechanism of disease provides the foundation for *Genetic Nutritioneering*. It is a view that has grown over time from the pioneering work of some of the world's most innovative and dedicated medical and laboratory scientists.

Drs. Joseph and Mary Goldberger are examples of the dedication that led to the discovery that nutrition influences gene expression. As a husband-and-wife team of medical microbiologists in the early 1900s, the Goldbergers were assigned by the federal government's Public Health Service to isolate and identify the communicable organism that caused the disease pellagra. The Goldbergers were well suited to this task; Joseph Goldberger had already successfully identified a number of disease-producing organisms that were causing public health problems. The early 1900s were the age of discovery of bacterially caused illnesses, and the Goldbergers were at the top of their game.

PELLAGRA: A clinical deficiency syndrome due to deficiency of vitamin B3 (niacin) or failure to convert tryptophan to niacin. It is characterized by dermatitis, inflammation of mucous membranes, diarrhea and psychic disturbances.

Each fall and winter in the Southeastern United States at that time, mental hospitals would fill with people with dementia, diarrhea and dermatitis (the 3 Ds of pellagra). Previous medical investigators had found that those who contracted pellagra were immigrants from Eastern Europe; therefore the condition was believed to be of genetic origin. The seasonality of the illness suggested that, like the flu, it was caused by an infection contracted by genetically susceptible individuals. Detailed family history diagrams had been drafted to show that pellagra had a genetic inheritance linkage.

The Goldbergers quickly became convinced from their observations that pellagra was neither genetic nor caused by an infection. Instead, they found it resulted from a nutritional deficiency. This discovery was remarkable because neither Goldberger was trained in nutrition; if they had a scientific bias, one would assume it would be to find a bacterial cause of the disease. They were model scientists, however, and through exhaustive studies they demonstrated the nutritional link to pellagra. They were so committed to this concept that they injected themselves with and ingested biological materials taken from people with pellagra to demonstrate it was not communicable. They were also able to demonstrate that they could treat pellagra with juice taken from beef liver squeezed through cheesecloth. Later research revealed that liver has a high level of vitamin B3 (niacin), the missing nutrient required for the prevention of pellagra.

The Goldbergers worked on the pellagra project for more than 15 years. In 1932 the federal government issued what it called the Pellagra II Report, more than 10 years after the Goldbergers first suggested that pellagra was caused by a nutritional deficiency. The only mention of their contribution was, "The Goldbergers have suggested that pellagra is caused by a nutritional deficiency, which has not as of yet been proven." The Pellagra II Report clung to the theory that pellagra had a genetic origin. Old concepts often die slowly. Only recently have scientists begun to amass overwhelming evidence that many diseases we previously ascribed to bad genes in fact result from nutritional inadequacy to meet the specific genetically determined needs of the individual.

This concept of how nutrients could modify the expression of a disease was advanced in the 1940s and 1950s by the pioneering work of Linus Pauling, Ph.D.,[9] and Roger Williams, Ph.D.[10] In his 1949 study of sickle cell anemia, Pauling, a recipient of two Nobel Prizes (one for chemistry and one for peace), described how a single alteration in genetic structure could result in a disease. Williams, a professor of biochemistry at the University of Texas in the 1950s, described what he called "biochemical individuality" and "genetotrophic disease," a disease resulting from the suboptimal intake of nutrients necessary to meet the genetically determined biochemical needs of the individual.

BIOCHEMICAL INDIVIDUALITY: The unique set of genetic factors a person possesses that control his or her metabolism, nutritional needs, and environmental sensitivities.

GENETOTROPHIC DISEASE: A disease appearing in midlife or beyond that is a result of poor nutrition that leads to suboptimal gene expression, e.g., heart disease, some cancers, adult-onset diabetes.

Just as countless thousands of people are now spared from pellagra through proper dietary intake of vitamin B3, in the future millions of people will be saved from premature illness and death by application of the concepts described in *Genetic Nutritioneering*. In this book you will learn how your genes work to control your health and function and how to modify the expression of your genes through the proper application of nutrients to meet your needs for the prevention of premature aging. You will learn to access and use to your health advantage the miraculous scientific and medical breakthroughs available today to modify genetic expression and help prevent such diseases of aging as diabetes, heart disease, dementia, arthritis and cancer. Above all, *Genetic Nutritioneering* will give you the tools you need to improve the way you function and how well you feel every day.

2

HOW YOUR GENES WORK

FOR AS LONG AS MEN and women have been producing offspring, parents have noticed similarities between their children and themselves. In the 1700s the Swiss naturalist Charles Bonnet advanced an early concept of genetic inheritance, suggesting a preformed miniature human being that resided in the sperm was transferred to the female egg at conception, took up residence there and grew into a human infant. This tiny embryo, presumed to reside within the sperm, was called a homunculus and was believed to be a completely formed person. This male-centered theory of genetics, which Bonnet promulgated in *Philosophical Palingesis, or Ideas on the Past and Future States of Living Beings*, was widely depicted in drawings and illustrations (as shown in Figure 1). For nearly a century, Bonnet's theory of evolution was a major influence on scientific thinking about the origin of acquired characteristics.

Early in the 19th century, however, observations of the reproduction of plants and domesticated animals led scientists to believe there was more to inheritance than simply what was provided by the male. The Augustinian monk Gregor Mendel, who lived from 1822 to 1884, bred pea plants in the monastery garden and made a remarkable discovery. He found that every pea flower had both

Figure 1. The Homunculus

male and female organs and under normal circumstances they fertilized themselves. If he used pollen from the male parts of one type of pea plant to fertilize the female part of another type of pea plant, however, he was able to produce hybrids or combinations of the two. He could predict the frequency of colors and sizes of the hybridized plants he produced based on the concept of what he called dominant and recessive characteristics. He suggested there was something in the pollen (i.e., sperm) of the stamen and the ovum from the female pistil that determined the characteristics of the offspring. This "something" is what we now know as genes.

The genes in our chromosomes are acquired in equal numbers

from our mothers and fathers. Some genes are dominant over others, which are called recessive. We may thus carry "silent" genetic characteristics that are not expressed in our phenotype because they are recessive to our dominant genes. Blue eye color, for instance, is recessive to brown eye color. If you have blue eyes, both of your parents gave you their recessive genetic characteristic for blue eyes, even if they themselves did not have blue eyes. Genetic scientists can predict the probability of expressing certain characteristics if they know the genetic history of the parents. This concept of the inheritance of dominant and recessive characteristics is shown in the following diagram.

Figure 2. Dominant and Recessive Genes

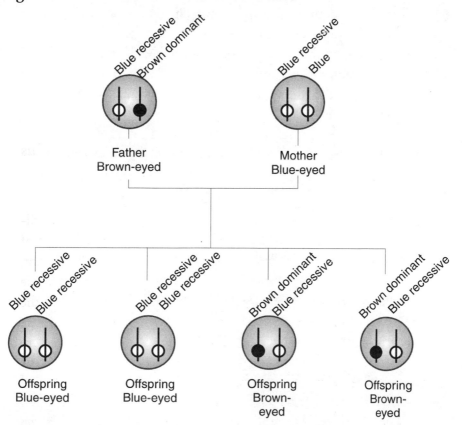

Geneticists used Mendel's research to uncover the basis of inheritance. They found that mother and father contribute equally to the material contained in the 23 pairs of chromosomes inherited by their offspring. Characteristics in genes contributed equally by both parents are called homozygous, and those contributed un-equally from each parent are called heterozygous. If a brown-eyed parent and a blue-eyed parent produce a blue-eyed child, for exam-ple, the brown-eyed parent must have carried a gene for both brown and blue eyes (heterozygous) because brown eye color is known to be dominant over blue. If one parent carried only brown eye char-acteristics on its two genes for eye color (homozygous) then the child could only have brown eyes. Characteristics associated with genes like the color of one's eyes are called "alleles." You get one allele from your mother and another from your father.

Another example of a dominant characteristic is that color vision is dominant over color blindness. A man could be a carrier of color blindness without being color blind; therefore, his children would not be color blind unless he conceived a child with a woman who also carried the color-blindness characteristic, thereby produc-ing a homozygous child.

HOMOZYGOUS: Possessing a pair of identical alleles (forms of a gene) at a given locus.

HETEROZYGOUS: Having a dominant and a recessive allele.

As genetics research progressed, scientists learned that cases of double possession of recessive characteristics (i.e., homozygous) were often associated with a number of rare genetic conditions, including hemophilia, sickle cell anemia, dwarfism, thalassemia and others.

The following rules of genetics evolved from this research:

1. Hereditary traits are governed by genes that retain their identity in the offspring. Genes are not "blended" together.

2. One form of a gene (an allele) may be dominant over another, but recessive genes will show themselves in future generations.

3. Each adult organism has two copies of each gene in every cell of its body except the sperm and the egg, each of which has one copy.

4. Different genetic characteristics are sorted out to the sperm and egg randomly.

Genetic scientists found that genes could undergo damage and their information could be altered. This was called a "mutation," and the result could be an altered characteristic in the offspring that neither parent shared. In most cases these mutations are not helpful, and in some cases they are harmful. Occasionally, however, they can result in a characteristic that makes the offspring more able than its parents to succeed in its environment. Favorable mutations are what scientists feel contribute to the evolution of the species over many millions of years.

GENETIC MUTATION: A permanent transmissible change in the genetic material, usually in a single gene.

Gregor Mendel's genetic research, and that of many geneticists who followed him, fostered a mechanical, deterministic view of heredity that persists today. Many people—scientists and lay people alike—feel we have no control over our genes. We got whatever resulted from the union of sperm and egg, and those genes control our destiny. The belief that our characteristics are "hard-wired" and cannot be changed is incorporated into our thinking about health, aging and disease. When a person lives a long, healthy life we say he is blessed with good genes. When someone succumbs to cancer or heart disease in the prime of life, we blame his death on bad genes.

When a person dies from smoking-induced lung cancer, alcoholic liver disease or malnutrition, however, can we blame the death on genes alone? Certainly not. In such cases, under optimal conditions the individual's genes may have allowed him or her to live a long, healthy life. In her book, *Living Downstream*, Dr. Sandra Steingraber describes her personal health challenges in dealing with bladder cancer.[1] She writes that whenever she lectured on this subject she explained that her mother, uncle and grandfather all had various forms of cancer. Her audiences always assumed she inherited "cancer genes," until she told them she was adopted. Her point is that families share common environments as well as genes. Diet, environment, lifestyle and the exposure to toxic substances all work together in modifying the way one's individual genes are expressed. Conditions to which genes are exposed contribute either to health or to premature disease and death. The deterministic view of genetics we inherited from Gregor Mendel, which would have us believe our health is predetermined by our genes, is not consistent with the revolution in the science of genetics that is taking place today.

Medicine was built upon the Mendelian principle of the deterministic gene. From this concept was born the philosophy that "you are well until you are proven sick." Medicine's responsibility under this belief system is to "fix" the results of bad genes by means of surgery, medications and replacement parts after a person is "broken." Because we have historically believed we could do little to influence the way our genes control our health, medicine evolved to focus on diagnosis and to be little interested in function or prevention. This philosophy is currently undergoing revolutionary change, however, as a consequence of breakthroughs in molecular biology and genetics.

THE AGE OF MOLECULAR BIOLOGY

The principal question, which remained until the 1950s, was how the information in the genes was captured. Scientists suspected the information was molecular in nature because the genes were composed of biochemicals. The chromosomes of cells were found to be made up of proteins and an unusual material called deoxyribonucleic acid (DNA). Until the 1950s scientists did not believe DNA was an important determinant in heredity because DNA was made up of only four chemical building blocks—adenine (A), thymine (T), cytosine (C) and guanine (G). It seemed there could be no way these four chemicals could account for the amazing diversity in structure and function of humans, animals and plants.

In the 1940s two biologists, George Beadle and Edward Tatum, discovered that each gene codes for the manufacture of one protein. The body uses proteins as building materials for bone, skin and connective tissue or, in the form of enzymes, to control biochemical function. Proteins, which are made up of more than 20 separate units called amino acids, are much more complex than DNA. Beadle and Tatum believed, therefore, that genetic information was probably comprised of nucleoprotein (specific proteins in the nucleus of the cell, which were associated with the chromosomes).

ENZYME: A protein molecule that catalyzes chemical reactions of other substances without itself being destroyed or altered.

In the early 1950s scientists were engaged in a race to discover the nature of the genetic material. When they isolated the genetic material from cells, they discovered to their surprise that it was DNA. In 1953, J.D. Watson and F.H. Crick, two young scientists at Cambridge University, made a discovery that has forever changed our view of nature and genetics. They found that DNA was arranged as a double-stranded helix made up of A, T, G and C. The strands were duplicates of one another, but arranged head to tail. In a paper they published in the prestigious scientific journal *Nature*, Watson and Crick revealed the molecular structure of DNA.[2]

With the publication of that article, the field of molecular biology began to explode. Scientists have found that the genetic characteristics Mendel described are encoded in the DNA by the combination of A, T, G and C in sets of three. There are only 64 possible combinations of A, T, G and C when they are combined three at a time, which means that all of the diversity we know in life of bacteria, plants and animals derives from these 64 possibilities in the formation of genes. Genes, therefore, are long strings of these triplet combinations. Specific genes reside on specific chromosomes (numbered 1 through 23) at specific places. The human genome is made up of more than 100,000 genes, all of which will be analyzed by the work of the Human Genome Project.

CHROMOSOME: In animal cells, a structure in the nucleus containing a linear thread of DNA, which transmits genetic information.

Watson and Crick's breakthrough discovery in the 1950s led to the development of both molecular and genetic medicine in the 1990s. According to a recent article in the *Journal of the American Medical Association*,

> Perhaps no scientific discipline is as fast-paced today as medical genetics. Fueled largely by the nearly 7-year-old Human Genome Project, the U.S. government-led effort to map the entire human genome, researchers now seem to isolate a new gene associated with a particular disease every week. To date, clinical tests have been developed for use in more than 450 human genetic disorders. The profound implications of actually seeing the molecular status of each patient's individual genome will affect virtually all medical disciplines.[3]

There are now computer sites on the worldwide web where human genetics and its relationship to health and disease can be studied and the progress followed daily.* The family history of genetic risk factors related to disease is being written as you read this book. The tools to diagnose these genetic uniquenesses are becoming available. What is most remarkable from these advances is the message that disease is not inevitable.

Analysis of the genome has indicated it contains a significant amount of what has been described as "junk DNA."[4] The major difference between the genomes of monkeys and humans may, in fact, be the presence of this genetic junk. "Junk" may be one of the poorest words that could have been chosen to describe what is actually genetic information for which no function has yet been defined.

The emerging view of medicine based upon these discoveries in molecular biology is that our genes control the manufacture within our cells of the substances that make us who we are— proteins, enzymes, nucleic acids and thousands of biochemicals. Not all of our genetic messages are being expressed at any one time. In fact, only a small portion of the genetic information in our cells is expressed at any given moment. Our diet, lifestyle and environment modify the nature of this information and how it is expressed. We are the products of what and how well our genetic messages are expressed. Healthy aging is accomplished when our genes continue to express healthy messages throughout our lives. Our phenotype is a result of how well our genes are expressed.

We do know that genes are polymorphic, which means there are differences in the structure and function of all genes among people.[5] We also know that some genes code for more than one type of a specific protein, and one message may be translated under one set of circumstances and another message under another set of circumstances. This understanding implies that biochemically or functionally we are pluripotential. There are many forms of "you"

---

* See *http://www.hhml.org/Genetic Trail/* and *http://healthlinks.washington.edu/ helix* and *http://www.ornl.gov/techresources/publications.html.*

encoded into your genes. The you who is reading this book right now is the result of the experiences of your life thus far bathing over your genes to produce the expression of who you are. Under a different set of experiences in life, a different "you" would be reading this book today. Your genes would be the same, but the way their message was expressed would be different.

POLYMORPHIC: Occurring in several or many forms; appearing in different forms at different stages of development.

PLURIPOTENTIAL: Possessing the power to develop or act in any one of several possible ways.

As you read this book, you are, in a sense, involved in an experiment called "your life." Scientists do not run this experiment, and it is neither placebo-controlled nor double-blinded. It is just your life, based upon the decisions you make about leading it. You are probably familiar with the outcomes of the "life experiment" of an individual you know, in the way that person's appearance changes when he or she is under extreme stress, has been a heavy smoker for many years or has taken excessive quantities of drugs or medications. The individual's genes have not changed, but the expression of those genes has changed.

Similarly, you no doubt know people who have eaten too many calories or relied upon high-fat, salty and sweet convenience and snack foods as their main sources of nutrition. Those individuals are typically overweight, have poor luster to their skin and hair and do not appear robust or vital. Again, their genes have not changed, but their gene expression has.

The possibility of changing the way genes are expressed has made it possible to use the information from the Human Genome Project in a different way. Reed Edwin Pyeritz, M.D., Ph.D. recently wrote in the *Journal of the American Medical Association*,

"Even when an individual's genome can be displayed on a personal microchip, interpreting that information will depend, in large part, on the biological and environmental contexts in which that genome is expressed."[6]

Using information that is rapidly becoming available about an individual's genetic blueprint, one can imagine a far different doctor-patient relationship from the fatalistic one that an individual would be forced to accept if the message within his genes were, in fact, immutable. A spokesperson for the National Human Genome Research Institute at the National Institutes of Health recently wrote,

> Imagine a physician discussing the results of a blood test with a patient that show the risk for colon cancer to be increased 4-fold and the risk for diabetes as twice normal. After discussing the meaning of the tests, the physician, the patient and the nurse design a preventive medicine program to maximize the patient's chances of staying well.[7]

This possibility for altering the expression of one's genes is the basis of the Genetic Nutritioneering Program. Your genes are polymorphic and pluripotential. There are many possible versions of "you" within your genes. You can alter the expression of your genetic potential through the foods you eat, the lifestyle you select and the environment in which you work and live. Regardless of your age, you can change the terms of the "experiment" of your life and get different results in the way your genes are expressed.

Gregor Mendel helped us understand our genetic inheritance, but he only got it partially right. Your genes alone are not responsible for your health. Instead, your health depends principally on the way you influence the expression of your genes throughout the collective experiences of your life.

You have a lot more control over your health than you may have believed. Scientists are developing tools both to assess your genetic uniqueness and to modify the expression of your genes with nutrition. Science is on your side, and you have the chance to participate in the greatest change in medicine and health care since the development of the germ theory of disease, antibiotics and immunization.

ROGER WILLIAMS AND BIOCHEMICAL INDIVIDUALITY

Roger Williams, Ph.D. was a pioneer in the use of individualized nutrition programs to benefit health. Working in the 1950s and 1960s at the University of Texas, Austin, Dr. Williams was one of the principal biochemists of this century. He discovered pantothenic acid, one of the important B vitamins, and published hundreds of articles on basic biochemical discoveries. Dr. Williams revolutionized medical thinking in the 1950s with his book, *Biochemical Individuality*.[8] In this book he explained there was much more diversity in human anatomy and physiology than science had previously acknowledged. And there was even greater diversity in individuals' biochemical makeup. Dr. Williams proposed that differences in biochemical function among individuals resulted from differences in genes and gene expression.

Molecular genetics was in its infancy when Dr. Williams advanced the concept of biochemical individuality. Because the ideas he described were expressed in biochemical terms, with which most doctors are not comfortable, his theory of biochemical individuality and the concept of "genetotrophic disease" did not gain favor. Dr. Williams defined genetotrophic disease as ". . . one in which the genetic pattern of the afflicted individual calls for an augmented supply of a particular nutrient (or nutrients), for which there develops, as a result, a nutritional deficiency."[9] He suggested that as research progressed many common diseases would be found to have this type of origin.

Over the past 40 years Dr. Williams has been proven right, and the concept of biochemical individuality stands as one of the great insights in the evolution of medical thinking. He was adamant in his belief that the standard American diet contributed to the diseases of our culture because people's genetic needs were not being met and flawed gene expression was the result. Diseases of overconsumption/undernutrition (eating too much food of too little nutritional value) include heart disease, high blood pressure and stroke, arthritis, dementia and nervous system disorders, lowered immunity and increased infection, digestive disorders including irritable bowel disease, chronic kidney disorders, adult-onset diabetes and adult cancers.

When he was asked what he thought of the Recommended Dietary Allowances and government guidelines for a balanced diet, Dr. Williams replied, "Nutrition is for real people. Statistical humans are of little interest." The establishment of dietary recommendations is based on the needs of a mythical "average" person. They do not take into account the range of genetic polymorphism within the human population.

Much of medicine and its relationship to nutrition is built upon this concept of "average" or "normal" humans. Using this type of reasoning, it would be possible to have a "normal" (meaning "average") blood cholesterol level in a society in which everyone gets heart disease or a "normal" blood sugar level at which everyone develops diabetes.

Dr. Williams proposed that as the science of molecular nutrition and genetics evolved, we would begin to recognize that many people who are considered "normal," meaning they are not presently sick, would be found to require much higher levels of specific nutrients to maintain health and prevent age-related diseases. He suggested that functional assessments of health would be more important than the definition or diagnosis of disease. Potentially useful functional criteria for judging nutritional adequacy, according to Dr. Williams, included recovery time after surgery, the ability to manage stress, wound healing, memory and hair growth rate.[10]

Functional health and its relationship to genetic nutritioneering is the basis for the practice of functional medicine, which is defined as the field of health care that employs assessment and early intervention to improve physiological, cognitive/emotional and physical function.*

LINUS PAULING AND THE BIRTH OF MOLECULAR MEDICINE

In addition to Dr. Williams, functional medicine owes its origin to Linus Pauling, Ph.D. Many people remember Dr. Pauling as a father of modern chemistry and, with his wife Eva Helen, as a leader in promoting world peace and nuclear disarmament. Some also associate his name with his advocacy for supplementation with vitamin C to prevent and treat the common cold and flu and to help prevent cancer and heart disease. Even more important than these accomplishments was the help he provided us in understanding that disease resulted from an altered molecular environment in the cell. He determined how molecules "fit" with one another and how this relationship controls function in the cell, which in turn gives rise to health or disease. Dr. Pauling believed the future of medicine would be to recognize how to create the optimal cellular environment using substances that are natural to our physiology, such as vitamin C and other nutrients.

In 1949, Dr. Pauling and Harvey Itano, M.D., his postdoctoral student at the California Institute of Technology, published a landmark paper on the origin of sickle cell anemia.[11] In the paper they used the term "molecular disease" for the first time. The concepts they wrote about represent the start of a paradigm shift in medicine. It has taken molecular biology some 50 years to take full advantage

---

* A description of functional medicine, its concepts, and its training programs can be found on the worldwide web at *http://www.healthcomm.com.*

of these concepts, which represent the intellectual heritage for the Genetic Nutritioneering Program.

MOLECULAR DISEASE: A disease caused by the alteration of a specific biochemical process in the body, e.g., sickle cell anemia, certain forms of heart disease, arthritis.

Sickle cell anemia is an inherited condition characterized by a defect in the structure of hemoglobin, which is the molecule that gives the blood its red color. In the sickle hemoglobin condition, the defect causes the hemoglobin in the red blood cell to stick to other hemoglobin molecules. The hemoglobin crystallizes in the cell, causing a change in the shape of the cell. Instead of its normal disc-like shape, the cell bends to resemble a "sickle." Like a sickle, the red cell with this shape cuts its way through the bloodstream and organs, resulting in damage and the pain of sickle cell crisis.

Dr. Pauling called sickle cell anemia a "molecular disease" because just one molecule was damaged due to a genetic uniqueness (i.e., a genetic mutation). He proposed that in the future a method would be found to modify the expression of this sickle cell genetic characteristic to prevent the disease.

In 1994, some 45 years after Dr. Pauling made this prediction, researchers discovered two substances that do just that. These substances are hydroxyurea and butyrate. Both substances are capable of waking up the sleeping message in the genome for the production of fetal hemoglobin.[12] When a fetus is in the womb, its hemoglobin is unique in its structure and ability to capture oxygen from the mother's blood supply. After birth, the genetic message for the production of this type of hemoglobin goes to sleep and is replaced by the message for the production of adult hemoglobin. The fetal hemoglobin message is still on the genome; it is just not being expressed.

Administering hydroxyurea or butyrate to an individual who carries the genetic message for the production of sickle hemoglobin

Figure 3. Red-Cell Sickling

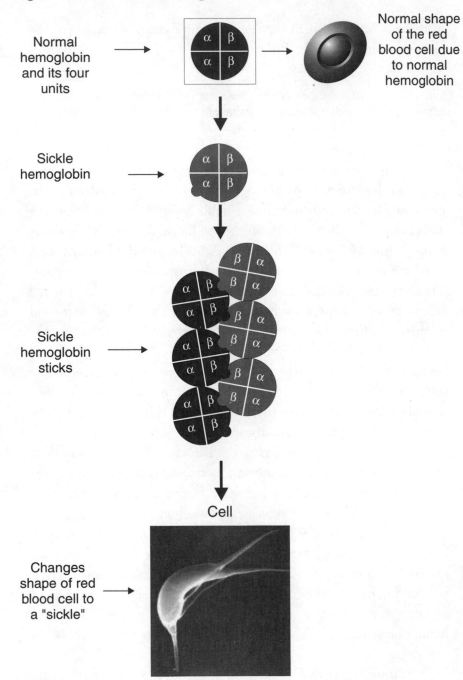

Normal hemoglobin and its four units

α | β
α | β

Normal shape of the red blood cell due to normal hemoglobin

Sickle hemoglobin

α | β
α | β

Sickle hemoglobin sticks

Cell

Changes shape of red blood cell to a "sickle"

awakens the message to produce the normal fetal hemoglobin. The newly produced fetal hemoglobin dilutes the sickle hemoglobin, preventing it from crystallizing. This nutritional intervention is a classic example of the genetic nutritioneering approach. By using a substance that modifies genetic expression, it is possible to alter the course of a genetically determined illness.

In sickle cell anemia the degree of expression of the genetic mutation is severe because it is homozygous (i.e., present on both alleles). In many other age-related diseases, however, the genetic condition is not as severe; therefore, the nutritional modification of gene expression is easier to accomplish.

Both Dr. Williams and Dr. Pauling were decades ahead of their time. The concepts of genetotrophic disease and molecular medicine are just now gaining enough support to become generally applicable for the prevention—and in some cases the treatment—of health problems and diseases of aging.

In the next chapter we will see how diet and specific nutrients can be used to modify gene expression in preserving health and reducing symptoms of aging.

3

CAN FOOD IMPROVE THE EXPRESSION OF YOUR GENES?

IT SEEMS MIRACULOUS WHEN YOU consider that you originated from a single cell, which combined the genetic message from your father's sperm and your mother's ovum. That single cell contained all the genetic information necessary not only to develop a fully formed infant but to code for the changes in your life that occurred with development, maturation and the changing rhythms of your life. Every cell that is derived from that initial fertilized ovum carries the same set of genetic information with the single exception of the sperm you produce if you are male or the eggs you produce if you are female.

As the fetus develops in the womb, cells differentiate into their specific tasks, which will be seen in the fetus and later in the infant. First to develop is the nervous system, then the gastrointestinal system, the heart and lungs, and, much later, the immune system. Deep within the nucleus of each of the cells that make up the specialized organs is the genetic information that can encode for the development of every other cell in the body. Therefore, the liver cell contains the information to make a heart cell, and vice versa. The process of differentiation and developmental biology is what causes cellular specialization to occur. Any one cell expresses only a fraction of the genome. You are the sum of the genetic messages expressed. This differentiation process is further complicated by the fact that, with time, maturation occurs, and cells undergo changes as a consequence of aging. All of these messages are locked within the genetic code and have the potential to be expressed at any moment.

During the course of your life, many events alter the way your genetic characteristics are expressed in individual cells, tissues or organs. In some cases these alterations are natural responses to your changing environment, such as your response to stress, cold or heat, heavy exercise or exposure to environmental chemicals. In other cases, however, changes in gene expression may reflect changes in phenotype that indicate disease or the loss of health and vitality.

An extreme example of this change in phenotype is the case of J.M. Barrie, the author of *Peter Pan*.[1] As a child, Barrie witnessed the traumatic death of his brother. He was subsequently isolated from his parents, and his mother continued to focus on the beautiful dead brother's memory. At this point, young James stopped growing and maturing. When he died in his 60s, he was only 4 feet 10 inches tall and apparently had never gone through puberty. He was, in essence, Peter Pan. This phenomenon occurred in the absence of any known disease or genetic abnormality. In the medical literature of today, this appears to be a case of arrested maturation due to a psychological trauma so severe that it altered gene expression of the hormones required for development.

Our environment and experiences can play a significant role in modifying our phenotype. This most remarkable case of stress-induced dwarfism in J.M. Barrie demonstrates the power of the environment to control the activity of our genes.

In most cases, however, the first manifestation of this type of gene expression is generally a loss of function that could be as simple as sleep disturbance, mood swings, low energy and fatigue, chronic pain, changes in body temperature and weight or poor exercise tolerance. These changes may be the early warning signs or what are called "biomarkers" of altered gene expression. If you do not pay attention to those early warnings, the result, after many years, could be the expression of disease.

Most people who undertake a physical fitness improvement program notice their energy improves, the shape of their body changes, their appetite normalizes and they sleep better. It is easy to explain these changes by saying, "Exercise is good for you." The complete explanation is that moderate regular exercise is one of the factors that improves gene expression and alters your phenotype.

Regardless of gender, race, age, likes or dislikes, all human beings share three activities in common—movement, breathing and eating. All are extremely important in modifying gene expression. Sedentary individuals who do not engage in movement, such as the institutionalized elderly or, in past years, astronauts in space, lose muscle mass and bone. They have reduced heart and lung function and altered hormone levels. These body functions change as a consequence of the alteration in gene expression that occurs with lack of movement or exercise.

Similarly, if you don't drink enough water your body becomes dehydrated, and a number of adverse cellular effects can result. If dehydration is extended for a period of time, some of these cellular responses are seen as altered gene expression. Water is an essential nutrient that not only hydrates the body but also provides the proper cellular environment so cells can engage in biochemical reactions associated with gene expression, protein synthesis and metabolic function.

Nutrition also plays an important role in modulating gene expression. This fact, which gives new meaning to the saying "You are what you eat," places increased responsibility on the decisions you make about foods. One meal does not make a difference in the expression of your genes, but over the course of many years your dietary choices can influence your gene expression in such a way as to modify your phenotype, enhancing or diminishing your cellular function.

The idea that the foods you eat and the nutrients they contain have the ability to communicate with your genes may be new and strange to you. Information emerging from current scientific research, however, strongly supports that relationship.

This does not mean that food changes your genes in any way. The message you were born with remains intact, embedded in the nucleus of cells in every organ of your body. What does change is the way the message from your genes is expressed. The effect of the nutrients you ingest on the expression of messages within your genes is like the effect of hydroxyurea or butyrate on sickle cell anemia, which I described in Chapter 2. In that case, administration of those specific nutrients results in the awakening of a sleeping genetic message.

Genetic messages can either be put to sleep or awakened as a consequence of alterations in your diet. Putting to sleep the messages that result in increased risk of disease and awakening those messages that enhance health and help prevent premature aging is the focus of the Genetic Nutritioneering Program.

How Diet Influences Genetic Expression

Chronic diseases, including heart disease, high blood pressure, diabetes and cancer, are significant health problems in the United States and the developed world. Although the rate of death from heart disease has declined throughout the past four decades, it remains the leading cause of death in the United States, followed by stroke and cancer. According to the American Heart Association, roughly one of four Americans currently suffers from some form of cardiovascular disease. The Third National Health and Nutrition Examination Survey (NHANES III) revealed that at least 43 million U.S. adults have high blood pressure.[2] Although the death rate from

Figure 1. How Food Affects Gene Expression

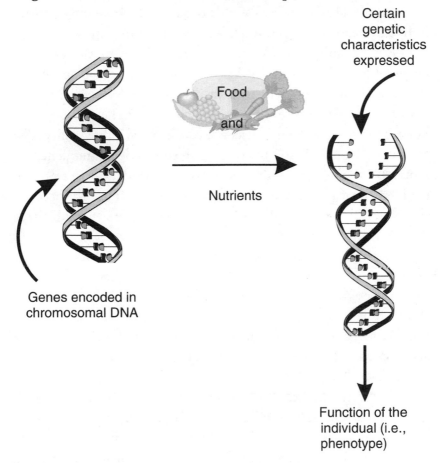

cancer has decreased slightly in recent years, the age-adjusted rate of cancer in the years 1987 to 1991 was 19 percent higher in men and 12 percent higher in women than it was in the years 1975 to 1979. In the United States we are currently witnessing a virtual epidemic of adult-onset diabetes, with its attendant kidney failure, blindness and neurological disorders.

Government-sponsored public health education programs emphasize that all of these diseases have lifestyle and nutrition components, reducible risk factors that, if we manage them properly, should lower the risk of these diseases. Yet most of us know of someone who had a fatal heart attack at an early age who had moderate cholesterol and blood pressure, did not smoke, had no family history of heart disease and was not diabetic. We may also know someone who had a healthy lifestyle but was struck down by cancer in the prime of life. Why, you may ask, if we know so much about risk factors and we work to reduce those risk factors, do so many people still end up with life-threatening or fatal diseases? The answer to that question goes back to the concept of biochemical individuality (discussed in Chapter 2) and the relationship of genetic uniqueness to individual health risks. Public health recommendations are fine for the hypothetical "average" person, but they don't meet the needs of those whose unique genetic characteristics require individualized programs.

Research now indicates there is significant variation among people in how their genes respond to diet and lifestyle. You have heard, for example, that if you have elevated blood pressure you should follow a low-salt diet. New research, however, estimates that only 30 to 50 percent of individuals with high blood pressure are actually "salt-sensitive."[3] For the rest, salt restriction is an unnecessary bother that produces no benefit.

You have also heard that eating too many foods high in saturated fats and cholesterol will raise your blood cholesterol levels and increase your risk of heart disease. As a result of this warning, many people have been placed on fat- and cholesterol-restricted diets. Although it may be a prudent course of action for most people, a low-fat diet is not necessarily the best for everyone. In a recent study, 41 percent of individuals with a certain type of elevated blood cholesterol (i.e., an increase in LDL subclass A) experienced *increases* rather than decreases in the type of blood cholesterol associated with heart disease when they were placed on a low-fat diet.[4] Researchers are learning that most chronic diseases associated with aging are "polygenic," taking their message from a number of different genetic characteristics.

POLYGENIC: **Pertaining to or determined by the action of several different genes.**

Scientists estimate that genetics explains only about 50 percent of the variation in blood cholesterol levels, 30 to 60 percent of the variation in blood pressure levels, and 20 percent of ovarian cancer risk. The other modifier of genetic expression and the appearance of these diseases is how we affect our genes through diet, lifestyle and environment.

Gregory Miller, Ph.D. and Susan Groziak, Ph.D., R.D. recently wrote,

> A genetic approach to dietary recommendations to help prevent chronic diseases will greatly improve the efficacy of dietary advice. Health professions need to rely less on the universal public health approach and more frequently utilize a selective, informed process that takes into account individual genetic differences in risk for specific diseases. By identifying genetic variables that affect chronic disease risk and by exploring gene-nutrient interactions, we can evolutionize dietary advice to best prevent, delay, and treat chronic diseases.[5]

The understanding that diet can modify gene expression achieved a new level of acceptance in the scientific community in the 1980s with the work of Michael Brown, M.D. and Joseph Goldstein, M.D. These researchers from the University of Texas Southwestern Medical School were awarded the Nobel Prize in Medicine in 1985 for their pioneering work on cholesterol and its relationship to heart disease.[6]

The pair set out to understand the basic defect in families whose members have high incidence of heart disease. This characteristic, which is associated with very high blood cholesterol levels, is a genetic trait that occurs in about 1 in 500 individuals worldwide. Affected individuals have elevated blood levels of the "bad" LDL cholesterol. Over time, cholesterol is deposited in arteries, resulting in plaque and a narrowing of the arteries which leads to heart disease, particularly in males with this genetic condition who are between the ages of 35 and 50.

The pioneering work of Brown and Goldstein led to the understanding that in these individuals the difficulty is not necessarily that they are consuming too much cholesterol in their diet. Instead, their bodies produce too much cholesterol as a consequence of a defect in the thermostat that regulates the manufacture of cholesterol in the liver. Through this pioneering work, agents called statin drugs were found that could turn off the thermostat that controls cholesterol synthesis. The result was a reduction in cholesterol and in heart disease incidence among these individuals. Significant side effects, including a potential increased risk of cancer, have subsequently been associated with these cholesterol-lowering drugs in some individuals.

A number of recently discovered dietary substances can also help regulate the cholesterol thermostat.[7] One such substance is tocotrienol, a nutrient found in high levels in rice, barley and palm oils. Tocotrienol, which is a member of the vitamin E family, seems to have a unique ability to help regulate the cholesterol thermostat in the liver. This is one example of a specific food that is enriched in a certain nutrient that can have an impact on physiological function in individuals with specific genetic risk. Studies are underway utilizing a combination of supplemental nutrients in individuals who have defects in their cholesterol thermostat. Among the nutrients being studied in an attempt to reduce the excessive production of cholesterol by the body are niacin, soluble fiber, tocotrienols and the mineral chromium.

Research has also been conducted into the management of high blood pressure with nutritional modulation of gene expression and function. Increased intake of fresh juices of fruits and vegetables rich in potassium and magnesium, along with calcium supplementation, has been found helpful in lowering blood pressure in individuals with essential hypertension who have not responded to sodium restriction.[8] Other research has shown that reducing saturated animal fats and partially hydrogenated vegetable oils in the diet and replacing them with fish oils and other unsaturated oils can lower blood pressure.[9]

In studying adult-onset diabetes, researchers have found that reducing excessive calories in the diet and altering the ratio of protein to carbohydrate and fat can improve the regulation of blood sugar levels.[10]

Since the combination of amino acids in vegetable protein is different from that of animal protein, some people's bodies respond much differently to these two forms of protein. Consuming vegetable protein in place of animal protein alters many aspects of metabolism and its relationship to gene expression, improving insulin sensitivity and reducing toxicity reactions.

The connection between diet, gene expression and diabetes will be explored in greater detail in Chapter 7.

PHYTONUTRIENTS AND GENE EXPRESSION

In addition to fat, protein, carbohydrate and fiber, plants contain a myriad of other nutrients, including vitamins, minerals and phytochemicals. *Phyto* means *plant*, and phytochemicals are plant-derived substances that modify gene expression or physiological function in individuals who consume them. Americans have been told to eat more plant foods and for good reason. A diet that contains "five-a-day" fruits and vegetables will be rich in phytochemicals. Nuts, whole grains, fruits and vegetables contain an abundance of phenolic compounds, terpenoids, pigments and other natural antioxidants, including carotenes, vitamin E and vitamin C, all of which are associated with protection from and/or treatment for chronic diseases like cancer, heart disease, diabetes and high blood pressure. In 82 percent of 156 recently published dietary research studies, it was found that fruit and vegetable consumption provided significant protection against many cancers.[11] People who eat more fruits and vegetables have about one-half the risk of cancer and less cancer mortality than those who are not vegetable eaters.

PHYTONUTRIENT: A specific nutrient derived from a plant.

The average American currently eats only about one-and-one-half servings of vegetables and less than one serving of fruit a day. A recent survey of American eating habits showed that only one in 11 Americans met the guidelines for eating at least three servings of vegetables and at least two servings a day of fruit. In fact, one in every nine Americans surveyed ate no fruit or vegetable on the day of the survey, and 45 percent reported eating no fruit that day.[12]

More than $20 million has been spent in the past few years on research to evaluate the anticancer potential of plant foods. The foods and herbs with the highest anticancer activity are garlic, soybeans, cabbage, ginger, licorice and the umbelliferous vegetables (including carrots, celery, cilantro, parsley and parsnips). Foods and spices with a modest level of cancer-protective activity are onions, flax, citrus, turmeric, cruciferous vegetables (including broccoli, Brussels sprouts, cabbage and cauliflower), the solanaceous vegetables (including tomatoes, eggplant and peppers), brown rice, whole wheat and barley. Other foods and herbs with a measure of anti-cancer activity included oats and barley, mint, rosemary, thyme, sage, oregano, basil, cucumber, cantaloupe and berries.

Researchers have identified a host of active substances in these anticancer plant foods that modify gene expression and help protect against age-related diseases. The following phytochemicals and their sources have been subjects of research:

- Allyl sulfides in garlic and onions (antioxidants, detoxification)

- Phytates in grains and legumes like soy (anticancer agents)
- Glucarates in citrus, grains and tomatoes (improve detoxification)
- Lignans in flax and soybeans (normalize metabolism of estrogen/testosterone)
- Isoflavones in soybeans (normalize activity of estrogen/testosterone)
- Saponins in legumes (anticancer agents)
- Indoles, isothiocyanates and hydroxybutene in cruciferous vegetables (improve detoxification of carcinogens)
- Ellagic acid in grapes, strawberries, raspberries and nuts (antioxidants)
- Bioflavonoids, carotenoids and terpenoids in various other plant foods (modify inflammation and immunity)

Most of these substances influence specific aspects of gene expression and help either to induce anticancer genes or put cancer genes to sleep. Cancer prevention through genetic nutritioneering will be discussed in greater detail in Chapter 10.

One example of the power of phytochemicals is the recent report that the flavonoid naringenin, which is found in grapefruit but not in orange, lemon or lime, can assist the costly prescription drug cyclosporin in preventing organ transplant rejection after surgery.[13] Reports in surgery journals have recommended that, after kidney or liver transplant surgery, patients be given a pint of grapefruit juice to drink to improve the usefulness of cyclosporin in protecting against organ rejection. Naringenin suppresses the gene expression for a detoxifying enzyme in the liver that eliminates the drug cyclosporin from the body. By inhibiting the expression of this enzyme, naringenin helps patients get more benefit from cyclosporin by preventing its detoxification, thereby slowing its elimination from the body.

Used in this way, is grapefruit juice a food or a drug? That is a good question. As research on nutrients and their effects on gene expression increases, the distinction between foods and drugs is being blurred. A number of biologically active substances in foods help regulate gene expression. Over the course of the lifetime of an individual these substances may be much more important in determining health and disease patterns than the drugs he or she may take for a short period of time.

Regular consumption of citrus fruits is a good example of the benefits to be derived from foods. In addition to providing an ample supply of vitamin C, folic acid, potassium and the soluble fiber pectin, oranges contain an array of active phytochemicals. In fact, more than 170 phytochemicals have been identified in oranges. The more than 60 bioflavonoids found in oranges have a wide range of properties that modify gene expression; they serve as anti-inflammatories, inhibit blood clots and activate the body's detoxification system.

Limonene, a monoterpene nutrient found in grapefruit and orange juice, inhibits tumor formation by stimulating the gene expression for a detoxifying enzyme called glutathione S-transferase. Glutathione S-transferase is an important enzyme that promotes the detoxification of cancer-producing chemicals and their elimination from the body as nontoxic derivatives. Citrus pulp and the white of the orange are rich in a family of phytochemicals called glucarates. These substances are being studied for their potential to alter the gene expression associated with breast cancer and to lower the risk of symptoms of hormonal imbalances associated with premenstrual syndrome in women.

MONOTERPENES: Essential oils from spices, herbs, and fruits, such as essence of orange, mint and clove.

More than 20 carotenoids are also found in oranges. These include not only beta-carotene, but also other members of the carotene family, including lutein, zeaxanthin and cryptoxanthin.

These other carotenoids are associated with a lower incidence of age-related macular degeneration (ARMD), the leading cause of blindness in the United States after the age of 65.

CAROTENOIDS: The orange-red pigments found in fruits and vegetables such as carrots, tomatoes, winter squash and yams.

Garlic is another food that contains a number of phytochemicals that can help modulate gene expression. The sulfur compounds in garlic help protect against carcinogenic chemicals, lower blood pressure and blood cholesterol levels and help boost immunity.[14]

Phytochemicals in spices also have important influences on gene expression. The substance curcumin, found in the spice turmeric, for example, is a powerful antioxidant that reduces gene expression associated with inflammation.[15] Curcumin helps soak up harmful substances produced within the cell that can damage the genes, and it serves as a switch to control the expression of certain genes that provide anti-inflammatory function to the body. A combination of the capsaicin from hot peppers, curcumin from turmeric, and fish oils helped lower the inflammatory response after exposure to inflammation-producing substances when administered to animals.[16]

Ginger is another spice that contains phytochemicals that modify gene expression and help to reduce inflammation associated with arthritis and other inflammatory disorders. Active phytochemicals called gingerols work along with curcumin to reduce the genetic expression associated with the inflammatory response.[17, 18]

Another phytochemical that is associated with alteration of inflammation is the flavonoid quercetin. High concentrations of quercetin are found in onions and garlic. This phytochemical helps normalize gene expression in conditions of inflammation associated with allergy and arthritis.[19] Quercetin can be taken as a supplement or is reasonably well-absorbed from the diet, and it can be distributed in the bloodstream throughout the body to help regulate and control gene expression associated with inflammation.

BIOFLAVONOID: A class of thousands of related phytonutrients that include subclasses of isoflavones, flavonones, flavones and flavonols, all of which act as antioxidants, hormone modulators and anti-inflammatories.

Quercetin is one member of the bioflavonoid family. More than 1,000 different bioflavonoids have been found in various foods. As a class of phytochemicals, bioflavonoids have important gene response-modifying effects and are also antioxidants. One large study found that the reason consuming fruits and vegetables helps protect against stroke is that it increases the intake of bioflavonoids from these foods. This study concluded that the regular intake of bioflavonoids from food may help protect against stroke.[20] Tea is the major source of bioflavonoids in the average diet. Both black and Chinese green tea contain high levels of bioflavonoids. Since these bioflavonoids are not found in coffee, tea drinkers derive significant additional benefit from their beverage of choice. Chinese green tea contains a class of bioflavonoids called catechins.[21] These bioflavonoids have very powerful antioxidant and gene-protective effects.

The so-called "French paradox," which has received considerable media attention in recent years, notes that individuals in France who consume a traditional high-fat diet seem to have lower incidence of heart disease than their counterparts in other developed countries. Recent research indicates that the protection against heart disease by consumption of the natural French diet is conferred, at least in part, by the increased intake of protective flavonoids from fresh vegetables, as well as red wine.[22] Red wine contains a number of phytochemicals called phenolics, including resveratrol and quercetin, both of which alter gene expression in such a way as to protect against blood clot formation and heart disease.

VITAMINS, MINERALS AND GENE EXPRESSION

In addition to phytochemicals, protein, carbohydrate, fat and fiber, vitamins and minerals can be important modulators of gene expression. Vitamins that rank at the head of this list include the B vitamins, particularly vitamin B6 (pyridoxine), vitamin B12 (cobalamin) and folic acid. As I will explain in Chapters Nine and Ten, these B-vitamin nutrients play important roles in modulating gene activity through their ability to mask certain portions of the gene that should not be expressed in adults. Through this masking effect, messages related to the risk of both heart disease and cancer can be put to sleep.

The essential trace mineral zinc is important in modulating gene expression as well. Zinc is a pivotal nutrient in supporting immune system function and it helps regulate the way that the genetic message is translated into protein synthesis in the cell. One of the first signs of zinc inadequacy is the loss of taste or smell. Older individuals who have become zinc-deprived and whose gene expression is modified as a consequence of zinc insufficiency frequently have a poor sense of taste or smell. Zinc is found in abundance in lean meats and fish, foods that children and the elderly may not consume in sufficient quantity. Zinc inadequacy in the diet can produce loss of immune function. In adolescents it may be seen as acne, and in the elderly as increased risk of infection.

Scientists have learned during the past decade that the nutrients found in foods engage in complex interactions with our genetic machinery. Your food and beverage selections play a significant role in determining aspects of your gene expression. Over the years, altered gene expression signals a message to your body, telling it how to perform. A poor-quality diet results in poor physiological function, reduced vitality, and increased risk of age-related diseases. Each of us carries different genetic sensitivities to these nutrients, and therefore a diet that may be optimal for someone else may not even be adequate for you. In the next chapter I will explain how to recognize aspects of your biochemical uniqueness and how to use dietary principles to "talk to your genes" in a way that increases your healthy life span.

4

How Your Diet Communicates with Your Genes

In the 1950s and 1960s, scientists from around the world traveled to Guam to study an extraordinary disease epidemic called lytico-bodig. This disease could manifest itself in a variety of ways, from the classic "lytico," characterized by a progressive paralysis that resembled amyotrophic lateral sclerosis (ALS or Lou Gehrig's Disease), or sometimes as "bodig," a condition resembling Parkinson's disease, occasionally occurring with dementia. Researchers assembled in Guam to study these conditions, determine their cause, and design a therapy for them.

Extensive research over the last 40 years has uncovered the potential source of this strange condition, which is seen not only in Guam, but also in surrounding islands in Micronesia. The unifying theme appears to be exposure through the food and water supply to a toxic substance that affects individuals with specific genetic susceptibility. The culprit in the food supply is a unique type of flour derived from the cycad plant.

The cycads are some of the most ancient plants in the world. They resemble what you might imagine palm trees looked like in the Jurassic period of prehistory. Their seeds can be ground into fine flour that is highly prized by individuals in Micronesia for its unique taste. The association between consumption of cycad flour and neurological diseases was first reported in 1888 in the *Journal of the American Medical Association*.[1] Since then, a number of toxic substances have been identified in cycad flour. They include 2-amino-3-(methyl amino) propanoic acid (BMAA). Exposure to cycad flour that contains potential neurotoxins and the consumption of water that is high in aluminum and manganese are the suggested contributors to the neurological diseases characterized as lytico-bodig.

The most interesting aspect of this disease is not that these toxic substances are present in the diet and the water consumed by people in Guam, but that the condition seems to afflict only those individuals with specific genetic susceptibility.[2]

Lytico-bodig is an extreme example of a theme that is emerging from research around the world. Scientists are identifying certain genetic characteristics that make individuals more susceptible to food-induced disease and chronic health problems. Those genetic characteristics are related to digestive function, detoxification ability and the unique sensitivities of the nervous and immune systems to substances in specific foods. Lytico-bodig disease, therefore, reminds us that food and the nutrients within it speak in very personal ways to our genes and may result in increased susceptibility to specific diseases.

Moving from Micronesia to the Mediterranean region of the world, we find that many people there are very sensitive to fava beans. Consumption of these beans results in potentially life-threatening damage to their red blood cells, spontaneous bleeding and anemia. Fava beans contain a specific substance that can poison the activity of a very important enzyme called glucose-6-phosphate dehydrogenase (G6PD), which is found in red blood cells and is very important for the maintenance of their structure and function. People of Mediterranean heritage who inherit a genetic deficiency of the G6PD enzyme are much more susceptible to this toxic substance found in fava beans. Interestingly, geneticists have found the G6PD deficiency characteristic is the most common human genetic variation that has yet been identified. It is found in many forms and degrees. Some individuals whose genes express much more G6PD deficiency than others may be much more sensitive to fava beans.[3] Not all individuals will react in the same way. Fava bean sensitivity is another example of the way a specific food and substances within it influence the function of the gene products of individuals who carry certain inheritance factors. Fava beans, which are considered a nutritious food for many individuals, are consumed in large quantities in the Middle East. For those who carry the G6PD deficiency inheritance factor, however, eating fava beans can be dangerous.

The genes do not change in these instances. What does change when an individual consumes these potentially toxic food substances is the way his or her genetic uniqueness is functionally expressed. We carry genetic polymorphism within the human population. There is a wide variation in the way specific genetic inheritance factors are described in the chromosomes of each of us. As I explained earlier, the unique nature of your genes describes your genotype. The exposure of your genotype to specific foods, stress, and environmental and lifestyle factors, such as smoking and alcohol consumption, result in altered function of your genotype as expressed in your phenotype. Certain genetic characteristics can be induced by exposure to specific foods and nutrients, and other genetic characteristics may be suppressed. The communication between the food you eat and your genotype contributes to your health by modifying your phenotype or function.

GENETIC POLYMORPHISM: The occurrence together in the same population of two or more genetically determined phenotypes.

SUGAR SENSITIVITY

In her book, *Breaking the Vicious Cycle: Intestinal Health Through Diet*, Elaine Gottschall describes individuals with serious digestive problems, including colitis, irritable bowel syndrome and Crohn's disease.[4] These conditions are characterized by inflammation of the intestinal tract and intestinal bleeding, and, in extreme cases, surgery may be required to remove a portion of the damaged intestinal tract. She describes extensive international research that has found that many individuals experience a remission of their digestive disorder when they adhere to a low-carbohydrate diet.

How could the carbohydrate in foods lead to serious digestive inflammation and ulceration? One answer that is emerging from research is that individuals with specific genetic inheritance factors are more sensitive to fructose, a form of sugar. There are a variety of genetic uniquenesses in the way that individuals metabolize sugar and absorb it from their intestinal tract. Fructose sensitivity, which results from the altered absorption and metabolism of fructose, can result in inflammation of the intestinal tract.

Another sugar that produces digestive difficulty in individuals with specific genetic inheritance factors is the milk sugar lactose. Individuals who complain of diarrhea, gas and intestinal pain after drinking milk may suffer from the genetic inheritance of lactose intolerance. This genetic characteristic is found much more frequently in individuals of Asian and black ethnic extraction. In addition to potential digestive problems, those who have a genetic difficulty in metabolizing lactose may also, if they continue to consume dairy products throughout their lives, run a higher risk of developing cataracts because of their inability to metabolize another component of milk sugar, galactose.

Some people have a genetic sensitivity not to milk sugar but to the milk protein casein. Casein sensitivity can result not only in digestive problems but also in ear infections in children, respiratory congestion, mucus formation and activation of the immune system that produces symptoms of a low-grade flu with sore muscles and joints, low energy and what some people call "foggy brain."

Dairy products are not the only foods that impact the genes in such a way as to induce allergic responses. Another food family that has this capability is the gluten-containing grains, which include wheat, rye, oats and barley. A great many people are sensitive to gluten, some of them to such an extent that it produces serious inflammation of their intestinal tracts which can eventually result in intestinal disease. Gluten-sensitive individuals sometimes lose the ability to absorb proper nutrition from their diets and start suffering from malnutrition even though they eat high-quality foods.

We are not really what we eat but what we absorb from what we eat. Inflammation of the intestinal tract and impaired intestinal function from continuous exposure to foods to which the genes respond adversely can result in poor absorption of nutrients. The result can be vitamin and mineral deficiencies, excessive weight loss, and anemia. Medical geneticists have found there is a wide range of severity in sensitivity to gluten.

In extreme cases, genetic sensitivity to these food proteins in dairy products and grains, as well as to peanuts and certain fish, may be so dramatic that it produces a life-threatening anaphylactic response. Anaphylaxis is a shock-like response to exposure to something that puts the body's function in jeopardy. It may result in heart attack, coma, respiratory failure or death. Although these extreme examples of genetic susceptibility are rare, they indicate how important the relationship between food constituents and our genetic messages can be. In one case, a 10-year-old boy had a near-fatal respiratory response to a muffin that he had eaten for breakfast, which contained peanuts, to which he was allergic.[5] His mother had known he was sensitive to peanuts and had rigorously excluded any peanut- or peanut oil-containing products from his diet. Later analysis revealed that the muffin he had eaten listed walnuts among its ingredients, although it actually contained peanuts that had been bleached and flavored with walnut extract. Consumption of only a few peanut fragments sent a message to the boy's genes to respond as if his body was under attack from a foreign invader. This response was so strong that it produced near-fatal anaphylaxis.

The message from these examples is clear. Don't underestimate the power of your genes to control your specific sensitivity to your environment, food and lifestyle. Much of what you may accept as your genetic lot in life is really a consequence of the exposure of your genes to agents that induce the expression of a phenotype of disease.

DETOXIFICATION AND YOUR GENOTYPE

The body protects itself against potentially injurious toxic substances through a complex process called metabolic detoxification. Nearly every organ of the body contains specific enzymes that participate in this detoxification process and help protect that organ against toxins that originate in the outside world or are produced inside the body. The message for the construction of these detoxifying enzymes is buried in the genes. Depending on their genetic inheritance factors, individuals have very different detoxification abilities. One remarkable recent medical discovery in the area of metabolic detoxification is that the detoxification abilities of apparently healthy people may vary by a factor of between three- and fivefold. In other words, when two people with different genetic capabilities for detoxification are exposed to the same substance for a period of years, one may be five times as likely to develop disease as the other. Two passengers in a car may be exposed to the same rush hour traffic-induced pollution. One may feel fine and the other may develop weeping eyes, a runny nose, irritation of the throat and lungs and a headache. The exposure to pollutants may be exactly the same, but one person is able to mobilize his detoxification enzymes while the other cannot do so and suffers a toxic reaction.

Figure 1. Nutrients and Liver Detoxification

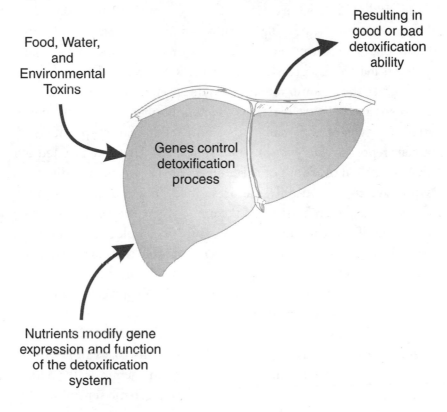

Resulting in good or bad detoxification ability

Food, Water, and Environmental Toxins

Genes control detoxification process

Nutrients modify gene expression and function of the detoxification system

---

METABOLIC DETOXIFICATION: The process by which the body transforms toxins from external or internal sources into substances that can be excreted from the body. Although detoxification takes place in a number of body systems, the principal organ of detoxification is the liver.

You no doubt are familiar with toxin sensitivity, because you or someone you know probably has had an adverse reaction to some medication. Adverse reactions of this type can arise from an inability to detoxify that specific substance. Doctors are now starting to recognize that adverse drug reactions may come from genetic characteristics that result in poor detoxification of specific families of drugs. New blood tests are being developed to analyze a patient's inability to detoxify certain substances before he or she is given a drug. Individuals who carry specific genetic characteristics may have difficulty detoxifying some anti-inflammatories, antibiotics, antidepressants, antiulcer medications or pain medications. These patients may have a greatly increased risk of adverse drug reactions.

Over-the-counter medications like acetaminophen and aspirin can also cause adverse reactions. Acetaminophen is the active ingredient in Tylenol and many other anti-inflammatory products. A recent report in the *New England Journal of Medicine* pointed out that accidental overdose of acetaminophen can occur in individuals who have consumed only the prescribed dose and have not overdosed.[6] The researchers found the unusual adverse reactions, which could be life-threatening, were a result of people's altered detoxification ability for the medication. The most extraordinary discovery in this research was that individuals who consumed alcohol or who were fasting when they took acetaminophen were much more susceptible to the toxic effects of the drug.

The breakthrough in understanding that emerged from this research is that foods contain specific nutrients that can help support the metabolic detoxification of drugs and chemicals. If a person who carries a specific detoxification-altering genetic sensitivity also has a poor-quality diet that is inadequate in specific nutrients, he or she may be at greatly increased risk of adverse reactions to these substances. Those reactions could range from chronic illness to severe, life-threatening responses.

The discovery that diet can modify detoxification function was a breakthrough in understanding the interrelationship between genes and diet. You are exposed to toxic substances throughout the course of your life. The question really is how your body will detoxify those substances before they produce injury. Responsibility for this detoxification process resides with the complex array of protective detoxification enzymes. Manufacture of these enzymes is determined not only by your genetic hard wiring, but also as a consequence of the foods you eat and the nutrients they contain. A few of the nutrients that play a role in promoting proper detoxification function are the amino acid glycine, the B-complex vitamin pantothenic acid, the sulfur-containing amino acids taurine and cysteine, and the minerals magnesium, selenium and zinc as well as the substance glutathione.

Some genetic characteristics are "constitutional," which means the expression of the genes that encode for these characteristics is not easily modified by changes in diet, lifestyle or environment. Other genetic characteristics, however, are inducible: their expression can be activated or suppressed by dietary, environmental or lifestyle exposures. Inducible genetic characteristics, which are sensitive to what you eat, form the basis of the genetic nutritioneering approach.

CONSTITUTIONAL: Characteristics produced constantly or in fixed amounts, regardless of environmental conditions or demand.

INDUCIBLE: Characteristics produced in varying quantities depending upon modification of gene expression.

Many specific detoxification processes in the body are tied to inducible genetic characteristics. This means the foods you eat and the nutrients within those foods have profound potential influence on how well your body can protect itself against toxins from the outside world or those produced by your own metabolism.

Alcohol consumption provides an illustration of the inducible nature of the genes. At modest levels of intake, alcohol is metabolized in the liver by action of the enzyme alcohol dehydrogenase. At high levels of intake the genes are induced to express a different detoxification enzyme (i.e., cytochrome P450 1e2), which, in its alcohol-metabolizing activity, releases oxidants that can damage the liver. Liver damage that is observed as a result of excessive alcohol intake is caused in part by this inducible factor from altered gene expression. A person can defend him/herself against the damaging effects of oxidants released after alcohol consumption by increasing his or her dietary intake of antioxidants like vitamin E, cysteine or glutathione, thereby providing protection against this inducible process.

DETOXIFICATION, GENOTYPES AND THE RISK OF DISEASE

A number of chronic health disorders may be a consequence of increased exposure to toxins and the body's reduced ability to promote the expression of genetic factors that provide detoxification. Scientists have identified specific genotypes that have a higher risk of certain diseases as a consequence of reduced detoxification ability. Cigarette smokers who carry in their genes poor detoxification may have a more toxic response and a greater cancer risk from smoking than those who got the genetic luck of the draw and have better detoxification ability. A study of breast cancer in women found a much higher incidence of breast cancer in smokers who had very poor detoxification ability as a consequence of the poor genetic expression of a detoxification enzyme called N-acetyltransferase.[7] Similarly, lung cancer risk in smokers is increased in individuals who have a genetically sluggish detoxification enzyme called glutathione transferase.[8]

Individuals who have these genetically sluggish detoxification enzyme systems may be at much higher risk of disease as a consequence of exposure to toxins in specific occupational or environmental situations. One recent study found that individuals who worked in foundries where they were exposed to gases that contain potentially toxic cancer-producing chemicals had a higher risk of cancer if they had poor detoxification abilities. This risk was further increased if they consumed other known toxic substances, such as those present in charbroiled meats.[9]

This brings up the concept of "total load." A single exposure or a single substance may not overburden the body and induce damage. It is the total exposure to toxic substances and how effectively they can be detoxified that determines relative health risk. A man who lives in a very polluted environment, pursues an occupation that exposes him to toxic substances, smokes cigarettes, drinks excessive alcohol, has a poor-quality diet and eats foods like charbroiled meats that are high in toxic substances adds constantly to the total load on his detoxification machinery. Eventually, it can be overwhelmed. If he has a sluggish detoxification system as a consequence of specific genetic uniqueness, he definitely becomes a potential candidate for heart disease, cancer, arthritis or neurological disease.

The medical and scientific communities now recognize that diet plays an important role in modifying detoxification ability. Poor-quality diets that are very high in toxic substances and low in nutrients that help support gene expression of detoxification enzymes result in increased risk of toxic reactions. Diets that are low in toxic substances and high in the nutrients that support the expression of inducible genes associated with detoxification, on the other hand, can make individuals much more tolerant of exposure to various toxins. Charbroiling meat, fish or poultry, for example, promotes the formation of a family of toxic substances called heterocyclic aromatic amines (HAAs).[10] These toxic substances can become cancer producing or alter the function of the immune and nervous systems. An efficiently functioning detoxification system provides protection against these toxic HAAs. High-fiber foods and those that are enriched in specific nutrients, such as antioxidants and bioflavonoids, can help protect against the damage induced by HAAs.

Toxic substances from foods, water or environment may also induce nervous system damage if they are not properly detoxified. Glynn Steventon and Rosemary Waring at the Neurology Department, University of Birmingham Medical School in England have found that individuals who are poor detoxifiers have increased risk of developing either Parkinson's or Alzheimer's disease.[11] The association between poor detoxification and Parkinson's disease was further confirmed by recent work at the Department of Clinical Neurology at the University of London School of Medicine.[12]

In children, susceptibility to infection and failure to thrive may also come from the reduced ability to detoxify foreign substances. A recent research study of children in Zimbabwe found that low detoxification ability was characteristic of children who had more severe infections and poor health prognosis. The researchers attributed this poor detoxification ability to chronic parasitic infections, generally poor nutrition and nutrient deficiencies that reduce genetic expression of detoxification enzymes and their function.[13]

DIETARY MODIFICATION— GENE EXPRESSION OF DETOXIFICATION

Research that links diet, genetic characteristics and disease susceptibility helps us understand that chronic diseases may not be mysterious or unexplainable. They may be the logical outcome of interactions among diet, lifestyle, environment, gene expression and detoxification ability. This research is pointing to a better understanding of the reactions to cycad flour in Guam. Residents of Guam who carry in their genetic inheritance factors the message for specific defects in detoxification may be much more sensitive to the substances in cycad flour that produce toxic nervous system reactions than those with better detoxification ability.

Although much of the metabolic detoxification process takes place in the liver, virtually every organ in the body carries out some level of detoxification. Organs other than the liver that play a major role in detoxification are the lining of the intestinal tract (called the gastrointestinal lumen) and the lining of the lungs. This makes obvious sense, because these two areas of the body are continually exposed to toxins that must be detoxified. Genetic characteristics related to poor detoxification in the liver also affect detoxification in the gastrointestinal lumen and lungs. A variety of methods have been developed to evaluate an individual's detoxification abilities. One useful method is to give a person a dose of a specific substance whose detoxification pathways are known and then to examine in the urine or saliva how effectively he or she has detoxified the substance. This tells the physician about the patient's relative detoxification ability and to which substances he or she may be sensitive as a consequence of altered detoxification.

One substance used in this type of challenge testing is caffeine. The detoxification of caffeine occurs principally in the liver, and the mechanism by which it occurs is very well understood. The genes that control the detoxification enzymes for caffeine (and other substances with similar characteristics) are well-known. If a person consumes a standard dose of caffeine and then his/her saliva is collected at intervals thereafter, the patient's relative detoxification ability can be determined by measuring certain substances in the saliva. This caffeine analysis method has been used to evaluate patients who are suffering from various diseases to determine whether poor detoxification is playing a role in the progression of the disease.

One study, which looked at patients with liver disease, found the severity of the disease and its future course could be predicted on the basis of how effectively individuals could detoxify caffeine.[14] Liver disease patients with very poor caffeine detoxification were thought to have a very poor prognosis, and those who had better caffeine detoxification, indicating improved genetic expression of detoxification enzymes, had a much better prognosis.

One of the first studies that indicated the important role of dietary substances in modifying detoxification ability occurred in 1954, when investigators from the University of Wisconsin reported that detoxification of caffeine-like substances could be enhanced by specific dietary factors.[15] These dietary factors included increased levels of protein, adequate levels of the B vitamins, improved antioxidant intake and proper mineral nutrition.

According to recent research conclusions, a variety of adjunctive or supplementary nutrients, along with the diet, can increase the genetic expression of detoxification enzymes or enhance their activity. Supplemental intake of the amino acid glycine, for example, has been found to be very helpful in assisting the detoxification of a variety of drugs and toxic chemicals.[16]

In the 1930s, A.J. Quick, M.D., a pathologist at a major New York university hospital studied the role of glycine supplementation in the recovery of individuals with a variety of chronic diseases, including liver disease. He concluded that oral daily doses of approximately 3,000 mg of glycine greatly improved aspects of detoxification function and resulted in improved recovery from liver disease and other illnesses.[17]

Since this pioneering work on the nutrient modification of detoxification ability took place, information about specific foods that can promote genetic expression of detoxification enzymes has advanced very rapidly. The food family that has received the most attention in this area is cruciferous vegetables, including cabbage, cauliflower, broccoli and Brussels sprouts. The unique phytochemicals in cruciferous vegetables cause them to give off a sulfur-like odor.

The phytochemicals in cruciferous vegetables include indole-3-carbinol, phenylisothiocyanate and 3-hydroxybutene, all of which are in the category of substances called glucosinolates. The cruciferous vegetable plant manufactures these phytochemicals while it is growing, for use in its development and defense mechanisms. When humans consume them, specific digestive enzymes break down these phytochemicals, and the release of these enzymes helps promote the genetic expression of human detoxification enzyme systems. Research has shown that glucosinolates are extraordinarily important in supporting proper detoxification system activity. The enhanced detoxification of potentially cancer-producing substances may be the reason cultures that have consumed higher levels of cruciferous vegetables have a lower incidence of cancer.

A controlled study at the gastroenterology department at University Hospital in the Netherlands found that individuals who consumed Brussels sprouts had considerably increased genetic expression and activity of the important detoxification enzyme glutathione S-transferase. When these individuals ate the same quantity of food that did not contain the same amount of glucosinolates from these vegetables, they did not have increased activity of glutathione S-transferase.[18] This important detoxification enzyme helps protect against the harmful effects of cancer-producing chemicals. The protective function of glutathione S-transferase may help explain why populations that eat more cruciferous vegetables have a lower incidence of colon cancer.

Another recent study found there are a variety of nutrients that might help promote proper gene expression of the detoxification enzyme systems.[19] This study evaluated the detoxification function of individuals with various ethnic backgrounds in Hawaii. It found nearly a 20-fold difference in detoxification ability from one individual to another. The data indicated that nearly one-third of the variation in detoxification ability from one individual to another was associated with dietary differences. Vitamins that were associated with better detoxification ability included vitamin C, vitamin E and the carotenoids (the red-orange pigment in vegetables).

This study also found the control of estrogen hormones in women was linked to the expression of various detoxification enzyme systems. Estrogen is synthesized principally in the ovaries of women, but it is detoxified and eliminated in the body through the genetic expression in the liver of detoxification enzymes. The toxic effects of estrogen, therefore, can result not just as a consequence of excessive production of estrogen from the ovaries or from the consumption of estrogen-containing medications, but also from the poor expression of detoxification enzymes in the liver. Estrogen hormones were better metabolized and regulated by women in this study whose livers expressed proper detoxification enzyme activity, and this characteristic could be linked to diet. Women who consume a nutrient-deprived diet that is low in B vitamins, trace minerals and antioxidants (such as vitamin C, vitamin E and carotenoids) may have much more difficulty metabolizing estrogen hormones. As a consequence, they may be at increased risk of hormone-related health problems, such as fibrocystic disease of the breast, premenstrual tension or even estrogen-induced cancer.

The discovery that diet and various nutrients play a role in promoting the genetic expression of detoxification enzymes has sparked keen interest on the part of scientists in many disciplines, including toxicology, molecular genetics and nutrition. Researchers in these disciplines have been working to identify foods that help promote proper balance of detoxification enzyme systems. One food family in the research spotlight is soy products. Recently published work at the department of food science and nutrition at the University of Minnesota found that feeding soy protein supplements to animals induced the genetic expression of important detoxification enzymes.[20] The fact that soy contains important properties that help protect against disease and promote good health is now well-recognized. Scientists have found soy contains a variety of phytochemicals, including antioxidants, enzyme inhibitors and hormone normalizing substances, all of which help protect against various diseases.

The most remarkable discovery is that soy also contains phytochemicals that communicate with the genes and assist in the genetic expression of detoxification enzyme function.[21] The soy phytochemicals that stimulate the genetic expression of detoxification enzymes may include such things as bioflavonoids, indoles, vitamin E, isothiocyanates and thiocarbamates. These natural substances that are produced by the soybean may work synergistically as antioxidants and as regulators of gene expression that help control the production of detoxification enzymes. This study concluded the intake of soy that would be required to produce this beneficial effect on detoxification enzymes in humans would be equivalent to a four-ounce serving of tofu or a six-ounce serving of soy milk or soybeans daily. Nutrition experts like Mark Messina, Ph.D., believe the evidence accumulating about the benefits of soy is so strong that the government should be recommending an intake of four to six ounces of soy products per day.[22] This is a practical level that most individuals can achieve by incorporating soy flour, soy milk, soybeans, textured soy protein, tempeh, miso, or tofu into their diets.

The bioflavonoid family heads the list of phytochemicals that research shows help promote gene expression of detoxification function. Bioflavonoids are a diverse family of phytochemicals found at some level in nearly every plant food. Certain bioflavonoids appear to have a much greater ability than others to influence the genetic expression of detoxification enzyme systems.[23] Green and black tea contain a variety of bioflavonoids that seem to have a significant influence on promoting the genetic expression of detoxification enzymes. Coffee does not contain meaningful levels of bioflavonoids.

Detoxification enzymes are classified in two general families: phase I and phase II enzymes. Toxicologists have determined that optimal detoxification occurs when these two systems are in balance with one another. Exposure to a toxic substance may communicate with the genes in a manner that increases the expression of phase I of the detoxification enzyme system without increasing phase II expression. The result can be an imbalance of detoxification that can be very harmful to the individual because the intermediate, partially detoxified substances produced by this imbalance are frequently more toxic than the initial substance to which the individual was exposed. Complete detoxification of a toxic substance requires balanced increases in the gene expression for the components of both the phase I and the phase II systems. The bioflavonoids promote the genetic expression of phase II detoxification enzymes, which helps balance the overall detoxification system and reduces the risk of accumulation of partially detoxified intermediate substances.

Bioflavonoids come not only from green and black tea, but also from such foods as grapes, onions, garlic and the fleshy inner peel of citrus fruits, particularly oranges.

The most important point to remember from this discussion is that foods interact with our genetic inheritance factors in very meaningful ways to express various phenotypes. We all carry unique genetic sensitivities to specific foods and the nutrients contained within them. You can design your diet to promote improved function if you know something about your genetic inheritance factors and your sensitivities to various foods, or you can regularly consume foods that are poorly matched to your genotype and thereby express function associated with disease. The remarkable conclusion emerging from research in laboratories and clinics around the world is that our genes are in constant communication with the foods we eat and are taking their orders from the nutrients and phytochemicals in our diet. The translation of your genotype to phenotype, therefore, depends intimately upon the foods that bathe your genes over the course of your life.

You cannot change your genes by the foods you eat, but you can change the expression of those genes and the way they relate to your health or disease patterns as you age. This new association between diet and genetic expression puts a much greater responsibility on you in selecting the foods you eat. In most cases, the impact of foods on your health is not like that of a drug. The effects of a drug can be felt immediately, but the impact of nutrients on genetic expression occurs over time, through a lifetime of dietary patterns and habits. Some individuals have such high genetic sensitivity to specific principles in foods that a one-time exposure to a food can cause a severe adverse reaction. This is sometimes the case with dairy or gluten sensitivity. For most individuals, however, reactions to foods are subtle and not well-recognized. Many people assume that because they do not immediately have a bad response from eating some food that everything is okay. They may be mistaken. The foods they have consumed over the years of their lives may speak to their genes in such a way as to promote an inappropriate phenotype. After several years, when they are middle-aged or older, this phenotype may result in the appearance of a disease of "unknown origin."

In the past, we did not understand our genes and how the expression of their characteristics could be influenced by environment and diet. This is no longer the case. Now we know that virtually thousands of substances in foods impact the genes in such a way as to either promote or suppress specific expressions. Your phenotype, therefore, is the result of your dietary history and the experiences you have had throughout your life.

Once again it is important to point out that not all genetic characteristics are inducible and capable of modification in the phenotype by your dietary habits. As we stated earlier, certain genetic characteristics are constitutional or hard-wired, and their expression cannot easily be modified. Many genetic characteristics are inducible, however, and their expression can be modified by the way the genes are treated with dietary factors, lifestyle and environmental exposures. These characteristics are the foundation of the Genetic Nutritioneering Program. Fortunately, most of the characteristics that determine health and vitality after mid-life are related to the inducible or modifiable genetic factors and not the hard-wired or constitutional factors. In fact, gerontologists now state that 75 percent of an individual's health after age 40 is dependent upon what the person has done to his or her genes, not to the genes themselves.

5

Genes, Blood Type and Disease

GENETIC NUTRITIONEERING IS BOTH A way of thinking about your health and a blueprint for designing your own health promotion program. It is built on key concepts derived from research in genetics over the past several decades. These concepts, which have been described in the first four chapters of this book, can be summarized in the following way:

1. Your genes don't change. Their expression does.
2. Specific characteristics may differ from individual to individual as a result of genetic polymorphism.
3. Each individual is biochemically unique, but family history is important in identifying general inheritance patterns.
4. Your genotype, when it is influenced by diet, lifestyle and environment, results in your phenotype.
5. Your overall dietary patterns and the vitamins, minerals, phytonutrients and accessory nutrients you consume modify gene expression.
6. Not all genetic characteristics can be changed. Some are constitutional and cannot be modified by diet and lifestyle.

7. Genetic characteristics are not "all or nothing." They can be seen in varying degrees of expression among individuals.

New genetic screening tests are being developed to help individuals determine their unique characteristics. The National Institutes of Health (NIH) recently convened a task force to examine the legal, ethical and social implications of genetic testing.[1] The NIH cautions that these tests should not be used to subject people to unfair discrimination. It points out, however, that scientifically valid tests can and should be used in the future of medicine for full predictive testing of an individual's modifiable health risks. Using the tests in this way will facilitate the development of personally tailored health promotion/disease prevention programs that will result in the prevention of disease and the improvement of function.

Many currently available tests have predictive value for determining genetic uniqueness. We may not think of the cholesterol-screening test as a genetic test, but in a sense it is. Regulation of cholesterol in the body is closely controlled by unique genetic characteristics, and cholesterol has an impact on the risk of heart disease, dementia and, potentially, even cancer. I will discuss the association between cholesterol and these conditions in later chapters of this book. Other commonly applied laboratory tests, such as the test for A, B, AB or O blood type, are also closely linked with genetic uniqueness.

Blood typing originated with the pioneering work of Karl Landsteiner, M.D. at the turn of the century.[2] Using properties in their blood, he was able to classify individuals into A, B and O groups. In a 1907 study, J. Jansky found a fourth group, which became known as AB.[3] Collectively, the blood types became known as ABO blood groups. Researchers found ABO blood groups were genetically transmitted from parents to children.

The classification of an individual's blood type is made possible by the fact that blood cells clump together or agglutinate when exposed to specific substances. Substances on the surface of red blood cells give those cells a unique chemical personality and are responsible for the unique pattern of agglutination that results in blood typing. Manufacture of these substances is controlled by the genes.

These substances that sit on the surface of red blood cells are also found in secretions throughout the body, as well as on the surface of many tissues, such as tissues of the intestinal tract, lungs and liver. These substances, called antigens, are specific proteins that impart a chemical message to the surface of the tissue or in the biological fluids, creating a unique reaction between the antigen and the external world.

Further study of the ABO blood groups revealed that not all individuals secrete their ABO antigens into biological fluids such as saliva. Therefore, there are what are known as "secretors" and "nonsecretors." We all carry the genetic characteristics of our ABO blood group on our red blood cells, however, and in specific tissues, regardless of our secretor or nonsecretor status.

For years scientists knew the ABO blood groups were of general interest in characterizing differences in the blood between one individual and another. It was of great value in determining the compatibility of blood donation from one individual to another. Giving blood of the wrong blood type could induce a toxic reaction because of the different chemical personalities of the blood cells. The blood cells of the recipient of the transfusion would signal his or her body to fight back against the foreign blood cells of the donor. The type O blood group has no antigens on the surface of the red cell. People with this blood type are considered "universal donors" and can give blood to those with type A, B, AB or O without risk of adverse reaction.

One remarkable observation that has been made over the years of studying the ABO blood groups is that the genotype of a specific blood type can be modified in its expression to the phenotype. For example, a woman with type A blood who has cancer or another serious illness may lose or suppress her A blood type and undergo a conversion to another phenotype such as type O. This is an example of how the genotype can be modified in its expression as a consequence of environmental factors to exhibit a significantly altered phenotype. In the 1920s a variety of medical researchers found that specific blood types could be correlated with various diseases.

Both W. Alexander, M.D. from University College Medical School in Scotland and J. Arthur Buchanan, M.D. from the Mayo Foundation in Minnesota independently noted a significant correlation between type O and peptic ulcers and type A and gastric cancer.[4,5] These observations have been supported by the pioneering work of many other medical investigators over the past 70 years. J.A. Fraser Roberts, M.D. from the London School of Hygiene and Tropical Medicine carried this research forward in the 1950s and 1960s and identified more specifically how the genetic factors that are related to the ABO blood groups are linked to specific disease risks.[6] Studies have linked ABO blood groups to a wide range of health problems, including toxemia of pregnancy, various cancers, diabetes and arthritis. As a whole, this research shows that ABO blood groups can be used to predict susceptibility to certain diseases.

Researchers have wondered about the connections among ABO blood type, an individual's secretor or nonsecretor status and disease risk. The answer seems to be that the antigens sitting on the surface of cells are part of a chemical recognition system used by various agents in the body's immune system to determine how to respond to an infectious organism. The "stickiness" of the surface of various organs and tissues to bacteria, viruses and other disease-producing agents is related to the ABO antigens that reside on its surface. Different bacteria have different degrees of stickiness on their surface and can either bind with specific ABO antigens or be repelled. This reaction is analogous to two bar magnets that are brought into proximity to one another. When two north or south poles of magnets are brought together they repel, but when the north and south poles are brought together, they attract. The A or B antigens on the surface of the cell are like a magnet, either attracting or repelling the attachment with certain surface proteins that sit on bacteria and other foreign invaders, such as parasites.

The intestinal tract is coated with protective mucus and secretions that can contain A and B blood group antigens, depending upon the individual's genetic uniqueness. For this reason, the intestines can be a home for infection with specific disease-producing bacteria or other toxic substances that enter through diet. The digestive tract, therefore, could be the place where the ABO blood types are in most direct contact with the external environment and can signal a reaction to the rest of the body that indicates there is an invader on board.

In the 1960s medical researchers found a relationship between ABO blood group type and alcoholism and heart disease, and they wondered how a blood type could be related to the origin of two health problems that appeared to be distinctly different.[7,8] Individuals with type A blood had a much higher incidence of both alcoholism and heart disease than those with type O, suggesting there was something unique about the type A antigen and the risk of these disorders.

In 1993 investigators at the Department of Clinical Immunology and Internal Medicine at the University of Copenhagen Medical School in Denmark reported an increased risk of heart disease in men with not only type A but also type B blood. They also found a close correlation between these blood types and alterations in blood sugar control and the risk of diabetes.[9] There was a much closer correlation between alcohol consumption and heart disease among these individuals with A and B blood types than among type O individuals. This was an interesting observation because it was a general belief that modest alcohol consumption reduces heart disease risk by increasing the level of favorable HDL cholesterol. In individuals with specific blood type characteristics, however, alcohol consumption seems to increase the risk of heart disease as a consequence of inducing diabetes.

NUTRITIONAL RELATIONSHIP TO ABO GROUP AND DISEASE

In 1997, Peter D'Adamo, N.D. made a significant contribution to understanding the clinical importance of ABO blood type in his book, *Eat Right for Your Type*.[10] He suggested that individuals with a specific blood type react to specific foods because of an imbalance between the molecules in the food and the cell surface antigens of the digestive tract present in various blood groups. This incompatibility leads to the body's fighting itself, and the result is increased risk of various diseases. As Dr. D'Adamo points out, research indicates that various blood types are also more susceptible to infections with specific bacteria, worms or amoebic agents. Scientists found, for example, that blood type A antigen is identical to the *Pneumococcus* bacteria, while type O is more closely related to infection with *Yersinia* bacteria. Type B has been found to be much more susceptible to urinary tract infections with *Pseudomonas, Klebsiella* and *Proteus* as a consequence of the increased attachment of these bacteria to tissues that are coated with type B antigen.

Diet plays a role in these risks of infection, not only because contaminated food is a source of infection, but also, and more significantly, because food contains substances that can initiate attachment of bacteria or adverse reactions with blood group antigens that are associated with disease.

One class of dietary substances that creates this reaction with blood group antigens that coat the digestive tract is the lectins. Lectins, which are found in the seeds of various plants, have a chemical personality similar to the blood group antigens. In a sense, specific plant lectins can crossreact with the A or B antigens that line the digestive tract. The result can be specific, genetically linked food sensitivities that increase the probability of adherence of an infectious bacterium to the digestive lining, creating infection or amplifying an immune reaction that can result in digestive inflammation and generalized inflammation throughout the body.

LECTINS: Any of a group of hemagglutinin proteins found primarily in plant seeds which bind specifically to the receptor sites on the surface of cells.

In a sense, conditions like rheumatism and chronic inflammation could be aggravated by an adverse reaction between a blood group antigen lining the surface of the digestive tract and a specific lectin from foods. In the past some individuals have called this a "food allergy," but it would be more accurate to call it an adverse food reaction. Some lectins can induce an insulin-like effect on the body, altering the body's control of insulin and blood sugar and creating diabetic-like responses. It seems surprising that principles such as lectins in foods can communicate through the cell surface antigens on the digestive tract to the body's immune system and to hormones such as insulin, thus regulating overall body function and the risk of disease. But results of research that have accumulated during the last 40 years have continued to support this association.

The connection of food lectins to ABO blood type and disease risk is further amplified when an individual is exposed to potentially infectious bacteria. Bacteria have antigens sitting on their surface, and those antigens can crossreact with either type A or type B blood antigens and food lectins. This association indicates that diets that contain lectins that are incompatible with a specific blood type antigen could increase the risk of bacterial adherence to the digestive tract and subsequent infection. A number of factors that help control the immune function of the digestive tract may indicate why one individual develops a digestive infection when exposed to a tainted food and another individual does not. The lectin connection to ABO blood type is certainly one of the contributors to this risk of infection.

Similarly, infection with worms and amoeba such as *Giardia* is also related not only to ABO blood type but also to dietary lectins that can increase the potential adherence of these organisms to the lining of the digestive tract.

Plant lectins, some level of which are found in nearly every plant food we eat, are a group of specific proteins called glycoproteins (which means the protein is bound to a specific type of sugar), which display a wide range of properties. They share in common with A and B blood type antigens the ability to recognize and combine with specific substances on the surface of cells. In a sense, they are the tiny "bar magnets" that attach to compatible magnetic sites of the ABO blood type on the cell surface. Potatoes, peas, beans, soybeans, a variety of nuts, wheat germ and tomatoes contribute significant amounts of lectins to the diet. Lectins are released as you chew and digest foods, and they can survive passage through the gastrointestinal tract. They can also survive cooking and food processing.

Because it is so common, the tomato lectin is one of the most studied lectins. Exposure to tomato lectins in the U.S. population is significant, because every American eats approximately 74 pounds of tomatoes a year. Thus the average person ingests about 100 mg of tomato lectins a year.[11] Because their chemical personality is similar to that of blood group antigens, tomato lectins can interact with the lining of the intestinal tract and produce symptoms ranging from gastrointestinal inflammation, to malabsorption of nutrients, to alerting the body's immune system to produce inflammation. Some individuals with specific genetic inheritance factors may therefore be very sensitive to food products containing tomatoes and should avoid them in their diet.

How do you know if you are sensitive to tomato lectins? By eliminating tomato products from the diet and seeing if arthritis-like symptoms go away you can analyze your own sensitivity to tomato lectins.

VEGETABLES AND FOOD SENSITIVITY

The fact that lectins are found primarily in vegetable foods has caused confusion for some people. Many health-conscious individuals have tried to increase the grain, seed and vegetable components of their diets only to experience allergic reactions, intestinal discomfort and chronic inflammation. Some of these reactions could be caused by specific food allergies, such as the reactions caused by gluten in grains. Some people, however, may have specific blood group antigens that line the surface of their intestinal tract making them more susceptible to food lectin reactions.

Our sensitivity to certain vegetables and grains may be tied to our genetic inheritance and to its linkage to our ABO blood group type. In *Eat Right for Your Type*, Dr. D'Adamo pointed out that individuals with type O blood, in contrast to those with type A, B or AB, more often have reactions to lectin-containing foods. Type O is the most common blood type in the United States, suggesting that many people may be ill-suited to adopting a vegetarian diet, with its higher levels of lectins.

This information does not suggest that no one with type O blood should be a vegetarian and no one with type A blood should eat meat. Instead, it indicates that response to specific foods is an individual matter. We should not designate foods as "good" or "bad" but should tailor our diet to our unique genetic needs. "Food for one may be poison for another," as the old adage goes. ABO blood types are only one indicator of the unique way an individual could respond to specific characteristics in the diet.

Most people would do well to increase the vegetable component of their diets and reduce their intake of animal products. The vegetables you include in your diet should reflect your individual immune tolerance to these foods. Because we are genetically so different from one another, there is no such thing as a food that everyone can tolerate. If you have problems of arthritis-like pain of unknown origin, you should evaluate the possibility that certain foods in the diet may be contributing to the problem. Start by evaluating wheat, corn, oats, citrus, tomato, dairy, beef and chicken to see how your symptoms respond after eliminating these foods one at a time for three or four days.

This discussion also has particular meaning for you if you have chronic digestive disorders or inflammation, even after you eliminate the common food allergens like dairy and wheat from your diet. If that description fits, you should also consider eliminating specific lectin-containing foods, such as wheat germ, tomatoes, navy beans, soybeans, green peas and lentils from your diet to see if the reduction in lectins results in a reduction of symptoms of digestive disorders or chronic inflammation.[12]

More than 10 years ago, Dr. D.L.J. Freed, a lecturer in immunology at the University of Manchester in England, wrote about lectins in the *British Medical Journal.*

> Having survived at least partially the assaults of cooking and digestion, can ingested lectins cause disease? We do not know for sure, but many lectins are powerfully poisonous or inflammatory or both. They are particularly suited to evoke autoimmune responses, since they can bind for very long periods of time to tissues with a slow turnover, altering their antigenic composition, and virtually all body cells and most enzymes are susceptible to lectin binding. Lectins have been used to produce animal models of chronic rheumatoid arthritis, extrinsic allergic alveolitis, malabsorption of vitamin B12, and acute enteritis [digestive inflammation] with cachexia. But the idea [that lectins cause disease] is too new to have been seriously evaluated by science; lectins are still causes in search of diseases.[13]

Several new drugs are now being tested as anti-inflammatory and pain medications whose principal mode of action is to block the sites of attachment of lectins and molecules that sit on the surface of bacteria from their attachment to antigenic substances that coat the surface of the digestive tract. It is remarkable that a message initiated by the binding of a foreign substance to the lining of the intestinal tract could trigger a cascade of events that result in pain. This story is not as remarkable as it might seem, however. I will discuss the topic at greater length in Chapter 8.

One lectin-blocking pain medication that has been studied is a carbohydrate-like molecule called amiprilose. Research has shown that this synthetic carbohydrate has anti-inflammatory effects, and in human clinical trials it reduced the pain of inflammatory arthritis. Its mode of action is not completely understood, but it appears to work by blocking the binding sites on the lining of the intestinal tract to molecules like lectins and bacteria, which could induce an inflammatory immune response.[14] Given this research, it is not unreasonable to suggest that designing the appropriate diet to match the chemical personality of your intestinal tract makes good sense.

ULCERATION OF THE INTESTINAL TRACT AND ABO BLOOD TYPE

One of the most remarkable medical examples of this concept of an intestinal bacterium's attaching itself to the lining of intestines and triggering inflammation is peptic ulcer disease. Until very recently the medical community believed that ulceration of the portion of the upper intestinal tract called the duodenum was a result of stress, alcohol consumption and a high-fat diet which resulted in excessive secretion of stomach acid and, in a sense, burned a hole in the intestinal lining. The result, peptic ulcer disease, causes pain, bleeding and potentially life-threatening perforation of the intestines. To respond to this disease model, drug companies developed what are called H2-blocking drugs, which worked specifically by reducing the production of stomach acid, thereby lowering the risk of damage to the intestines.

H2-blocking drugs were hailed as major breakthroughs in pharmacology because before they became available the only treatment for inflammation of the intestinal tract was drinking milk or taking antacids. Although milk and antacids could relieve some symptoms, they did not prevent ulceration of the intestinal tract and serious disease in many people. The new drugs were hailed as medical miracles, however, because they really did prevent intestinal inflammation and bleeding. Because intestinal inflammation is so common, H2-blocking drugs rapidly became the most prescribed medication in developed countries around the world. For a time, drug companies, gastroenterologists, ulcer patients and hospitals were all satisfied with the use of these medications.

The status quo was shattered by a family doctor in Australia named Barry Marshall, M.D. Working with a colleague who was a pathologist, Dr. Marshall discovered a very strong association between ulceration of the intestines and infection with a bacterium called *Helicobacter pylori*.[15] Because Marshall was not a research scientist, his observations of the connection between the bacteria and stomach ulceration were not taken seriously by his medical colleagues, who were convinced that ulceration of the intestinal tract resulted from stress, alcohol consumption and high-fat diet. It had nothing to do with bacterial infection. Marshall, however, was a tireless and undaunted investigator, and he threw himself wholeheartedly into understanding the continued association between *H. pylori* and intestinal ulceration.

Marshall finally identified the specific organism that was associated with this inflammation. He believed so strongly that this organism could create the disease that he consumed billions of these organisms and produced the disease in himself. Respected gastroenterologists who followed the progress of Marshall's disease confirmed that by self-administering an oral dose of the bacterium he had transformed his healthy digestive tract into an inflamed one.

Once the cause of the disease had been observed, there was a need for treatment. Over the past 70 years antibacterial medications have been developed to treat different types of infections. Marshall's doctors tested the sensitivities of *H. pylori* to different antibiotics and designed a treatment regimen using a combination of medications. When Marshall undertook this multiple antibiotic program his stomach ulceration cleared up and the infection disappeared.

The result was a revolution that occurred almost overnight in thinking about the origin of peptic ulcer disease.

Over the next five years, Marshall's hypothesis was confirmed. An industry that had been selling three and one-half billion dollars of H2-blocking drugs each year contracted rapidly as they were replaced by treatment that employed antibiotics to kill *H. pylori*. This is one of the most remarkable stories in recent medicine. It shows the power of observation and the strength of conviction of an investigator who worked against all odds to change accepted thinking. H2-blocking drugs may have been very profitable for the drug companies because individuals had to continue taking these drugs indefinitely. Their use did not lead to optimal patient health outcomes, however, because they did not deal with the cause of the disease.

The lingering question is why some people get *H. pylori* infection and peptic ulcer disease and others do not. This bacterium is universally present in our environment, and we are all exposed to it. In fact, *H. pylori* grows around the teeth and gums in many individuals. Part of the reason why some people develop infection and most others do not despite constant exposure to *H. pylori* is related to the immune function of the digestive tract. When individuals have the proper mucous lining in their intestinal tract and good immune function, the *H. pylori* organism has less opportunity to adhere to the mucous membranes, grow and create the inflammatory response.

Another part of the explanation is that the *H. pylori* organism is more likely to adhere to the intestinal lining of individuals with type O blood than those individuals with blood type A, B or AB. The relationship to blood type helps explain the very low incidence of peptic ulcer disease in equatorial Africa despite the very high level presence of *H. pylori*. Type O blood is very uncommon in this region so the organism has less opportunity to adhere and multiply in the digestive tracts of these individuals.

This research has led to the understanding that intestinal infection with specific bacteria, which could produce both localized digestive disorders and general inflammation that could be called "allergic arthritis," may be prevented. Prevention of these disorders is possible by improving digestive function, bolstering the immune defense of the lining of the digestive tract and blocking the adherence of bacteria to the digestive lining. Studies now indicate that a number of nutritional substances may help block the adherence of bad bacteria like *H. pylori* to the digestive lining. These nutritional substances, called oligosaccharides, are starchy substances that are present in foods like chicory and Jerusalem artichoke flour. Preliminary studies indicate that oral consumption of these nondigestible carbohydrates in supplement form can help protect against adherence of these unfriendly bacteria and reduce the risk of infection.[16]

The discussion in this chapter indicates the power of the genetic nutritioneering concept. By understanding something about your family health history, your own personal response to your diet, and your genetic uniqueness as expressed by such things as your ABO blood type and food reactions, you can design a diet that will become your friend, not your foe.

Many people do not understand the extraordinary relationship between their health and disease patterns and the messages communicated to their genes by substances in their diet. The example of the ABO blood type and its relationship to food lectins is just one of many examples we will discuss in the following chapters that relate the concept of genetic nutritioneering to prevention of age-related diseases. Research in molecular biology and genetics is making it possible to reinterpret old information, such as the ABO blood group, and use it to help design specific nutritional programs to promote health and prevent disease. In the next chapter we will explore how these concepts can be used to prevent premature aging.

RESISTING THE AGING PROCESS

MOST OF US BELIEVE WE age by genetically predetermined processes that are beyond our control. We admire those people who are still healthy and vigorous in their 80s and shake our heads over others who begin to look old and tired by age 50. And all the while we cross our fingers and hope we have gotten the genetic luck of the draw that will place us in the former category. However, recent scientific breakthroughs indicate that there are actually steps we can take to shape our own aging processes.

James Fries, M.D., a professor of preventive medicine at Stanford University Medical School, pointed out that, like other animals, humans do lose certain aspects of physiological function as they age.[1] The ability of the heart and lungs to transport oxygen in the blood to the various organs of the body diminishes. The kidneys become less able to filter poisons from the blood. Strength declines. Short-term memory and the ability to analyze complex situations become compromised. Eyesight, hearing and skin elasticity grow poorer with age. Before you become too discouraged, however, read on. Dr. Fries also pointed out that almost every one of the characteristics we associate with aging can be modified by nutritional, lifestyle and environmental factors.

Irwin Rosenberg, M.D. and William Evans, Ph.D. are professors of nutrition and medicine at Tufts University in the Human Nutrition Center on Aging in Boston. They believe these so-called biomarkers of aging can all be improved if an individual takes control of the expression of his or her genes and uses the tools we describe in the genetic nutritioneering approach. As they succinctly state, "You can adopt a pattern of activity and eating that maximizes your ability to age much more slowly."[2]

Taking responsibility for your own healthy aging will not only benefit you, but it will also help reduce unnecessary medical expenditures. Previously unimagined numbers of people are living to be very old in America. At the turn of the century, only 4 percent of the U.S. population was over the age of 65. Today that number is 13 percent. Life expectancy at birth in the United States has climbed from 47 years in 1900 to more than 76 years today. Gerontologists indicate it is likely to reach 83 years by the year 2050.[3]

If we plan to live longer, we should also plan to live healthier as we age. Incidence of a number of chronic disorders, including arthritis, dementia, high blood pressure, stroke and emphysema, is falling. These indicators of lower disease incidence in older age have been attributed to a combination of improved lifestyle, diet and environment, coupled with better medical care for the elderly. We are also redefining what it means to grow older. We are not satisfied to retire to rocking chairs and bingo games. In the "new gerontology," we want to travel, remain active in social pursuits and sports, and go back to school to develop new skills. These expectations require a greater functional ability than simply the absence of disease.

Dr. John Rowe stated recently,

There are significant qualitative as well as quantitative differences between age-related (senescent) and disease-related (pathological) processes . . . Health and functional status in late life are increasingly seen as under our own control. The stage is set for major community-based intervention studies designed to enhance the likelihood of older persons not only to avoid disease and disability, but to truly age successfully.[4]

The key, as Dr. Fries pointed out, is to maintain functional reserve in the organs of the body so they can resist the inevitable stresses of life that can cause loss of function and disease.

ORGAN RESERVE

Young people have considerable reserve of function in every organ beyond what they need to maintain basic life processes. They mobilize these reserves when their bodies are under stress from infection, trauma or injury to help them remain healthy. With age, however, organ reserve declines, and the stresses they could formerly accommodate by mobilizing their reserves now overtake them and produce the "disease" of aging. According to Drs. Fries, Rosenberg, Evans and other medical investigators, however, individuals can regain that lost organ reserve with the right health promotion program, matched to their genetic need.

According to a recent article in the *British Medical Journal,*

Taking all diseases together, the total death rate in developed countries such as Britain is 500 times greater at the age of 80 than at age 20. Why? What biological mechanisms account for this vast difference in mortality between old and young adults? And since so many major diseases are much more common in old than in young adults, does this imply that there must be some common biological process called "aging" that causes all of these large differences in mortality? Our answer, particularly for cancer, is that it need not do so.[5]

Writing in a recent issue of *Science* magazine, Dr. Caleb Finch, a professor at the Andrus Gerontology Center at the University of Southern California, described the complex role of genetics in determining life span, health and disease patterns. He points out, however, that extensive research in the past several decades indicates the heritability of life span is relatively minor. Our genes alter how our metabolism functions in response to certain environmental and lifestyle factors, which then control our disease patterns and our life expectancy. He concludes, "The relatively minor heritability of human life span at advanced ages, and the variable penetrance of genetic risk factors imply that choice of lifestyle profoundly influences the outcomes of aging."[6]

Older-aged individuals are frequently blamed for placing a disproportionate burden on medical services by their illness and functional disability, causing healthcare costs to soar. Recent research indicates this belief is factually incorrect. Aging itself is not to blame for the increasing costs of health care. That responsibility belongs instead to those individuals who are very ill and are moving toward premature death. Chris van Weel, M.D. and Joop Michels, M.D. from the Department of Social Medicine in the Netherlands, recently wrote, "Aging is, in our view, a powerful marker of the health of a population, and it should not be stigmatized as a waste, a burden on society. Our hypothesis is that it is dying rather than old age that implies high costs."[7] More and more research over the past decade has indicated that we carry a number of myths concerning aging, with the most powerful myth being that we can do nothing about it.[8]

In this book we provide some powerful tools to modify the way your genes express their function throughout the whole of the aging process. Proper application of the concepts presented here can increase not only your life expectancy but also your functional ability throughout life. Although she is unfamiliar with the concepts of genetic nutritioneering, Ella Scotchmer is an example of the success of such a program.[9] At age 102, Ella lives independently in

London. She attributes her longevity, which is not common in her family, to a healthy diet and "never having borne a grudge." She is still actively involved in community affairs, assisting people who are much younger than she is and teaching at a senior center. By following a lifelong diet of unrefined whole foods, remaining active, keeping a positive outlook and controlling stress, Ella Scotchmer has enabled the genes she inherited to be expressed into a healthy phenotype for more than a century. Without access to complex science and the understanding of molecular biology, she has designed her own genetic nutritioneering program and applied it throughout her adult life. And she continues to reap the rewards.

AGING AND OUR HORMONES

Some people believe the secret to aging is as simple as protecting against the loss of hormones that are associated with youth, such as testosterone in men and estrogen in women. A recent *Newsweek* cover article featured the headline, "Testosterone—Super Hormone Therapy: Can It Keep Men Young?"[10] Other publications have described the benefits in maintaining youth by supplementing with the hormones dehydroepiandrosterone (DHEA), melatonin, pregnenolone, insulin-like growth factor (IGF) and human growth hormone (human chorionic gonadotropin, or HCG). The assumption is that because younger people have higher levels of these hormones and older people have lower levels, providing these hormones in supplemental doses to older people will keep them young.

Supplementation with hormones in specific cases can, without question, produce remarkable benefits in the function of older individuals. Hormone replacement therapy in postmenopausal women, for example, can help them maintain bone reserve and prevent osteoporosis, improve memory and mental function, and even help reduce the risk of heart disease. Similarly, testosterone supplementation can help certain older men improve their muscle strength, vitality and quality of life. The following three hormonal systems definitely show decreasing levels throughout the aging process:

1. Sex hormones (estrogen in women and testosterone in men)
2. DHEA
3. Growth hormone and insulin-like growth factor

It is questionable, however, whether the decline in these hormones to levels that reduce quality of life and functional ability is a natural consequence of aging or a result of altered gene expression through poor choices in lifestyle, diet and environment.[11]

You should not treat the subject of hormone replacement therapy lightly. Your body's hormones are complex messenger molecules that "talk to your genes" to awaken some genetic messages and put others to sleep. They are what are called signal transducers. Hormones communicate messages from the organs in which they are produced (for example, estrogen from women's ovaries and testosterone from men's testes), to all the other organs and tissues of the body, including the brain. If hormone replacement therapy is given incorrectly to older individuals and not properly balanced, it can overwhelm the body's messenger system and have adverse effects, including increased risk of cancer, heart disease, arthritis or other health disorders we associate with aging.

SIGNAL TRANSDUCER: A substance that translates messages from one cell to another.

A few years ago people got very excited about replacement of human growth hormone in older individuals. Early reports told of men achieving miraculous improvements in muscle tone and strength after just a few injections. Human growth hormone became the miracle drug of the aged, and sales soared. As information accumulated, however, many of the optimistic stories proved to be misleading. Improvements in strength and vitality after prolonged administration of HCG diminished, and side effects, such as the onset of diabetes, appeared.

Similarly, if it is not very carefully controlled, estrogen replacement therapy in postmenopausal women can increase the risk of endometrial and breast cancer. Testosterone replacement therapy in men can increase the risk of heart disease and prostate cancer. Considered as a whole, the pharmacological modification of aging may have inherent risks. The body's genetic messages may be overwhelmed by the administration of too high a level of hormones or an imbalance of hormones that delivers the wrong messages to the genes.

The result is a dilemma. Research has shown that improving hormone levels in older individuals can reduce the risk of a number of age-related diseases and improve general health and vitality. Estrogen replacement, for example, has led to marked improvement in the cognitive skills of women with memory disabilities.[12] Similarly, in men, low blood hormone levels of testosterone, IGF and HCG are predictive for poor health and vitality with aging.[13] Balancing hormones, therefore, can have a dramatically positive impact on aging and help the genes continue to express their full potential throughout life. The $64 question is: can the genetic messages that exist in a younger person that go to sleep as we age be awakened so that hormones can be maintained naturally rather than depending upon pharmacology for their replacement?

As I pointed out earlier, the genetic messages for all phases of your life, including youth, will remain locked into your genes, even when you are 80, 90 or 100 years old. Gerontologists believe that in the near future we will find ways to unlock these youthful messages from our genes and discover a whole new approach for the treatment of age-related diseases. Those technologies are not yet available, but you do have the tools of nutrition, lifestyle, exercise and environmental modification with which to enhance genetic expression, provide yourself with more youthful messages and reduce your biological age.

As a woman moves into menopause, she typically experiences symptoms of hot flushes, sweating, mood swings and low energy. These symptoms are particularly likely to occur if she is under considerable emotional stress, has poor exercise tolerance, is a smoker, consumes alcohol in excess, eats a poor quality diet and takes a number of medications. These differences occur, in part, because a woman's body produces estrogen not only in the ovaries, which lose function at menopause, but also in the adrenal glands. The factors mentioned above place considerable stress on a woman's body. As a consequence, her adrenal glands cannot produce estrogen because they are being used almost exclusively to manufacture the stress hormone cortisol. The result is that the woman experiences a much more difficult transition to menopause. Ironically, she then may require more medications and early hormone replacement therapy. She could have avoided these complications by reducing stress in her life, improving her diet and exercising regularly. This is another example of the power each of us has to control gene expression and ensure optimal function.

Thyroid function provides a good example of the relationship between the function of organs that produce hormones and the aging process. Your thyroid gland is your body's thermostat. It controls your metabolic activity and your cellular vitality. Located at the base of the neck, the thyroid gland secretes a variety of hormones, including thyroxin (T_4) and triiodothyronine (T_3). If the thyroid gland malfunctions and cannot control the release of these hormones, the body's metabolism is adversely affected. The affected individual can experience low energy, poor muscle function, altered digestive function, constipation, hair loss, loss of skin integrity, menstrual irregularities if she is a woman, and alterations in heart function.

A recent study found the thyroid glands of healthy 100-year-olds functioned like those of much younger individuals.[14] In contrast, the thyroid function of much younger individuals who were ill was significantly altered. Most important, these ill individuals' bodies were producing proteins (i.e., antithyroid antibodies) designed to destroy the thyroid gland. In these unhealthy people the immune system produced the proteins as if the thyroid gland were a "foreigner" that the body must attack and destroy. In medical terms, this is called autoimmunity; the individuals became allergic to their own thyroid glands. The healthy 100-year-olds did not display this characteristic. This suggests that an important feature of healthy aging is to prevent the body from becoming allergic to itself and from developing autoimmunity. Disorders associated with autoimmunity include rheumatoid arthritis, lupus erythematosus and myasthenia gravis. Chronic autoimmunity, however, seems to be associated with lowered organ function and increased biological aging.

AUTOIMMUNITY: A condition characterized by a specific humoral or cell-mediated immune response against constituents of the body's own tissues.

How does the body become allergic to itself? Researchers all over the world are actively seeking the answer to this question. We will consider that question in greater detail in Chapter 8, but the evidence suggests that when inappropriate gene messages are uncovered by exposure to toxic substances, stress or agents that activate the immune system, the risk of autoimmunity increases. Healthy aging is associated with keeping the function of the immune system properly balanced and allowing hormone-producing organs like the thyroid gland to engage in their proper function.

FREE RADICAL–INDUCED AGING

The explanation for the loss of certain hormones and the development of autoimmunity with age may emerge from the work of doctors like Dr. Rajindar Sohal and his colleagues in the Department of Biological Sciences at Southern Methodist University.[15] For many years these scientists have been working on the genetics of fruit flies and examining how these lowly insects age. To the casual observer this research may appear to have no relevance to human aging, the loss of hormone function and autoimmunity. The fruit fly, *Drosophila melanogaster*, however, is an important animal model for human aging. It is one of very few animals whose cells are all of the same chronological age. The aging of the whole animal, therefore, can be studied by looking at the individual cells of its body. This is very different from the human. Our cells are of different ages, depending upon when they are replaced. Our skin is sloughed off and replaced by new cells every few days, for example, so the age of our skin cells may be very different from that of our brain or liver cells.

Researchers have found the aging of the cells of the fruit fly is directly related to the ability of those cells to protect themselves from damage by free radicals. A free radical is an unstable and therefore highly reactive molecule. It is missing an electron and is constantly searching for another molecule with which to pair up. If it can't readily find one, it steals an electron from another molecule, thereby damaging that molecule which itself becomes a free radical. Unless it is detoxified, the reaction continues, damaging tissues and organs. This process occurs rapidly in animals that are undergoing accelerated biological aging.

The theory of free radical aging was first advanced by Denham Harman, M.D., Ph.D. at the University of California at Berkeley in 1956. In a landmark article titled "Aging: A Theory Based on Free Radical and Radiation Chemistry," Dr. Harmon described research indicating that various free radicals produced in biological systems could be the chemical substances that cause the damage we see in the aging of cellular proteins, genetic materials and the membranes that hold cells together.[16] He pointed out that animals possess sophisticated antioxidant systems to help defend against free radical damage. A number of antioxidants occur in the diet as essential nutrients. They include vitamin E (tocopherol), vitamin C (ascorbic acid) and beta-carotene (pro-vitamin A). Animals with low antioxidant protection, Dr. Harmon explained, experienced increased damage by free radicals and had accelerated biological aging.[17]

A number of enzymes work with antioxidant nutrients to defend against free radical damage. These enzymes include superoxide dismutase, glutathione peroxidase, glutathione reductase and catalase, each of which is manufactured in cells from a message taken from the genes. These enzymes are also activated by specific nutrients, including the trace minerals zinc, manganese, copper and iron. The antioxidant defense system of your body, which helps protect you against accelerated aging from free radical damage and oxidant stress, is a combination of your genetic inheritance coupled with your diet, lifestyle and environmental exposures.

Dr. Sohal found that if a fruit fly's genes carry the inherited message for producing more antioxidant enzyme protection it will experience a much lower rate of biological aging and a one-third extension of life span. This is in contrast to the shorter lives of those fruit flies that have poor expression of antioxidant protection.[18]

A diet that is rich in antioxidants, including vitamins E, C, carotenoids and flavonoids, plus trace minerals like zinc, manganese and copper, can help defend against free radical-induced oxidative stress.

If the organs of your body are not defended by sufficient antioxidants against oxidative stress, they lose function over time, and their ability to produce hormones or control immune function is lost. After several years, free radical-induced organ damage can result in the appearance of "twisted molecules." These unnatural twisted molecules can activate the body's immune system to combat misidentified foreign invaders, resulting in damage to organs like the thyroid from autoimmunity.

The effects of free radical-induced damage can be seen in all organs of the body, but particularly in those organs that have the highest levels of oxygen, such as the brain, heart, liver, gastrointestinal tract, kidneys, immune system, hormone-secreting system, lungs and blood. If the body's antioxidant systems are not able to keep up with the production of free radical substances, over years the genes will modify their expression, and a new phenotype of accelerated aging results. This new phenotype is associated with the loss of hormone function, increased autoimmunity, decreased skin elasticity and reduced organ reserve in the brain, heart, lungs and liver.

Even excessive skin wrinkling is related to accelerated free radical production. Medical studies have shown that wrinkling of the skin occurs many times faster in smokers than nonsmokers.[19] Smoking increases the blood level of free radicals, which create damage to collagen and elastin, the proteins that hold the skin together. Smoking-induced free radical damage to these proteins causes small puckers or gathers to develop in the protein which pull the skin with the protein that lies beneath it, resulting in what we observe as a wrinkle. The same phenomenon occurs with sun-induced damage to the skin. The sun's ultraviolet rays penetrate the top layers of the skin, damage the collagen and elastin that lie below the surface and cause them to become crosslinked, producing wrinkles. The genes of the individual do not necessarily encode for the message of accelerated skin wrinkling. Instead, lifestyle and dietary factors that accelerate or retard the effects of free radicals contribute extensively to aging of the skin and wrinkling. These modifiable factors include cessation of smoking, minimal use of alcohol, lower-fat diets and increased antioxidants in the diet (including vitamins E, C, carotenes and flavonoids). Lowering stress also reduces the level of free radicals in the body.

The mitochondria are the source of most free radical substances produced in the body. The mitochondrion is the furnace or energy powerhouse of the cell. Mitochondria exist within the cells as the sites where food is converted into energy in the presence of oxygen. They might be thought of as the lungs of the cells, the organelles where oxygen is taken in, combined with the protein, carbohydrate and fat components of diet, and converted through the process of aerobic metabolism (respiration) into metabolic energy. This energy is used for all functions of the body, including muscle contraction, nervous system activity, reproduction, cell repair, digestion and immune defense. The structure of the mitochondrion and its relationship to other cellular organelles is shown in Figure 1.

Douglas Wallace, Ph.D., professor of molecular genetics and director of the Center for Molecular Medicine at the Emory University Medical School, has proposed that the function of the mitochondrion and how it processes oxygen may be the key for understanding aging and age-related diseases.[20] Dr. Wallace describes the example of a seemingly healthy five-year-old boy who inexplicably began to lose his hearing. He was entirely deaf by age 18. From ages 5 to 18 he was diagnosed as hyperactive and he suffered occasional seizures. By the time he was 23, his vision had declined.

Figure 1. The Mitochondrion

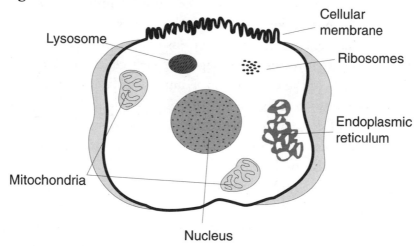

Mitochondria . . .

1. generate energy for detoxification process.

2. produce reactive oxygen species (oxidative stress).

He had cataracts, glaucoma and progressive deterioration of the retina. His seizures became severe, and his kidneys failed. He died at age 28 from conditions we would normally associate only with the very elderly. The root of his problems was found to be an alteration in the way the mitochondria utilized oxygen and manufactured cellular energy. His mitochondria were producing extraordinary levels of free radical oxidants which damaged his entire body.

Research on this case history and others like it has led to the recognition that the human aging process may be tied to the function of the mitochondria throughout life.

MITOCHONDRIAL DNA AND AGING

In 1963 researchers made the revolutionary discovery that the mitochondria harbor their own genetic information. Until then scientists believed all genetic information of the body was locked into chromosomes and genes found in the nucleus of the cell. (See Figure 1.) Geneticists at first resisted the suggestion that genetic information existed outside of the chromosomes, but it was later proved to be correct. Mitchondrial DNA is very different from the DNA within the nucleus of cells. Mitochondrial DNA is simpler in structure, arranged not like our chromosomes but in a circular pattern. It reminded scientists of the inheritance factors of primitive organisms like bacteria. Dr. Lynn Margulis has proposed that millions of years ago mitochondria were actually bacteria living on their own. They "infected" primitive animal cells and have been coinhabitants within the cells ever since.[21] This symbiotic relationship has been beneficial to the animal cell because the mitochondrion produces more energy by using oxygen and it is advantageous to the bacteria (now called the mitochondria), which thus have a nutrient-rich, safe environment in which to live.

The bacteria that infected cells and later became known as mitochondria brought their own genetic information in the form of unique DNA. This DNA has continued to reside within animal cells throughout the centuries of evolution, making possible the animal's metabolic ability to utilize oxygen efficiently.

The mitochondrial inheritance factor comes exclusively from the mother, and therefore our inheritance factors are more than 50 percent derived from our mothers. There are many thousands of mitochondria in a woman's egg, and only a few in the sperm, localized in the sperm's tail. Following fertilization, the tail of the sperm falls off. Therefore, mitochondrial inheritance factors are contributed exclusively by the maternal egg. In a sense, our biochemical energy process came from our mother.

Mitochondrial DNA does not communicate closely with the chromosomal DNA in the nucleus, but their activities are closely interrelated. The simple structure of mitochondrial DNA, which is similar to bacterial DNA, is much more vulnerable to damage by free radical oxidants than nuclear DNA. It is in physical proximity to the mitochondria, where most of the oxygen is processed. The processing of oxygen by the mitochondria produces oxygen free radicals that can damage the mitochondrial DNA if it is not protected by the adequate presence of antioxidants. These antioxidants include not only vitamin E but also substances like glutathione, lipoic acid, coenzyme Q10 and superoxide dismutase. All of these mitochondrial protective factors are derived, in part, from specific dietary nutrients.

The vulnerability of mitochondrial DNA once again reinforces the message that diet can play an important role in protecting gene expression not only through regulation of chromosomal function within the nucleus of cells but also by protecting mitochondrial DNA from damage.

Dr. Wallace and his colleagues in molecular genetics found that many individuals may be born with genetic abnormalities in their mitochondrial DNA, placing them at increased risk of oxidative injury and free radical aging. This was the case with the five-year-old boy who underwent an accelerated aging process. His death at age 28 was due to a severe imperfection in his mitochondrial DNA. In most individuals, however, the genetic inheritance factor is not the major determinant of how the mitochondria will function over the course of their lives. It is what they do to their mitochondria in the form of exposure to toxins, radiation, pollutants, drugs and diet that makes the difference.

One remarkable example of the role of mitochondria in function is the story of the elite, world-class bicycle racer Greg Le-Mond.[22] Mr. LeMond was at the top of his game in long-distance bicycle racing when he suddenly began to have performance difficulties in his sport. Extensive medical evaluation revealed he was suffering from what was called "mitochondrial myopathy." The mitochondria in his muscles were not able to manufacture energy efficiently, and their function declined. The symptoms of mitochondrial myopathy are fatigue, loss of muscle integrity and reduced exercise performance. Mr. LeMond did not suffer from genetic impairment that reduced his mitochondrial function. He seemed to have acquired his reduced mitochondrial function over his years of competition.

In a recent article in the *New England Journal of Medicine*, Donald Johns, M.D. wrote that loss of mitochondrial function with age arises from what we do to the mitochondrial DNA through our lifestyle and dietary choices rather than just from our inheritance factors.[23] According to Dr. Johns, "I do not know the basis of the diagnosis in the case of Mr. LeMond, but given the ever-expanding phenotypic spectrum of the mitochondrial disorders, one must not be dogmatic and rigid about these emerging diseases."

With this statement he was alerting his medical colleagues to the fact that age-related dysfunction and loss of performance with increased biomarkers of aging might be the result of induced mitochondrial damage. Although no one knows for certain how Mr. LeMond sustained mitochondrial damage, there has been speculation about the relationship between long-term heavy, demanding exercise, diet quality and the adequacy of antioxidant intake. Individuals who expose themselves to a considerable amount of oxidative stress, such as with long-term heavy exercise, and do not increase their intake of nutrients that protect the mitochondrial DNA against damage might incur cumulative damage that results in mitochondrial aging and the loss of performance. Research in the area of mitochondrial function indicates it is not just the inheritance of specific mitochondrial DNA that results in the risk of age-related disorders. What we have done to the mitochondrial DNA and how we have modified its expression through our lifestyle, diet and environmental choices are the determining factors.

The most common signs of premature aging and loss of function in individuals are fatigue, loss of energy and chronic pain. These symptoms are associated with the impairment of mitochondrial function and the resulting loss of energy production in the organs of the body. In a sense, fatigue is the body's statement that it cannot manufacture and control adequate energy to meet its needs. Fatigue of the brain leads to confusion; fatigue of the muscles is exhaustion; and fatigue of the immune system results in increased susceptibility to infection or autoimmunity.

This simple model of aging has broad-reaching significance. Scientists are finding the message locked in the mitochondrial DNA may be as important in determining how we age as the message of the chromosomes in the nucleus of cells.

Analysis of mitochondrial DNA is now being used not only to assess risk of disease and aging, but also for identification. Because a single cell contains hundreds or even thousands of mitochondria, more mitochondrial DNA is available for analysis than with nuclear DNA. Mitochondrial DNA is being used for forensic testing in criminology. It was used recently to identify the bones of Czar Nicholas II and to prove that the body in Jesse James's grave is truly that of the outlaw. Since 1991, the military has used mitochondrial DNA to identify soldiers' remains.[24]

The analysis of mitochondrial DNA has revealed it can readily sustain damage by free radicals. This damage can accumulate over time as an individual ages until it reaches such an extent that the mitochondrial DNA can no longer function properly. Bruce Ames, Ph.D., chairman of the department of biochemistry at the University of California at Berkeley, recently determined that mitochondrial DNA is about 15 times more susceptible than nuclear DNA to free radical oxidative injury.[25] If nuclear DNA is damaged, sophisticated repair enzymes present within the nucleus can help "put it back together." When mitochondrial DNA is damaged, however, there are no repair enzymes within the mitochondria to correct the defect. As a result, damaged mitochondrial DNA passes on its mutation to the daughter mitochondria that are derived from it. The error is thus perpetuated in new cells.

The free radical oxidants produced within the mitochondria as a consequence of reduced antioxidant protection can serve as stimulators for altered gene expression in nuclear DNA. Increasing evidence indicates that if they are not properly trapped by antioxidants, the oxidants produced within the mitochondria can create an alteration in gene expression from the chromosomal message within the nucleus.[26] This alteration in cell signaling and messages that are transmitted to the genes seems to play a very important role in determining the phenotype of aging. Many of the biomarkers we associate with unhealthy aging may result from increased oxidant production in the mitochondria and the effect it has on gene expression. Those biomarkers include loss of heart and lung function, reduced kidney function, and even cataracts and loss of skin elasticity.

Free radical oxidant substances produced within the mitochondria include hydrogen peroxide, superoxide, singlet oxygen and hydroxyl radical. All of these substances can contribute to altered gene expression. Through their ability to trap and defuse reactive oxygen species before they modify gene expression, dietary antioxidants play an important role in improving gene expression.[27] Reactive oxygen species, which are produced within the mitochondria, have been implicated in a number of diseases associated with aging, including heart disease, cancer and Alzheimer's disease. The most recent research provides a strong link between antioxidants and the protection against the damage by reactive oxygen species. It illustrates how dietary antioxidants may be important modifiers of messages that communicate with the genes.

Proper implementation of the genetic nutritioneering concept uses appropriate balance of dietary antioxidants, including vitamin E, vitamin C, carotenoids and flavonoids, to help communicate the correct messages to the genes and inheritance material found both in the mitochondria and in the nucleus of the cells. Vitamin E is just one member of a family of antioxidants with powerful abilities to help regulate genetic expression in the oxygen-rich tissues of the body, including the brain, heart, lungs, liver and immune system. By consuming a balanced blend of dietary antioxidants, an individual can bring about significant improvement in genetic expression over the course of his or her life. This improved genetic expression reduces the threat of mitochondrial DNA damage and accelerated biological aging.[28]

VITAMIN AND MINERAL SUPPLEMENTATION AND AGING

Edward Schneider, M.D., who was formerly associated with the National Institutes on Aging, wrote an article with his colleagues describing the role of vitamins and minerals in defense against age-related diseases. In this article, published in the *New England Journal of Medicine*, they suggested the Recommended Dietary Allowances (RDAs) for older individuals were inadequate to provide optimal levels of vitamins and minerals to defend against age-related diseases. They gave the following reasons for this conclusion:

1. The RDAs for older-aged groups had not been aimed at the maintenance of optimal physiological function.

2. The effects of nutritional factors on physiological function throughout the life span have not been considered in formulating the RDAs for all age groups.
3. The optimal blood or tissue level of nutrients, as well as the balance of all nutrients, has not been taken into account in establishing the RDAs.
4. There is much more biochemical individuality in human populations than was recognized when the RDAs were established.
5. Information concerning the interaction of nutrients with drugs and medications was not properly incorporated in establishing RDAs for older individuals.
6. The recent information concerning the value of nutritional supplements on functional health in older individuals was not taken into account in establishing the RDAs.[29]

The last modification of the RDAs occurred in 1989. Since then, the Reference Daily Intakes (RDIs) have been published. The RDIs actually reduced the suggested daily intake of some nutrients (e.g., folic acid, vitamin E) below the RDAs. These changes were not made on the basis of Dr. Schneider's suggestion or what researchers have learned about nutrient effects on gene expression or function. For this reason, the present information made available to the general public regarding the level of intake of specific nutrients to promote healthy aging is woefully inadequate.

We are standing on the threshold of a revolution in the way we view the aging process and the role of diet, lifestyle and environment in its modification. By itself, aging is not a prescription for disease or loss of function. The maintenance of genetic messages associated with youth is a primary objective in the application of the principles of genetic nutritioneering. Diet and the nutrients contained within it play an important role in modulating the genetic messages we associate with youthful function. Regular exercise, modifying your diet to meet your individual needs, increasing the levels of specific nutrients within your diet (including the antioxidants) and lowering your exposure to toxic factors such as stress, drugs and pollutants, will help enhance the performance of your genes and promote the continued expression of youthful characteristics. This concept will frame the specifics of how genetic nutritioneering can be applied to the prevention and even the remediation of such age-related disorders as diabetes, arthritis, heart disease, dementia and cancer in the chapters that follow.

7

DIABETES: DIET, INSULIN AND GENETIC EXPRESSION

DISCOVERIES ABOUT HUMAN HEALTH COME from remarkable places. In their laboratory at the Massachusetts General Hospital and Harvard Medical School in Boston, geneticist Dr. Gary Ruvkun and his colleagues made a discovery that seems at first glance to be obscure and unrelated to human aging. On closer inspection, however, it may have opened the door to understanding how aging relates to gene expression and, indirectly, to diet.[1]

Dr. Ruvkun and his colleagues were working with a lowly worm, *Caenorhabditis elegans*, which has the ability to "extend its life span" in response to stresses such as overcrowding or starvation. For years scientists have studied this worm's ability to extend its life span 20 to 30 percent under stressful conditions. They have wondered if it could be related to the ability of animals like rats and mice to extend their life spans when they are deprived of calories.

Is there something about the amount of food we eat and its nutrient composition that speaks to the genes and influences life span? This question spurred scientists in their investigation of *C. elegans*. They identified a specific gene in the worm's inheritance factors that helped it enter a state of suspended metabolism. This gene codes for the manufacture of a specific protein, hibernin, or DAF-2, which turns out to be the equivalent of the human insulin receptor protein, the molecule that "listens" for the hormone insulin, which is secreted in response to a rise in blood sugar. This protein sits on the surface of the cell, communicates with insulin circulating in the bloodstream and can translate an insulin message deep into the interior of the cell, influencing the way genes are expressed. Similarly, the protein discovered in C. elegans is a "switch" that helps shift the metabolism to a "suspend" mode, dramatically lengthening the life span of the worm when times are bad.[2]

Jim Thomas, a geneticist at the University of Washington in Seattle, notes that, "Simply finding an analog to the human insulin receptor in C. elegans is a surprise. Scientists weren't anticipating that the fundamental genetic circuitry that regulates glucose metabolism in mammals would be evolutionarily that ancient" and tied to such lowly organisms as the worm.[3]

Medical investigators are now interested in determining whether this genetic characteristic in worms can also describe the process that relates to life extension in animals when their diet is restricted in calories but adequate in nutrients. Geneticist Don Riddle, Ph.D., at the University of Missouri in Columbia, is an investigator in this field. He stated, "If some of the same genetic circuitry triggered in the worms by the DAF-2 signal accounts for the life span extension seen in rats and mice under conditions of caloric restriction, that would be a phenomenal discovery."[4]

The discovery of the connection between life span and the hormone insulin is extraordinarily interesting. It has long been known that individuals who have the disease diabetes, in which there is a defect in either the production or the activity of insulin, undergo changes associated with accelerated biological aging. The recent discoveries may lead to a greater understanding of how control of blood sugar through diet and lifestyle may help reduce biological aging. Control of blood sugar and its companion hormone insulin is a major focus of the genetic nutritioneering approach, because insulin plays a principal role in communicating with the genes and altering their expression.

The poor control of insulin and blood sugar that is associated with diabetes contributes to high medical costs, early-age disability and shortened life expectancy. Individuals who developed diabetes as adults (as contrasted to juvenile-onset diabetes) typically develop a range of health problems we associate with accelerated aging. One common problem is damage to the retina of the eyes, which is the major contributor to blindness in the adult. Another is damage to the kidneys, which is the major cause of chronic kidney disease and kidney failure in the adult. Finally, poor control of insulin and blood sugar in the adult (associated with maturity-onset diabetes) increases the risk of heart disease and disorders of the nervous system, including pain in the hands and feet.

Diabetes takes a tremendous toll on human life and health. A study of the impact of adult-onset diabetes on the U.S. population revealed that in 1996 the disease resulted in the loss of 920,000 person/years of sight. It led to 691,000 person/years of kidney disease and 678,000 years of lower extremity amputation. A total of 611,000 years of life were lost due to premature death from the disease. The cost was more than $4 billion in medical expenditures.[5]

Long before a diagnosis of diabetes can be made, poor management of blood sugar and insulin can alter function and produce a wide range of difficulties. Menstrual irregularities in women, loss of libido and erectile dysfunction in men, blood pressure disorders, weight gain and loss of elasticity in connective tissues (which makes the body stiff and susceptible to injury) are all related to poor blood sugar control. All could be called "age-related disorders," but they are not a part of healthy aging. They result instead from poor control of the hormone insulin and the way it influences gene expression.

Every cell in your body is nourished by the blood sugar

glucose. Glucose is the principal source of metabolic energy for most organs in the body. Control of glucose, through appropriate diet and hormonal management, has a critical influence on the way your body performs. Your brain, which represents less than 3 percent of your total body weight, consumes nearly 20 percent of the blood sugar in your body. Poor blood sugar control can result in altered learning and memory and can even be a factor in diseases of the nervous system, such as Alzheimer's disease.[6,7,8]

Dietary complex carbohydrates (or starches) and sugars provide the body's main sources of blood sugar. Starch in the diet is made up of long chains of repeating glucose units called "polysaccharides," which means "many sugars." Through the process of digestion, your body breaks down starch to release glucose that can be absorbed into the blood and help control energy demands. Table sugar or sucrose is a much simpler source of glucose than starch. It is smaller and more rapidly digested and assimilated into the bloodstream. Sucrose is made up of two sugars (glucose and fructose) and is therefore called a disaccharide. When sucrose is broken down and absorbed very rapidly, it delivers both glucose and fructose to the blood. In addition to having other metabolic uses, fructose can be converted into glucose in the liver. It is important to remember that your body uses starch and sugar in ways that are similar but not identical. Starch is composed of only glucose, while table sugar (sucrose) contains both glucose and fructose.

Starch is made up of long chains of glucose molecules linked together in linear or branched forms, depending on the source of the starch in the diet. Starches, or complex carbohydrates, are much more slowly digested and assimilated by the body than simple carbohydrate, or sucrose. This difference in the rate of absorption plays an important role in the way insulin responds to a meal. If glucose is absorbed more slowly into the body, as it is when you consume starch, then insulin, which is one of the principal hormones secreted to help control sugar levels in the body, is released more slowly from the pancreas where it is produced.

When you eat simple sugar, or sucrose, on the other hand, glucose and fructose are more rapidly absorbed. The body demands insulin more quickly and it can exaggerate the demand or "over-shoot the mark" and produce too much insulin. The result can be either a low blood sugar effect after eating, which is called hypo-glycemia, or the excessive circulation of insulin through the body, which is called hyperinsulinemia.

Scientists have learned that the hormone insulin does more than simply control the level of sugar in the blood. It is a hormone that can indirectly "speak to the genes" and alter gene expression. In doing so, it can influence a variety of other hormones and metabolic functions, including the effects of estrogen in women and the way the body utilizes calories for energy or deposits them as fat.[9]

Individuals who suffer from poor insulin and blood sugar control typically have a number of characteristics in common. They crave sugar or sweet foods and beverages, tend to gain weight in their upper bodies and have a "pear shape" (which means their waist-to-hip measurement ratio is greater than 1-to-1). They have marginally elevated blood pressure and cholesterol levels and are apt to feel they can't control their weight no matter what diet they try. Poor control of insulin influences gene expression of charac-teristics that shift the metabolism into a "calorie storage" state when the body stores calories as fat rather than using them effectively as a source of energy.

We have described this metabolic characteristic as "switched metabolism," because it seems the switch that controls the way the body converts calories from food into metabolic energy is turned off. It seems paradoxical that individuals who are overweight, meaning they are storing too much fat, appear to have too much energy because fat represents a storage form of energy. But when you look at their behavior, they are often tired, listless and fatigued, which appears to result from having too little energy. It is as though when they eat, their bodies don't know how to create metabolic energy from food calories. Therefore, those calories are stored as fat to be used for a rainy day that never comes. This "switched metabolism" has a significant relationship to the poor control of blood sugar and its companion hormone insulin.

Practitioners in the past believed that all the problems related to diabetes could be alleviated by regular administration of insulin to diabetic individuals. Now we know that many people with maturity-onset diabetes suffer not from too little insulin but from their bodies' insensitivity to the insulin they are producing. This condition is called insulin resistance. Administration of insulin to these individuals does not help resolve the problem and may actually make it worse.[10]

George Reaven, M.D., a professor emeritus from the Department of Medicine, Stanford University School of Medicine, was the first to identify and use the term "Syndrome X" to describe this characteristic of insulin resistance. His discovery led medicine to recognize that the ability to control blood sugar and insulin levels varies widely from person to person. These differences, and the individual's efforts to compensate for them by diet, environment and lifestyle modification, are major factors in determining the risk of developing premature, age-related diseases like heart disease, stroke, gout, arthritis-like changes and hormonal difficulties.[11]

SYNDROME X AND INSULIN EFFECTS

Insulin resistance occurs when cells become insensitive to the insulin message. When cells don't respond effectively to insulin, blood sugar is not properly managed, and the pancreas is required to secrete more and more insulin. When insulin levels in the blood become very high, they influence gene expression, altering cellular effects and promoting accelerated aging. The link between Dr. Ruvkun's discovery about the longevity message in the worm and insulin sensitivity in humans has caused medical scientists to recognize one of the cornerstones of the genetic nutritioneering approach. That cornerstone is the regulation of blood sugar and insulin and the message they communicate to the genes.

Syndrome X, which is characterized by insulin resistance and elevated insulin levels in the blood, alters metabolism and creates the switched metabolism phenomenon also found in *C. elegans*. This change results in an individual's gaining weight as body fat, often when he or she has never had a problem with weight control. Suddenly, normal eating or even a calorie-restricted diet causes the person to gain weight. The switched metabolism diverts calories from energy reserves and stores them as fat in body cells.[12]

It seems like a cruel trick. What the body has done is to become very hungry for calories it will store as body fat. Thus it robs Peter to pay Paul and produces less metabolic energy for function. As body fat increases, insulin resistance continues to increase as well. It is like a dog chasing its tail, with the individual gaining weight more easily, having more signs of accelerated aging and lowering functional vitality. Frustrated, a person with this condition may turn to starvation diets, weight-loss pills, metabolic activators, or a diet that relies on one specific food in a desperate effort to burn off the fat.

During the past decade, from studies by Dr. Reaven and many other specialists in this field, we have learned that control of insulin sensitivity and blood sugar regulation may hold the key to unlock the genetic message for controlling the metabolism of calories.

We have just gone through another episode in the weight-loss story with the weight-loss drugs Redux and the Phen-fen. The heart valve problems experienced by many individuals who took these diet drugs raised questions about the safety of pharmacological modification of metabolism.[13]

The concerns arise from the realization that hormones that control appetite and metabolism have more than one effect on the body. They influence many cellular functions. Although a person might experience a beneficial effect in one aspect of function, the pharmacological modification of these hormones might produce an adverse effect in another part of the body. Hormones, their signaling of gene expression, and the subsequent influences on metabolism exist in a complex web-like interaction. We cannot easily determine the effects of intervention at one level on the functioning of the whole.[14]

Control of insulin is related not only to the control of blood sugar but also to the interaction with many other hormones, including insulin-like growth factor, human growth hormone, cortisol, somatostatin, serotonin, noradrenaline and leptin. All of these hormones that help to control blood sugar are in part controlled through the modification of gene expression by stress, diet, exercise patterns and environment.[15]

Diet and exercise may be the most important tools available to individuals for resetting the sensitivity of their cells to insulin and recovering the healthy function of their genes. Thomas Wolever, M.D., Ph.D., from the Department of Nutritional Sciences and the Division of Endocrinology and Metabolism at the University of Toronto, found that some foods create greater insulin demands on the body than others and cause more havoc in the control of blood sugar. He classified these foods by a "glycemic index," which rates foods based on their blood glucose and insulin-raising potential.[16] Foods like table sugar and refined potato starch have a high glycemic index, which means they greatly increase blood sugar and insulin levels after eating. On the other hand, lentils, mung beans and soy have a low glycemic index and a much smaller adverse impact on blood sugar and insulin after eating.

Dr. Wolever and other investigators in this field, including David Jenkins, M.D. have developed glycemic index tables. Table 1 lists some commonly eaten foods and their glycemic index (GI). (Early studies used glucose as the reference food, but later studies found white bread to be more reliable. For comparison, we have included the GI using both glucose and white bread.) As Table 1 shows, foods like basmati rice, barley, lentils, split peas, dried beans, and whole fruits exhibit a low to moderate glycemic response.

Table 1. Glycemic Index of Commonly Eaten Foods[17]

Food	GI-Glucose Standard	GI-White Bread Standard
rye bread	63	90
white bread	69	100
whole wheat bread	72	99
white rice	72	81
brown rice	66	81
brown rice, high amylose		66
potato (new), boiled	70	80
sweet potato	48	70
shredded wheat	67	97
milk (skim)	32	46
corn flakes	80	109
oatmeal	49	93
green peas, frozen	51	65
kidney beans	29	43
lentils	29	38
pearl barley	25	36
spaghetti	50	61
apple	39	53
banana	62	84
orange	40	59
fructose	20	31
glucose	100	138
sucrose	59	89

Whole, unrefined, carbohydrate-rich foods that do not contain sugars have a lower glycemic index and appear to be more desirable in controlling blood sugar and insulin than those that are highly refined and have higher sugar and fat levels.[18] Whole-starch foods that contain what are called "resistant starch" are more desirable for insulin control than other starchy foods because resistant starch is more slowly metabolized and causes even less demand for insulin release. Resistant starch-containing foods include certain types of rice, corn, grains (such as millet) and legumes like soybeans and lentils.

Extraordinary as it may seem, emerging research confirms that the carbohydrates we eat do influence the expression of our genes. If the sensitivity of your genes to blood sugar and insulin is related in part to your family history, then you can look at your siblings, parents and grandparents to determine whether you might carry this carbohydrate sensitivity and tendency toward insulin resistance. The following characteristics identify insulin resistance:

1. Tendency to gain fat in the upper body.
2. Menstrual irregularities and polycystic ovaries in women.
3. Marginally elevated LDL cholesterol.
4. Marginally elevated blood fats (triglycerides).
5. Marginally elevated blood pressure.
6. A "sweet tooth."
7. Symptoms that resemble hypoglycemia.
8. A family history of maturity-onset diabetes.

Extensive published medical and biochemical research indicates that carbohydrates influence the regulation of gene expression through their effect on the secretion of insulin, glucagon and other cell-signaling hormones.[19,20] This new research places a unique burden on you every time you sit down to eat. It gives you new responsibility in selecting the foods you will consume. If you have a family or personal history of carbohydrate sensitivity and insulin resistance, then you need to be cautious about the types and amounts of carbohydrates you eat. You have to consider how they might ultimately talk to your genes, modifying gene expression and increasing your risk of biological aging.

If you are an insulin-resistant individual, a calorie-restricted diet may not help you lose weight because your body may still be suffering from "switched metabolism;" thus, whatever calories you consume will be preferentially converted into body fat for storage.

In cases of insulin resistance, the genetic nutritioneering approach focuses first on factors that can help improve insulin sensitivity and the control of blood sugar and cellular metabolism. It begins with reducing fat, sugar and refined foods in the diet and increasing consumption of the unrefined starches found in legumes, whole grains and low-glycemic starchy vegetables.

The second step is the recognition that improved insulin sensitivity can be achieved when the diet is higher in dietary fiber. Dietary fiber accompanies unrefined grains, legumes and starchy vegetables when you eat the whole foods. To add fiber to your diet, you should eat whole vegetable products and fruits rather than juiced or concentrated forms of these foods. Carrots, apples, broccoli, cauliflower, almonds and figs are all very high in dietary fiber. Juicing or concentrating these foods leaves behind the valuable fiber and reduces their benefit in helping the body control blood sugar and insulin.

Regular activity also plays an important role in helping the body control blood sugar and insulin levels.[21] A sedentary lifestyle increases the risk of insulin resistance and problems of weight gain. Some people argue that exercise is not an efficient way to burn off fat because you would have to run many miles to burn off a pound of stored fat. Burning off fat during exercise is not the reason why regular activity is encouraged. When you implement a regular activity program your body's sensitivity to insulin increases and your genes can express the proper message for controlling metabolism, thereby regulating the way calories are switched between fat and energy for activity.

In a sense, regular activity helps unswitch your metabolism and put you back into a more youthful physiological state in which your genes are expressed in such a way as to help control your body weight. Most young people do not worry about extra calories because their bodies work overtime to burn calories as energy. Only when their metabolism becomes "switched" in mid-life do they become concerned about their diet and their weight. Switched metabolism can come about as a consequence of insulin resistance. Dietary modification and regular activity are two principal tools employed in the genetic nutritioneering approach to wake up the messages that are still present in genes to regulate the expenditure of calories and prevent their storage as body fat.

THE 40-30-30 APPROACH FOR IMPROVING INSULIN SENSITIVITY

In addition to dietary carbohydrate, dietary fiber and activity, another principal tool that helps regulate insulin sensitivity and blood sugar levels is the amount and type of dietary protein you consume. In his recent best-selling diet book, *The Zone*, Barry Sears, Ph.D. described a dietary approach using higher protein, lower carbohydrate and modest fat for controlling insulin levels.[22] Sears advocates a daily diet of 30 percent of calories from protein, 40 percent from carbohydrate and 30 percent from dietary fat. He specifies that most of the dietary fat should be polyunsaturated fats from corn, safflower, sunflower and canola oils, as well as the oils derived from flaxseeds and fish (the omega-3 oils). His advocacy for increased levels of dietary protein to help stabilize insulin at the expense of lowered carbohydrate levels is based on the presumption that protein does not increase insulin needs, but carbohydrate does. Sears suggests that increasing the amount of protein in the diet of the average person, while limiting his or her carbohydrate intake, can have significant benefit in controlling the effects of insulin on gene expression.

Recent research indicates that the belief that carbohydrate increases insulin and protein protects against it is simplistic and misleading. A controlled study found that when individuals consumed protein-rich food their insulin output was *greater* than when they consumed an equal amount of carbohydrate-rich food. Some of the volunteers for this study did have a lower insulin output after protein-rich meals, but they were the exception, not the rule. The conclusions of this study once again support the genetic nutritioneering concept of tailoring the diet to the individual's genetic need. No single diet is optimal for all people.

Thirty percent of calories as protein, in individuals who consume 1600 to 2000 calories per day, translates to 120 to 150 grams of protein. For anyone who has poor liver, kidney or digestive function, this could be an excessive level of dietary protein. A more prudent diet, using the genetic nutritioneering approach, would be to eat more vegetable protein in the form of soy protein and soy products, unrefined, high-fiber fruits, vegetables and cereals, and modest amounts of fish and lean cuts of meat, including poultry without the skin. Encouraging people to eat too much protein might actually create more problems than it solves. Gene Spiller, Ph.D. found that a protein-enhanced diet might actually increase insulin resistance rather than decrease it.[23]

A balanced diet would result in a ratio of 15-25 percent protein (principally as vegetable protein and fish); 50-60 percent carbohydrate (principally unrefined vegetables, grains and legumes), and 20-25 percent fat (principally from unrefined vegetable oils and fish). Specific focus for all people on a "zone" of 30 percent protein, 40 percent carbohydrate and 30 percent fat, as if it were the body's requirement for proper metabolism, is based neither on reasonable interpretation of medical science nor on clinical reality. Instead, a range of type and amount of protein, carbohydrate and fat in the diet is more important in determining insulin sensitivity and control of blood sugar. It is the type of protein, carbohydrate and fat, not the percentages alone, that is most important in establishing your body's response. Unrefined diets produce a much lower insulin response than do refined diets. Vegetable proteins and unsaturated vegetable and fish oils produce a lower insulin response than fatty cuts of meat that are rich in saturated animal fats. Unrefined vegetables and cereals containing abundant quantities of soluble and insoluble fiber also reduce insulin response. Foods rich in vitamin E, like soybeans and wheat germ, and minerals, such as chromium and magnesium, from foods like root vegetables, whole grains and brewer's yeast, also improve insulin sensitivity.

The specific diet for any person should be based upon his or her individual response as determined by genetic uniqueness and lifestyle factors. This is the underlying approach described in this book. Your uniqueness as an individual as described by your genes should be matched by your own individual diet, lifestyle and activity patterns for optimal influence on genetic expression.

The best information we have available to date supports not a specific zone but a range of alternatives desirable for individuals across the range of genetic variation we now recognize in the human population. By using these guidelines and monitoring your own response to your diet, you can overcome problems like switched metabolism from insulin resistance by reawakening genetic messages that have lain dormant due to altered lifestyle, diet and environment.

THE OXIDATIVE STRESS CONNECTION TO INSULIN

Poor control of insulin and blood sugar also has an impact on accelerated biological aging related to oxidative stress. In the previous chapter we talked about the free radical theory of aging of Denham Harman, Ph.D. and how over the past 40 years the medical and scientific communities have come to accept this concept as a contributor to accelerated aging. Recent research reveals that insulin resistance and poor control of blood sugar may increase the risk for oxidative stress as well.[24] Poor blood sugar and insulin control results in the chemical combination of glucose and proteins in blood and tissues to produce damaged proteins called glycosylated proteins.

Formation of these damaged proteins resembles the formation

of crust on the top of bread when it is baked. This crust formation results from a chemical reaction of sugars in the dough with the protein in wheat flour, causing both to be modified by glycosylation. Using the bread crust as a mental image of what can happen when sugars react with protein, you can envision the reaction of sugar with proteins in the body to form "crusts" of damaged proteins which alter function and create damaging messages to the genes.

These altered proteins in the body have been called advanced glycosylation endproducts (AGEs). The more AGEs accumulate in your body, the more you are at risk for accelerated biological aging.[25-29]

AGEs "poison" mitochondrial function, producing more oxidative stress.[30] Based on their genetic inheritance factors, some individuals are much more sensitive to AGEs than other individuals. The insulin-resistant individual may be carrying a "silent killer" he or she does not recognize which increases the production of AGEs and increases oxidative stress reactions at the mitochondria, resulting in increased biological aging.[31]

This technical complicated-sounding information can be distilled to a simple concept. Your genes carry messages that describe how sensitive you are to insulin and blood sugar. You can modify the expression of these messages that are locked within your genes by what you eat, how much exercise you get, the amount of stress you are under and the toxins to which you have been exposed, including drugs and alcohol. The risk of insulin resistance in individuals with certain genetic susceptibilities increases significantly when they eat a poor-quality diet, are under stress or are exposed to toxins or drugs. Inappropriate decisions about lifestyle can result in the expression of genes that increase the formation of AGEs in these individuals. Oxidative stress in their mitochondria thereby increases along with damage to their organs. Many years later this damage may be diagnosed as kidney problems, heart disease, dementia, loss of eyesight or arthritis.

Most doctors do not check for insulin resistance in a standard physical examination. Insulin resistance is an overlooked condition just as elevated blood pressure or blood cholesterol was before people started having their blood pressure and cholesterol levels measured regularly. No symptoms were associated with elevated blood pressure or elevated cholesterol, but we learned that the individual had a much higher risk of having a stroke or developing heart disease, respectively, with these conditions. We can do the right thing for a patient with insulin resistance only if we have asked the right questions. These questions relate to family and personal health history as well as an oral glucose tolerance test in which both blood sugar and blood insulin are measured.

If an individual is found to have insulin resistance, a genetic nutritioneering approach can be applied to help stabilize his or her body's response to insulin and regulate gene expression more effectively.

A number of recently published medical studies indicate that poor control of blood sugar and increased formation of AGEs result in conditions such as stiffening of the kinetic connective tissue. This stiffening causes a person to be less flexible,[32] increases his or her risk of skin aging and wrinkling,[33] heightens the risk of allergic and arthritis-like responses,[34-35] and increases the risk of disorders like periodontal disease, which is the major cause of loss of teeth from gum disease in adults.[36] All of these conditions are associated with increased aging. These examples of compromised function, including increased body fat, lower energy, reduced flexibility, chronic pain and increased allergies, are all precursors or warnings of severe disorders like heart disease or kidney disease, which may occur later.[37-39]

THE IMPORTANCE OF TRACE MINERALS IN INSULIN CONTROL

Insulin and blood sugar control head the list of objectives for implementing the genetic nutritioneering approach. In addition to modifying the type and amount of carbohydrate, fiber, protein and fat in the diet, a number of nutrients have been found helpful to improve gene expression in the control of insulin and blood sugar. Supplementation with the trace mineral chromium and its companion mineral vanadium is one beneficial combination. Chromium has long been recognized as an essential nutrient that helps the body regulate insulin and the message it communicates to the genes. Many studies indicate that supplementation with chromium chloride, chromium polynicotinate, or chromium picolinate in ranges from 100 to 600 mcg per day is beneficial in stabilizing blood sugar control for some individuals with defects in the control of insulin or blood sugar.[40]

Chromium is found in brewer's yeast, root crop vegetables and whole grains grown in soils in which chromium is adequate. Food processing and changes in the level of trace elements in agricultural soils have caused the level of chromium in the standard American diet to become quite low.

Vanadium is another trace mineral that helps regulate insulin and blood sugar. In one study of this mineral, daily supplements with 12 mg of sodium metavanadate resulted in significant improvement in blood sugar control in individuals with maturity-onset diabetes.[41] At this level, sodium metavanadate appears to be an insulin-like substance that helps stimulate blood sugar control. The most common adverse side effect of this level of oral supplementation with sodium metavanadate was mild gastrointestinal intolerance and diarrhea. Because sodium metavanadate helps stabilize blood sugar levels, investigators at the Joslin Diabetes Center at the Department of Medicine, Brigham and Women's Hospital and Harvard Medical School, who performed this study, believe it has potential as an adjunctive therapy for patients with maturity-onset diabetes.[42]

In addition, antioxidants like vitamin E were found to help protect against the oxidative stress that occurs with poor control of insulin and blood sugar.[43] Daily supplementation with 400 mg of vitamin E, along with adequate levels of vitamins C and A, and the minerals selenium (100 to 200 mcg per day), copper (1 to 3 mg per day) and zinc (15 to 25 mg per day) helped reduce oxidative stress in individuals who had insulin resistance and poor control of blood sugar.

A companion study found that vitamin B12 was also very helpful for maintaining proper function of the nervous system in individuals who had maturity-onset diabetes and poor control of blood sugar. Increased levels of vitamin B12 were closely correlated with reduced oxidative stress in individuals with poor blood sugar control.[44]

Supplementation with oil of evening primrose, borage oil or black currant seed oil, all of which contain a unique fatty acid called gamma linolenic acid (GLA), may also help improve the functions of both the nervous and immune system in individuals who have poor insulin control.[45]

Finally, supplementation with the amino acid L-arginine can be beneficial for individuals who have increased AGEs and free radical-induced aging that accompanies poor control of blood sugar and insulin. In a clinical study done at the University of Vienna Department of Medicine, 1 gram of L-arginine was given twice daily to individuals who had oxidative stress as a consequence of poor blood sugar control. Results of the study revealed significant reduction in oxidative stress reactions, and L-arginine supplementation also reduced the amount of damage to DNA and other important cellular materials, thereby reducing the processes associated with accelerated aging.[46]

In summary, evidence from medical research clearly indicates that poor control of blood sugar and its relationship to insulin and other hormones can modify the expression of genes, which in turn translates to accelerated aging. Obesity, allergies, arthritis-like changes, changes in eyesight and mental acuity, and increased risk of heart and kidney disease, all of which are associated with accelerated aging, are a consequence of poor regulation of blood sugar and insulin. The most powerful tools available to modify these risks over the course of a person's life are diet, exercise, lifestyle habits and environmental considerations.

Research from many areas of discovery is converging on a central principle of aging that relates to poor control of blood sugar and altered function of insulin. The genetic nutritioneering approach provides an effective means of assessing genetic predisposition and developing a tailored program to meet the individual's need to reduce the risk of age-related diseases that come from altered control of blood sugar.

After reading this far, you should not be surprised to learn that conditions like diabetes, which many people feel is a result of bad genes, are modifiable by treating your genes a different way. Nor should you be surprised to learn that arthritis and inflammation are also modifiable through application of the genetic nutritioneering concept.

A PROGRAM TO MODIFY RISK FACTORS FOR DIABETES

- Your diet should be as high in unrefined foods as possible, with starchy vegetables and cereal grains as principal foods.
- Include dried legume and soy foods each day.
- Limit your intake of fruit juices and foods high in sugar.
- Your major protein sources should be beans, grains, fish and poultry without skin.
- Avoid fried foods, partially hydrogenated oils, convenience foods and fast foods.
- Limit your intake of fat-rich spreads and dressings, whole-fat dairy products and fatty cuts of meat.
- Engage in 20 to 30 minutes of aerobic exercise or activity each day.
- Eliminate excess body fat and increase your lean body tissue.
- Find time each day to reduce stress by listening to music, relaxing or spending time being quiet and reflective.

Genetic Nutritioneering Daily Support

Chromium, 100–400 mcg

Vanadium, 400–2,000 mcg as metavanadate

Vitamin E, 400 IU

Vitamin C, 250–1,000 mg

Citrus bioflavonoids, 200–1,000 mg

Vitamin B12, 10–100 mcg

Folic acid, 400–800 mcg

Vitamin B1, 5–25 mg

Vitamin B2, 3–10 mg

Selenium, 100–200 mcg

Copper, 1–2 mg

Zinc, 15–30 mg

Evening primrose oil and/or fish oil, 2–6 g

L-arginine, 1,000 mg, twice daily

8

ARTHRITIS, INFLAMMATION AND NUTRITIONEERING

MOST PEOPLE BELIEVE THE ACHING, swollen joints and chronic pain of inflammation that begin to affect them sometime after their 40th birthday are a natural part of growing older. Their parents and grandparents had arthritis or inflammatory digestive disorders, and their bad genes are bound to plague them. They can't do anything about their genes or erase the years of wear and tear that have led to their pain. The only alternative, they believe, is to reduce the symptoms with medications which block the inflammation and pain, but do not treat the cause of the condition. The Genetic Nutritioneering Program offers a different course of action, which is based on evidence that the pain and inflammation of arthritis result from reactions of the intestinal tract to toxins, allergens or bacterial debris.

The "Focus on Your Health" section of a recent issue of *Newsweek* magazine contained an article titled "Gut Reactions," which described the health history of 27-year-old Michael Vonelli, a shipping supervisor.[1] For several years chronic diarrhea, abdominal pain, constant fever and severe weight loss had incapacitated

Mr. Vonelli. He had been diagnosed with Crohn's disease, a serious inflammatory digestive disorder. Crohn's disease is characterized by such severe inflammation of the small intestine that it can result in ulceration and require surgery to remove the damaged portion of the intestinal tract. Mr. Vonelli had tried numerous medications, including steroids and antibiotics, but his condition had not improved.

Fortunately for Mr. Vonelli, his continuing search for ways to manage his condition took him to the office of Leo Galland, M.D. Dr. Galland, a functional medicine practitioner, is a founding member of the Institute for Functional Medicine and a leader in the field of genetic nutrition. His book, *The Four Pillars of Healing*, describes the approach he has employed in his practice for many years to manage patients with chronic health problems similar to those of Mr. Vonelli.[2]

Dr. Galland determined Michael Vonelli was suffering from what is called a "leaky gut." His digestive tract had become so damaged that it was unable to prevent the leakage of toxic substances through the lining of his intestines into his bloodstream, aggravating his inflammation. Dr. Galland pointed out that diet and lifestyle could play important roles in reducing the inflammation that leads to leaky gut syndrome and in promoting healing of the gastrointestinal lumen, the sensitive lining of the intestinal tract.

Dr. Galland helped Mr. Vonelli construct a tailored diet that is consistent with the genetic nutritioneering approach described in this chapter. By following this diet Mr. Vonelli was gradually able to eliminate the anti-inflammatory medications he had been taking for years and regain both his health and the weight he had lost.

The irony of this story is that many of the medications people might be taking for inflammatory conditions are the very substances that help create a leaky gut and increase the persistence of inflammation. This observation was first made by Ingvar Bjarnason, M.D., a gastroenterologist in Scandinavia, who found that both alcohol and many anti-inflammatory medications can cause leakiness of the intestinal tract, which can activate the inflammatory process and exacerbate the problems it causes.[3]

The body produces inflammation as if it were responding to an alarm message that had been sounded in the intestinal tract. That alarm message originates with a genetic signal and is transferred throughout the body. The intestinal tract is connected to all the organs of the body through this signaling system which is turned on and turned off as a consequence of gene expression.

Although the scientific basis for explaining the inflammatory process is only a few years old, the understanding that the function of the intestinal tract is related to overall health has existed for more than 100 years. R.H. Dalton, M.D. described this relationship in the June 3, 1893, issue of the *Journal of the American Medical Association.* In an article titled "The Limit of Human Life and How to Live Long," Dr. Dalton wrote,

> The morbid influence of habitual constipation on an organism, otherwise healthy, is an interesting study, but easily understood. The fecal mass, having traveled through the long digestive conduit, finally subsides into the colon and rectum in a complete state of decomposition—a mass of ptomaines—to be seized by the active absorbency of these receptacles and thrown back into the general circulation, poisoning tissues wherever they go and defying the liver, kidneys or other emunctory to cast them out of the system. Congestions, inflammations, abscesses and all of the catalog of pathological complications are liable to ensue. Most likely, a large majority of chronic diseases take their origin from this cause.[4]

We now know the intestines are not merely a digestive organ involved only in the breakdown of food and the processing of nutrients. The intestinal tract is also an immune system organ, the site of nearly two-thirds of the body's defense system. Gut-associated lymphoid tissue (GALT), specialized tissue that surrounds the digestive system, is the source of much of the body's immune system function.[5] The GALT is responsible for producing the antibody proteins that travel through the bloodstream to defend against infectious agents. This same lymphoid tissue is also responsible for a mission to seek and destroy toxic substances released in the gut or potentially disease-producing toxic bacteria that are trying to travel from the interior of the intestinal tract into the blood.

A number of organisms can activate the GALT. Among these activators are toxic bacteria that reside in the intestinal tract, parasitic organisms like yeasts (including *Candida albicans*, the organism that produces oral thrush in children or vaginitis in women), and waterborne parasites such as *Cryptosporidium*, *Giardia* or *Entamoeba histolitica*. Activation of the immune system in the intestinal tract by this stimulator causes altered genetic expression and increased production of messenger substances that travel in the blood, signaling inflammation.

The mechanism by which this message is transmitted is through the expression of cytokines, genes that code for the production of these alarm molecules. Cytokines are released by the GALT and are the town criers that alert the entire body to the presence of an enemy agent that should be eliminated.

Inflammation and immune system activity are an important part of the body's natural recycling system. They help defend against foreign agents that could otherwise produce life-threatening disease and recycle dead tissues of the body that need to be regenerated. Inflammation in response to a trauma or infection is actually a desirable process. When infection is sustained over a long period of time and becomes a chronic problem, however, the organs can sustain damage. The result is chronic pain, swelling, immune dysfunction and the feeling of being always sick. Many people who suffer from chronic fatigue syndrome, fibromyalgia, chronic *Candida* infection, middle ear infections in children, chronic tonsillitis or even symptoms of joint pain of arthritis may be experiencing the effects of chronic immune system activation that started in the gut and triggered an inflammatory process throughout the body.

Nitric oxide is one substance that is produced as a consequence of this alarm reaction. A very small molecule produced by all cells of the body, nitric oxide has only recently been identified as a messenger molecule. It communicates a message of inflammation or immune activation from one cell to another. When the immune system is stimulated as a consequence of repeated exposure to a presumed foreign invader or toxic substance, nitric oxide production may increase. If this increased production occurs as a consequence of exposure in the intestinal tract to toxic substances, nitric oxide, which is produced by the GALT, can damage the intestinal lumen, leading to "leaky gut."[6]

Nitric oxide is one of the most important molecules that helps control the function of the immune system at the cellular level. It is a "good" molecule, because its presence is critical for signaling the cells to be on guard against foreign invaders. It becomes a "bad" molecule when it is produced in excess because it can lead to inflammation.[7]

The immune system clustered around the intestinal tract is critically important in the regulation of nitric oxide. The presence of unfriendly or toxic bacteria in the intestinal tract is a primary activator of the GALT, which results in excessive nitric oxide production. Nearly three pounds of living bacteria of hundreds of different species live in your intestinal tract. These bacteria are of three classes:

> **Class I** includes the beneficial, symbiotic bacteria that produce vitamins and other nutrients and help support the immune system. Members of this family are *Bifidobacteria* and *Lactobacillus*.
>
> **Class II** bacteria are commensals whose presence neither helps nor harms the body.
>
> **Class III** are the parasitic or toxic bacteria, including *Clostridia*, enterotoxigenic *E. coli* and *Salmonella*. These harmful bacteria produce caustic chemicals that can alter gene ex-

pression of GALT, activating the body's alarm system and creating a state of chronic inflammation.[8]

Agents other than the toxic bacteria that can cause chronic intestinal or whole-body inflammation include parasites like the yeast *Candida albicans* and water- and food-borne amoebic organisms like *Giardia*.[9]

It may be difficult to believe, but the intestinal tract actually does have its own immune system and it is hard-wired into the circuitry of the rest of the body through the release of the alarm substances called cytokines. The way the genes of your intestinal cells "talk" to the contents of your intestines, including food and living bacteria, may determine how the immune system of the rest of your body functions. Medical researchers have begun to define this relationship more accurately. Julian Bion, M.D. and Peter Mountford, Ph.D., from the Department of Intensive Care Medicine, University of Birmingham, England, recently reported that patients who have cardiac bypass surgery often do poorly in recovery as a consequence of exposure to toxic substances from their intestinal tract produced by bacteria.[10] Bion and Mountford found that the toxic reaction to certain bacteria in the intestinal tracts of patients undergoing bypass surgery creates increased intestinal permeability. The result is the release into the blood of toxic substances that adversely affect the immune system, reduce healing and impede recovery.

Abnormal intestinal permeability is associated with toxic reactions that influence the brain and nervous system as well. A number of studies have found that children who suffer from autism often have "leaky gut," and their brains are exposed to high levels of toxic substances that originate in their intestinal tracts.[11] Of course, this does not mean that all cases of autism are caused by immune system reactions to toxins from the intestinal tract. It does suggest, however, that one contributor to altered gene expression and its influence on the immune system is the extraordinary linkage among

intestinal contents, the function of the GALT and the body's inflammatory mechanisms, including brain function.

Dr. Galland believes leaky gut syndrome is nearly epidemic
among individuals who have chronic inflammation and pain. He
estimates that this syndrome plays a role in 70 percent of people
with chronic fatigue syndrome, eight out of ten aspirin or ibuprofen
users, most alcoholics and anyone who has been hospitalized. He
believes parasites like *Cryptosporidium* also contribute to leaky gut
syndrome. Through toxic or allergic reactions, even foods we consider "good foods" can participate in GALT activation and initiate
this inflammatory response. This follows from the discussion in
Chapter 5 of lectins and blood types, which demonstrated that
individuals who carry specific genotypes may be more responsive
to certain lectin-containing food families that activate the
inflammation-producing system.

A number of medical tests are now available to assess intestinal
permeability. One of the most common is the lactulose-mannitol
challenge test. This test requires a patient to consume a liquid that
contains two synthetic sugars, lactulose and mannitol. After the
person drinks the solution, he or she collects urine samples and
sends them to the laboratory. The laboratory analyzes the levels of
these sugars that have been absorbed and excreted in the urine and
provides a permeability index. Lactulose is not normally absorbed
across the healthy intestinal tract. Excretion of lactulose in the urine
indicates how "leaky" the intestinal lumen is.[12]

ARTHRITIS AND ACTIVATION OF THE GUT-ASSOCIATED LYMPHOID TISSUE (GALT)

When the GALT is aroused by exposure to what it perceives as toxic
substances from bacteria in the intestinal tract, food, water or toxic
chemicals, it releases alarm cytokines into the bloodstream. This
increases intestinal permeability, resulting in leaky gut, and activates

the rest of the body's immune system to be on guard. The over-vigilance of the immune system can trigger inflammation which is seen as inflammatory arthritis.[13] Certain bacteria that inhabit the intestinal tract are the most problematic in activating the immune system and producing arthritis. These bacteria include *Yersinia* and *Klebsiella*. People with specific genetic predisposition and a certain immune system personality in their genetic structure are very reactive to these organisms if they inhabit their intestinal tract. These bad bacteria in the intestinal tracts of individuals with genetic susceptibility—the HLA-B27 antigen genotype—result in significantly increased risk for inflammatory arthritis.

Here again, the concept of genetic nutritioneering can be beneficial. By understanding something about a family's genetic history and immune system function, one might be more concerned about the potential for infection with bacteria such as *Yersinia* or *Klebsiella* that could initiate arthritis-like inflammation. The presence of these bacteria can be assessed by having a medical laboratory do a bacterial culture of the stool to see if these bacteria are residing within the intestinal tract. A number of medical laboratories now provide this service, which helps the health practitioner to determine whether toxic bacterial overgrowth in the intestinal tract could be associated with the causation of arthritis.*

As the intestinal tract becomes more leaky, more toxic substances are released into the bloodstream to initiate increased inflammatory response. In genetically susceptible individuals this process increases the risk of joint inflammation, which might be seen as rheumatoid arthritis or osteoarthritis.[14] Evidence of reactivity to nitric oxide activation has been found in the joint spaces of individuals who suffer from osteoarthritis, suggesting their immune systems have been overly activated.[15]

The results of these recent scientific investigations go a long way toward dispelling the myth that arthritis is solely the result of

---

* Great Smokies Diagnostic Laboratory, Ashville, North Carolina, (800) 522-4762.

bad genes or wear and tear. No doubt genes and abuse to the joints throughout life do contribute to the risk of inflammation and arthritis problems, but they are not the only factors that cause these difficulties. We might say genetic predisposition and wear and tear are factors that require, in turn, other gene response modifiers to trigger the inflammation of arthritis. More and more rheumatology researchers are discovering the link between intestinal function, GALT activation and joint space inflammation.[16]

A recent study of hundreds of patients found gut inflammation and leaky gut in more than 80 percent of those with forms of reactive arthritis. This association was particularly true of patients with ankylosing spondylitis, an arthritic condition associated with severe loss of the integrity of the connective tissue and inflammation of joints throughout the body.[17]

Medical science is on the verge of a remarkable discovery in learning to treat the cause of rheumatoid arthritis rather than just its

Figure 1. Gut-associated Lymphoid Tissue and the Liver

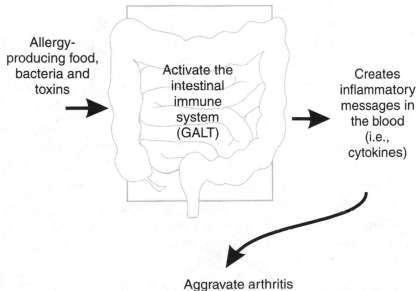

Allergy-producing food, bacteria and toxins

Activate the intestinal immune system (GALT)

Creates inflammatory messages in the blood (i.e., cytokines)

Aggravate arthritis pain and disability

symptoms. In the past, doctors used immune-suppressing or anti-inflammatory drugs like cortisone derivatives, gold and various pain medications to manage arthritis. Doctors who apply the latest research information in rheumatology will use a new class of agents to treat the *cause* of the inflammation rather than just the inflammation itself. Treating the inflammation alone might reduce pain and disability, but it might also allow the disease to continue to progress or produce adverse side effects. Side effects of some drug use, such as the long-term administration of cortisone-like drugs, can be life-threatening. A recent article in the *New England Journal of Medicine* described recent developments in the field and discussed treatment of rheumatoid arthritis with a specific gene-response modifier that altered the production of cytokines, the inflammatory messenger substances.[18]

Although this is still very experimental and new science, it clearly indicates that the same agents that activate the body's immune-inflammatory processes are the causative agents for inflammatory arthritis. These inflammatory disorders do not occur inevitably as a consequence of bad genes.

Only a few years ago we knew very little about the role of inflammatory substances or cytokines in the production of arthritis. We have now progressed to the point of recognizing that by applying the modification of gene response to the initiators of inflammation we can actually prevent the tissue destruction, disability and disfigurement associated with arthritis. Gary Firestein, M.D. and Nathan Zvaifler, M.D., renowned rheumatologists from the University of California San Diego School of Medicine, recently pointed out, "How anticytokine therapy will be used in rheumatoid arthritis remains to be defined.... The advances in anticytokine therapy are an important step forward both in therapy and in understanding the pathogenesis of chronic inflammatory arthritis."[19]

Pharmaceutical companies are competing to be the first to produce a new class of anti-inflammatories based on this new information. One class of these drugs, called "cyclooxygenase 2 inhibitors," blocks the inflammation message from the genes.[20] New drugs to modulate the inflammatory signals are the object of research at many of the world's most prestigious genetic engineering and pharmaceutical companies.[21] Most exciting, much of this benefit might be also achieved without drugs by applying the genetic nutritioneering approach.

NUTRITIONEERING AND THE INFLAMMATORY PROCESS

Once we accept the fact that inflammatory conditions, from intestinal inflammation to rheumatoid arthritis or osteoarthritis, might result from a combination of genetic, lifestyle and nutrition factors, the question of what to do with this information remains. Is it an academic subject for which there is no meaningful take-away message? Or are there things we can do to implement an anti-inflammation program by advancing the concepts of genetic nutritioneering?

Studies like those of Christina Surawicz, M.D. and Lynne McFarland, Ph.D., from the Department of Medicinal Chemistry at the University of Washington School of Medicine in Seattle, provide an affirmative answer to the second question. Surawicz and McFarland have reported that oral supplementation of friendly bacteria can help recolonize the intestinal tract with class I bacteria, which can then force out class III toxic bacteria. The result can be a reduction of inflammation of the intestinal tract or, in women, reduction of recurrent vaginal infections.[22]

This research helps expand the definition of nutrition to include consumption of substances that contain live cultures of friendly bacteria. This concept is not as strange as it may seem. You may regularly consume yogurt that contains live cultures of the friendly *Lactobacillus acidophilus* bacteria. These friendly bacteria, or "probiotics," promote healthy biological function. When you consume them as living organisms in beverages or foods like yogurt, they survive in your intestinal tract, recolonize it with friendly bacteria, and reduce the numbers of unfriendly toxic bacteria. Bacteria that can do this include not only *Lactobacillus acidophilus* but also *Lactobacillus casei, Bifidobacterium longum,* and *Saccharomyces boulardii*, a yeast that has very favorable effects on assisting the function of the GALT.

A number of companies now provide nutritional supplements or foods that contain live cultures of these friendly bacteria. Some people call this type of therapy "reflorestation." The bacteria that live in the intestinal tract are called flora, and by restoring the friendly bacteria, one has "re-florested." Adding supplemental levels of these friendly bacteria to the diet is one method of treating chronic *Candida* overgrowth associated with vaginal and other bacterial infections that activate the GALT and stimulate inflammation.

In addition to adding friendly bacteria to the diet, a person can also add selective foods that friendly bacteria can live upon in the intestinal tract. Theoretically, the objective is to feed the friendly bacteria and starve the unfriendly bacteria. To accomplish this, microbiologists have, through sophisticated detective work, studied the unique chemical personalities and food preferences of different bacteria. They then were able to identify foods that would selectively feed the good bacteria. This detective work led to the discovery of fructooligosaccharides (FOS), a class of carbohydrates found in certain plant foods, particularly soybeans and Jerusalem artichokes. The friendly bacteria in the intestinal tract readily use FOS as food, but the unfriendly bacteria cannot use these substances well. A substance called inulin in Jerusalem artichoke flour contains the favorable oligosaccharides, and soybeans and chicory can be commercially processed to concentrate FOS. Both inulin and FOS promote the growth of the friendly class I bacteria at the expense of the unfriendly class III bacteria.[23,24]

It takes only a small amount of FOS to produce favorable effects. Clinical studies indicate that one or two teaspoons of a FOS supplement daily along with supplementation with the friendly bacteria can bring about marked improvement in intestinal function and reduce intestinal permeability (leaky gut), chronic pain and infection.

The amino acid L-glutamine is another nutrient that is often included as part of a gastrointestinal supplementation program to reduce inflammation. According to Douglas Wilmore, M.D., a trauma care surgeon and researcher at Harvard Medical School, patients' intestinal permeability increases postoperatively. He found their intestinal integrity was improved by administering L-glutamine.[25] Judith Shabert, M.D., R.D. described the use of L-glutamine supplementation to improve intestinal function in her book *The Ultimate Nutrient, Glutamine.*[26] Studies indicate that 10 to 15 grams of supplemental L-glutamine daily can help preserve the gut lumen and heal a leaky gut.[27,28]

The message emerging from this research is that specific nutrients can speak to the genes of the gastrointestinal lumen. They can either put messages of inflammation to sleep or awaken them. The connection between nutrition and immune function is a rather recent breakthrough in understanding. Dr. Ranjit Chandra, M.D., at the University of Newfoundland, Canada, was a pioneer in the field of nutritional immunology. He described the role of specific nutrients in supporting the gene expression of function within the immune system. As we get older, or if we are under chronic stress from infection or trauma, nutrition becomes more important than ever in communicating with the immune system to provide adequate immune defense.[29]

Studies of older individuals show that inadequate amounts of vitamin E, zinc or carotenoids (the orange-red pigments in fruits and vegetables) can result in reduced immune function. Supplementary levels of these nutrients, sometimes in doses far in excess of the Recommended Dietary Allowances, bolster the immune function in these people. The research results suggest that enhanced levels of these nutrients talk to the genes to help improve immune defense. Work in nutritional immunology is advancing rapidly at the Tufts University Medical School and Human Nutrition Center on Aging in Boston, Massachusetts. A number of studies indicate that enhanced levels of vitamin E (up to 800 IU per day) can promote improved immune function and reduce some inflammatory markers in elderly individuals. A recent clinical intervention trial with vitamin C (1 gram per day) and vitamin E (400 IU per day) indicated the benefit achieved by giving the two nutrients together exceeded what one would expect by giving each of them independently. These studies indicate that combined supplementation with vitamin C, vitamin E and other antioxidants (including carotenoids and bioflavonoids) is more capable of improving immune function than supplementation with either family of nutrients alone.[30]

Vitamin E even helps trap damaging inflammation-initiating substances related to nitric oxide. Bruce Ames, Ph.D., chairman of the department of biochemistry and molecular biology at the University of California at Berkeley, and his colleagues recently reported that natural vitamin E, as contrasted to synthetic vitamin E, was helpful in deactivating the toxic effects of nitric oxide.[31]

Niacinamide (vitamin B3) is another nutrient that has received considerable attention because of its ability to help prevent inflammation. In the 1940s and 1950s, Connecticut physician William Kaufman, M.D., Ph.D. performed detailed evaluations of several hundred patients with both osteoarthritis and rheumatoid arthritis.[32] He treated them with very large doses of niacinamide, a form of vitamin B3 that does not produce the typical flushing reaction observed with niacin. He documented remarkable improvements in their joint function and range of motion, increased muscle strength and endurance, reduction in the inflammatory substances in their blood and a reduction in the amount of pain medication they were taking. He claimed the improvements occurred not just because of an anti-inflammatory effect of niacinamide, but because the increased level of this nutrient actually improved joint function and reduced inflammation, leading to healing of the joints.

Kaufman's observations and publications languished in the medical literature for nearly 50 years until they were reevaluated by Dr. Wayne Jonas and his colleagues at the Office of Alternative Medicine at the National Institutes of Health. The Jonas study, which duplicated the Kaufman supplementation program of 450 mg of niacinamide taken three times daily, confirmed the clinical benefit of this supplement in reducing the pain of osteoarthritis.[33] The mechanism of action of niacinamide is still not completely understood. It seems to work by reducing immune system activation and the resulting oxidant stress, which ultimately produces the pain, swelling, redness and tissue destruction of arthritis.

In addition to niacinamide, other natural substances are being investigated for their function as gene response modulators to reduce inflammation and help heal the joints. Chondroitin and glucosamine sulfate have been the focus of considerable media attention for their use in treating arthritis and healing damaged joints. Both are complex natural biochemicals. Chondroitin is derived from the connective tissues of animals, and glucosamine sulfate is derived from crab shells. These substances help promote reduction of the inflammatory process and assist in joint healing.

Finally, let's look at the rich 2,000-year history of the use of various herbal products in the field of Ayurvedic or Indian medicine for the management of inflammatory disorders. The Ayurvedic herbal product that has received most attention recently through pharmacological research is Boswellia.[34] Extracts from the *Boswellia serrata* tree in India yield a gum resin that contains what chemists call boswellic acids. These substances help reduce inflammation of the GALT and the messages it transmits to the rest of the body for chronic inflammation. Animal studies indicate that oral administration of boswellic acid helps reduce liver inflammation in hepatitis as well as joint inflammation in arthritis. Boswellic acid works by inhibiting the gene expression of the inflammatory messengers that promote chronic inflammation.[35]

In human clinical trials, supplementation with concentrates of Boswellia has resulted in significant reduction of inflammatory markers and recovery of function in individuals who have joint inflammation and other inflammatory conditions.[36]

An extraordinary chapter in the understanding of inflammation and arthritis is emerging. We now know that much of our inflammatory process is controlled at the gut level. We know that inflammatory alarm substances released into the bloodstream can trigger inflammation in the brain, muscles, joints, liver and even the heart. We recognize that certain agents can modify genetic expression to reduce the presence of these alarm substances. And finally, we understand that many of these modifiers of inflammation, which treat the cause of the inflammatory process and not just its effects, are natural substances derived from our diet. Some of these natural substances are fructooligosaccharides, L-glutamine, niacinamide and the antioxidants, including vitamins C, E and the flavonoids.

We also recognize that good foods for one person may be poisonous for another because the way the GALT speaks to the diet differs dramatically from one person to another. As stated in Chapter 5 regarding lectins and the type O blood group, any food or the principles within that food might react adversely with an individual's immune system to produce an inflammatory response. The following list of common allergy-producing foods is a good starting place for a trial elimination diet. You may be sensitive to one or more of the following:

- Wheat and other gluten-containing grains
- Corn
- Citrus
- Dairy products (lactose, casein)
- Shellfish
- Tomatoes and other foods in the nightshade family (peppers, potatoes, eggplant)
- Peanuts

- Yeast
- Soy

If you have a problem with chronic arthritis symptoms or other chronic inflammatory processes, your first course of action might be to utilize the genetic nutritioneering concept of looking for ways your genetic inheritance factors interrelate with your diet and lifestyle to produce the outcome of inflammation. By modifying your diet, lifestyle and medication use, you may be able to realize considerable improvements in your body's immune system function and thereby lower the level of alarm substances traveling in your bloodstream and triggering inflammation.

Most of us live time-urgent, compressed lives. We try to do more things than we are physically capable of accomplishing in finite periods of time. As a result, we subject ourselves to emotional trauma that makes our bodies tense and activates our nervous systems. This heightened activation combines dangerously with the increasing number of infectious organisms to which we are exposed in our food and water supplies, the presence of toxic chemicals in our environment, the increasing use of over-the-counter medications and alcohol and the poor quality of the typical diet. This can stress our genes into expressing the message, "I'm under siege and I need to fight back." The immune system fights back by becoming activated and promoting inflammation, which is the primary symptom of being at war with one's environment. The best way to treat inflammation may be to do all you can to unburden your immune system. Accomplishing this involves not only decreasing exposure to toxic substances and improving the function of your gastrointestinal system, but also lowering the load of stress and anxiety from your immune system. Although the genetic nutritioneering approach focuses principally on nutritional modification that can improve health and vitality, we do not want to minimize the importance of the impact of stress, anxiety, depression and despondency on the activity of the immune system.

A PROGRAM TO MODIFY RISK FACTORS FOR ARTHRITIS

- Your diet should be low in common allergy-producing foods such as wheat, dairy products, peanuts and corn.
- Evaluate your gastrointestinal/digestive function and determine the presence of intestinal parasites through a digestive stool analysis test.
- Supplement your diet with acidophilus and bifidobacteria along with fructooligosaccharides (FOS) and inulin.
- Avoid alcohol and anti-inflammatory medications.
- Take 5–15 g of L-glutamine daily.
- Increase rice and barley fiber intake.
- Introduce a stretching and body toning program along with stress management.

Genetic Nutritioneering Daily Immune System Support

Vitamin E, 400 IU
Zinc, 20–50 mg
Mixed carotenoids, 10–30 mg
Vitamin C, 1,000–2,000 mg

Genetic Nutritioneering Support for Symptom Relief of Chronic Inflammation

Niacinamide, 450 mg, 3 times daily
Glucosamine sulfate, 500 mg, 3 times daily
Chondroitin sulfate, 500 mg, 3 times daily
Boswellia serrata gum extract, 100 mg, 3 times daily

Beyond Cholesterol with Nutritioneering

In his recent book *Chromosome Six*,[1] medical mystery writer Robin Cook, M.D. describes a fictional genetic engineering company that has transplanted human chromosome 6 into monkeys. A monkey with the chromosome from a specific human, the reasoning went, could be used as an organ donor for that individual. Chromosome 6 carries the message for the inheritance of many aspects of immunity. Theoretically, by inserting the human characteristics on chromosome 6, the organs of the monkey could be made immunologically identical to the human's organs, eliminating the possibility of organ rejection. As the story unfolds, however, we learn that along with the characteristics for immunity, the monkeys received a number of other genetically linked characteristics in the transfer, giving them human personality characteristics.

Although this story takes liberties in describing molecular genetics and what is called transgenics (the insertion of the characteristics of one animal into the chromosomes of another), it does open our eyes to the fact that genetic characteristics are not necessarily compartmentalized and isolated. They are related in a weblike fashion, and the interactions within this complex whole are what give rise to the genotype—and ultimately the phenotype—of the individual. It is important that we understand this complexity, because for the past 50 years the tendency of medicine has been to isolate single disease characteristics of the individual and look for single agents to treat those characteristics.

The single cause/single solution concept no doubt originated with the discoveries in the early 20th century that specific diseases were produced by specific bacteria and could be treated by specific antibiotics. The medical successes in disease treatment with this philosophy fostered the belief that disease often had a single cause and a single treatment. The more we learn about the interrelationship of genes in the complex nature of the inheritance factors locked into our chromosomes, the more we recognize the limitations of this disease treatment model. Although it frequently is effective for bacterial diseases, it doesn't work well when it is applied to disorders that affect people in their middle and later years. Arthritis, digestive disorders, dementia, heart disease and cancer are too complex to submit to a single cause/single treatment solution.

A good example of the inadequacy of the single cause/single solution medical model is the recent focus on elevated blood cholesterol as the cause of heart disease. Research, diagnosis and treatment have all been directed toward cholesterol management. Low-cholesterol/low-fat foods are marketed to promote a "healthy heart." Cholesterol-lowering drugs are among the most prescribed medications of our time. And public health messages stress the importance of understanding the important role of elevated cholesterol in causing heart disease. Many people now mistakenly believe that, as long as they keep their cholesterol level below 200, they won't have to worry about heart disease.

Meanwhile, however, we keep hearing about someone whose blood cholesterol was "normal" and who seemed to be the picture of health who suddenly dropped dead of a heart attack. This couldn't happen if cholesterol were the whole story of heart disease.

The real explanation for heart health and disease is beginning to emerge from clinics, laboratories and research institutions around the world. It is based on the principles described in this book.

From 1979 to 1992 in Scandinavia, 15 young male athletes and one female athlete died of sudden cardiac arrest while they were competing in a sport called orienteering. Orienteering competitors run long distances through territory with no trails, using a map and compass as their only guides. This demanding sport requires agility, extraordinary fitness, strength and an uncanny sense of direction. The athletes who died had very low levels of blood cholesterol and none of the usual risk factors for heart disease. The 16 deaths of young, very fit athletes were considered to be an "epidemic" of unknown cause.

Swedish medical researchers spent several years trying to find the cause of death of these elite athletes. Postmortem examination revealed evidence of inflammation of the heart which seemed to be caused by a chronic infection with the parasite *Chlamydia pneumonia.*[2]

Following up on this discovery, investigators in the cardiology division at the University of Utah School of Medicine have confirmed the strong correlation between heart disease and infection with *Chlamydia.*[3] Investigators have now also found that other organisms, such as *Helicobacter pylori*, the bacteria that causes stomach ulcers, are also associated with an increased risk of heart disease.[4]

The organisms that cause chronic infection alter gene expression of the host individual and trigger the production of cytokines, the inflammatory markers described in the previous chapter. Laboratory analysis of individuals who have chronic infection reveal elevated levels of these markers of inflammation in their blood, including elevations of C-reactive protein and serum amyloid A protein, two well-known indicators of chronic inflammation.[5]

This research has led to the realization that factors other than cholesterol may play a role in heart disease. The interaction between agents that lead to inflammation and genes that express inflammatory markers like C-reactive protein and serum amyloid A protein increases the risk of damage to the heart and subsequent heart disease.

The importance of this interaction helps explain why routinely taking low-dose aspirin helps protect against heart attack. Statistically, although the reason was not previously known, taking the equivalent of a baby aspirin daily reduces the incidence of heart attack and heart disease in adults. Recently, medical investigators from the Division of Preventive Medicine and Cardiovascular Disease at Brigham and Women's Hospital at Harvard Medical School reported that aspirin might help protect against heart disease through its ability to reduce inflammation. When the researchers measured the levels of C-reactive protein in the blood of 543 apparently healthy men participating in a physicians' health study, they found those who had elevated levels of C-reactive protein had higher risk of heart disease. Those who took aspirin on a regular basis had a much lower risk. The investigators conclude that the reduction of heart disease risk associated with taking aspirin appears to be directly related to aspirin's ability to lower the level of C-reactive protein.[6]

According to renowned cardiologist Attilio Maseri, M.D., the new research linking inflammation and heart disease suggests that the current approach to heart disease prevention that focuses entirely on lowering cholesterol may be ill-advised. He believes we should be trying instead to identify individuals who would benefit most from specific therapies based upon their genetic need.[7]

Research is needed to explore the relationship between heart disease and multiple genetic susceptibilities, some of which may be related to inflammatory substances produced within the gut-associated lymphoid tissue (GALT). (See Chapter 8 for a discussion of GALT.) Many types of infection, toxic exposure or trauma could result in increased production of inflammatory alarm substances. These alarm substances, in turn, could interact with the genes in genetically susceptible individuals to produce heart inflammation and subsequent heart disease.[8] It has been only two years since medical investigators discovered that inflammation is related to heart disease, but we now understand that these markers for inflammation may be better predictors of heart disease than elevated blood cholesterol itself.[9]

DIETARY RECOMMENDATIONS FOR REDUCING HEART DISEASE RISK

If cholesterol alone is not responsible for heart disease, how important is diet in preventing heart disease? Once again, we must not throw the baby out with the bathwater. Extensive research continues to indicate that elevated levels of the "bad" LDL cholesterol are associated with increased risk of heart disease. In fact, studies indicate that for every 1 percent elevation in the bad LDL cholesterol there is a 2 percent increase in risk of heart disease. This statistic clearly supports continued monitoring of diet and lifestyle aimed at reducing levels of LDL cholesterol in the blood. As William Connor, M.D. and Sonja Connor, R.D. pointed out recently, studies around the world continue to indicate that a low-fat, high-fiber diet rich in unrefined, complex carbohydrates helps lower the risk of heart disease and improve heart health.[10]

Fat and cholesterol are not the only nutrition concerns that relate to an attempt to prevent heart disease, however. Although it is high in fat, the Mediterranean diet, in which the fats are primarily monounsaturated fats from olive oil, is associated with lower heart disease risk. Greenland Eskimos, whose diet is extraordinarily high in fat, also have a low incidence of heart disease, presumably because the fat they eat comes almost entirely from seals and cold-water fish. These fats are rich in omega-3 fatty acids, which seem to protect heart function.[11] It would be misleading, therefore, to say that simply reducing all fats in the diet and eating more unrefined carbohydrates and vegetable products could prevent heart disease. We have learned that the best approach to nutrition combines a reduction in saturated animal fats and partially hydrogenated vegetable oils from processed and convenience foods with increased intake of fresh fruits and vegetables, whole grains, lean meats, fish and monounsaturated, omega-3 rich oils.

In an article in the *New England Journal of Medicine*, Scott Grundy, M.D., Ph.D. from the University of Texas Southwestern Medical Center, and Walter Willett, M.D., D.P.H. from the Harvard School of Public Health cautioned about the current obsession with reducing fat. They wrote,

> The intense focus on total fat intake not only is unlikely to be beneficial but also distracts people from lifestyle changes that can have real benefits. These include specific dietary reductions in saturated and trans fats (partially hydrogenated oils), increases in the consumption of fruits, vegetables and whole grains, and the prevention of excessive weight gain by greater physical activity and reductions in overall calorie intake.[12]

Statistically, only about 10 percent of the population is genetically predisposed to have elevated blood cholesterol as a result of elevated dietary cholesterol. Most of the cholesterol in the blood does not come directly from the diet. The intestines and liver manufacture cholesterol from other sources of fat, carbohydrate and protein. Advising people to omit cholesterol-containing foods from their diet because cholesterol produces heart disease does not balance with the facts. Some people, because they are not genetically susceptible to dietary cholesterol intake, can eat dozens of eggs a week and still maintain low blood cholesterol levels.

Recent studies from Leiden University Medical Center in the Netherlands indicate that in people older than 85 years, high blood cholesterol levels are associated with longevity and good health, owing to a lower mortality from both cancer and infectious diseases. According to the medical report from these studies, the presumed protective effect of elevated blood cholesterol in the elderly indicates we should reevaluate the use of cholesterol-lowering therapy after a certain age. Lowering cholesterol may actually be increasing rather than decreasing the risk of disease.[13] The authors wrote, "Our study shows that a high serum blood cholesterol concentration is not a risk factor for cardiovascular disease in people aged 85 years and over—on the contrary, it is associated with longevity. On the evidence of our data, cholesterol-lowering therapy in the elderly is questionable."

Cholesterol has gotten a bad reputation in the past 10 years because of its presumed role in heart disease. We seem to have forgotten that cholesterol is an important substance in the body. It helps cells maintain their structure and function and it is also the substance from which the liver manufactures bile acids so we can digest and assimilate nutrients from food. It is also the material from which sex hormones are produced in the ovaries, testes and adrenal glands. In other words, cholesterol is valuable to the body. The difficulty arises when the body produces too much cholesterol or produces it in the wrong form, such as the LDL particles that increase the risk of heart disease. Medical investigators at the U.S. Department of Agriculture Human Nutrition Research Center on Aging recently reported that cholesterol plays an important role in protecting against aging of the brain as well as the heart.[14]

The USDA research indicates that cholesterol serves as an antioxidant in the body, retarding the effects of oxidative stress. As with many other substances in the body, proper cholesterol control can result in good health, whereas either too much or too little of it can produce increased risk of disease.

Blood cholesterol is no different from other measurable substances in the blood. All have optimal levels that are associated with good health and healthy aging. Most medical investigators agree the optimal level of total (LDL plus HDL) blood cholesterol is between 150 and 200 mg percent. In older people, however, in whom increased oxidative stress and free radical aging present a greater concern, higher blood cholesterol levels may have a protective effect against brain and heart aging.

For individuals whose LDL cholesterol levels exceed 130 mg percent, cholesterol-lowering therapies are still advisable, particularly if their HDL cholesterol level is lower than 35 mg percent. The objective of any prudent diet and lifestyle intervention program to reduce the risk of heart disease is to communicate with the genes in such a way that the ratio of total blood cholesterol to HDL cholesterol is five-to-one or less. This is undoubtedly one of the best markers available for determining one aspect of heart disease risk. If your total cholesterol is 200, your HDL cholesterol should be at least 40 to provide a ratio of five-to-one or less. The lower this ratio, the lower your heart disease risk related to cholesterol.[15]

BEYOND CHOLESTEROL

Although medical science is very clear in acknowledging that elevated LDL cholesterol is a risk factor for heart disease, it does not completely understand why this is true. The suspicion is emerging that cholesterol may be as much the *effect* of other processes going on as the *cause* of heart disease. This means cholesterol is like the body's smoke detector. The smoke detector does not cause the fire; it alerts us to the presence of a fire and forces us to look for its cause. Similarly, elevated blood cholesterol may not cause heart disease, but it may be very closely associated with the appearance of heart disease.

In the late 19th century, the German physiologist Rudolph Virchow proposed that the origin of heart disease was inflammation of the heart and the arteries that bring blood to the heart. His proposition was based on his detailed autopsy studies and pathology investigations of individuals who died of heart disease. He found their arteries looked as though they had been wounded inside, which suggested they had an inflammatory condition such as what would occur with a skin abrasion that became infected.

In the early 20th century, however, a Russian physiologist named Nikolai Anitschow proposed an entirely different mechanism as the origin of heart disease. He raised white rabbits on a high-fat, high-cholesterol diet and was able to produce serious heart and artery disease in these rabbits. He proposed that dietary fat caused fatty streaks and deposition of fat on the walls of arteries and in the heart, producing heart disease. The more investigators studied Anitschow's hypothesis, the more they became convinced that dietary fat was the cause of heart disease and the less they reflected on the pioneering work of Virchow.

In the 1980s, however, investigators at Harvard Medical School reevaluated the Anitschow concept.[16,17] Using the same type of white rabbits Anitschow had studied, they placed them on the same fat- and cholesterol-enriched diet and found they, too, could produce heart and artery disease in these animals. When they purified the cholesterol so it was 99.999999 percent pure before they fed it to the animals, they were unable to produce the same high level of heart disease. When they fed the rabbits a very low level of the impurity they had refined out of the normal cholesterol, suddenly the animals developed serious heart disease. The Harvard scientists concluded it was not the cholesterol itself that initiated the heart disease, but impurities in the cholesterol which were found to be cholesterol oxides.

Cholesterol oxides are forms of cholesterol that have been damaged by oxidative stress. These forms of cholesterol cause white blood cells to infiltrate the artery walls and initiate atherosclerosis or the heart disease process. The higher the level of blood cholesterol, the more cholesterol oxides are present. And the more oxidative stress a person is under, including inflammation, the more damage there is to cholesterol, leading to the formation of cholesterol oxides. Cigarette smoking, high serum iron levels, chronic infection and dietary antioxidant deficiencies can all increase cholesterol oxide formation and may be major contributors to heart disease.

ATHEROMA: A mass of plaque of degenerated, thickened arterial intima occurring in atherosclerosis.

Dr. Earl Benditt, a pathologist at the University of Washington School of Medicine, found these oxidized substances may be potential mutagens that react with the genes within cells on the artery wall. They can trigger a process of atheroma formation, by which the cells grow like a benign tumor on the inside of the artery.[18] Dr. Benditt believes the initial stages of heart disease may be caused by exposure of the arteries to these mutagenic substances that speak to the genes in ways that alter their function. We might consider the atheroma to be like a wart on the inside of the artery, a benign tumor that becomes inflamed, irritated and later infiltrated with cholesterol and calcium to become heart and artery diseases.

The process of atheroma formation might help explain why dietary antioxidants like vitamin E are helpful in preventing heart disease. Several studies have found that people whose diets contain more than RDA amounts of vitamin E have lower incidence of heart disease. A study of U.S. nurses and doctors found a 30 to 40 percent reduction in the incidence of heart disease among those who had the highest level of vitamin E intake over a four- to eight-year period. The benefit seemed to be greatest in individuals taking from 100 to 250 IU of supplemental vitamin E daily, which is an intake 6 to 15 times higher than the RDA for vitamin E.[19] Vitamin E is not the only important heart-protective antioxidant nutrient. Evidence suggests that vitamin C and the essential minerals magnesium, zinc, copper and selenium may also help protect against heart disease.

In addition to inflammation, elevations in C-reactive protein and serum amyloid A protein, elevated LDL cholesterol in the blood and oxidant stress factors, scientists have identified another heart disease risk factor. Nearly 30 years ago Kilmer McCully, M.D. suggested that an amino acid called homocysteine, which is found in the blood of some individuals, triggers heart disease. Dr. McCully recounts his discovery of the role of homocysteine and the history of its acceptance in his book, *The Homocysteine Revolution*.[20]

Old beliefs in the medical and scientific communities about the origin of heart disease change very slowly. Evan Shute, M.D., a cardiologist in London, Ontario, Canada during the 1950s and 1960s, can certainly attest to this fact.[21] Dr. Shute was the first cardiologist to talk about the benefit of vitamin E in the protection and even treatment of heart disease. He did fastidious clinical work and documented his observations of the benefits of vitamin E in heart disease, burn recovery and wound healing in thousands of patients. His medical colleagues not only would not accept his observations, they branded him a "kook." Nearly 50 years later, Dr. Shute's observations of the benefits of vitamin E are now being validated by the scientific community. Unfortunately, he and his brother, who was also actively involved in this research, did not live long enough to see the vindication of their efforts.

At age 63, on the other hand, Dr. McCully is still an active investigator at the Veterans Administration Hospital in New England. He is witnessing the acceptance of his idea that one of the major, unrecognized causes of heart disease is the elevation of the toxic amino acid homocysteine in the blood.[22]

This is not just an academic discussion. An article in a recent issue of *Time* magazine[23] told of the deaths of 64 men and women in Norway between 1992 and 1996. No one questioned the deaths. After all, all of the deceased had had heart disease, and many had undergone coronary bypass surgery. "Deaths like these are not the stuff of headlines." Retrospective analysis, however, revealed that the premature deaths of these Norwegians, like countless thousands of others around the world, resulted from the elevated levels of the amino acid homocysteine.[24]

Extensive medical research now indicates that at least 10

percent of the population (and perhaps even more) carries the genetic risk for production of elevated levels of homocysteine. Therefore, they are at increased risk of heart disease. Elevated levels of homocysteine in the blood are now universally accepted as a strong predictor of death from heart disease. Standard medical exams physicians have been doing for decades provide no information about homocysteine levels. In a sense, homocysteine has been a "silent killer" for years. Fortunately, however, many medical laboratories now offer cardiovascular screening tests that assess homocysteine level and provide information to the doctor and patient about genetic risk for this disorder.

Dr. McCully discovered the relationship between homocysteine and heart disease when he investigated the cause of death of an 8-year-old boy who died of a stroke in 1969. It is rare for a child of this age to have a stroke, and as a pathologist, Dr. McCully had his interest piqued by this case. It was not until years later, however, when the boy's sister developed what appeared to be heart disease in her 30s, that McCully began to put the pieces together. He believed homocysteine elevation, which was common to both cases, might be the cause of the stroke in the boy and heart disease in his sister. Although the link between homocysteine and heart disease had been known for some time, it was believed to be very uncommon and limited to a few unique genotypes. What Dr. McCully discovered was that there is a range of severity within this genotype. A number of genes interact to give rise to homocysteine elevation. Mild, moderate and severe forms of homocysteine elevation, therefore, resulted in varying risks of heart disease. An even more remarkable outcome of his investigations was the discovery that these characteristics of genetic risk to homocysteine could be modified through application of the principles of genetic nutritioneering.

Dr. McCully found that elevated homocysteine levels could be reduced by increasing the intake of specific nutrients that communicated with the genes and with the products of the genes in such a way as to reduce homocysteine levels to zero. These nutrients are folic acid, vitamin B12, vitamin B6 and the B-complex substance betaine.

Homocysteine and Aging

Following his discovery, Dr. McCully expanded his research to include a number of disorders associated with aging, including dementia, various forms of heart disease and alterations in connective tissue that are associated with arthritis. In all of these studies he found that elevated levels of homocysteine in the blood were associated with increased risk of age-related dysfunction. Therefore, they represented another genetically linked marker for biological aging.[25,26]

Many other investigators have confirmed the observations that elevated blood homocysteine is a marker for a number of genetically determined risk factors for accelerated biological aging. Measurements of plasma homocysteine throughout life are an important determinant of risk of heart disease and dementia.[27]

A recent collaborative investigation by European medical scientists resulted in a "consensus opinion," which they published in the *Journal of the American Medical Association* regarding the importance of elevated blood homocysteine levels. "An increased plasma total homocysteine level confers an independent risk of vascular disease similar to that of smoking or hyperlipidemia. It powerfully increases the risk associated with smoking and hypertension. It is time to undertake randomized controlled trials of the effect of vitamins that reduce plasma homocysteine levels on vascular disease risk."[28] By the same token, there is increasing evidence that the risk of dementia in the elderly increases in individuals with elevated homocysteine in their blood.[29]

The most amazing feature of these observations is not simply that investigators have identified a genetic risk factor that is related to a number of genes working in combination to control the levels of homocysteine. They have also found that common nutrients can be utilized to modify gene expression and activity to reduce the risk of dementia, heart disease and arthritis problems associated with elevated homocysteine.[30,31] This is an extraordinary example of the power of genetic nutritioneering. A number of genes control the phenotype we call elevated blood homocysteine. Different characteristics can make people more or less susceptible to the adverse effects of homocysteine, depending not only on the genes they carry, but also on the way they are expressed relative to their nutritional status.[32-35]

Some defects in homocysteine metabolism may be so mild they will not even show up in a standard blood test for homocysteine. They are observed only when the individual being tested consumes a supplement containing the amino acid methionine. Methionine is metabolized in the body through a process in which homocysteine is an intermediate. When someone has a very effective metabolism of homocysteine, there is no blood elevation of this amino acid when he or she is given a supplement of methionine. If the individual has a defect in homocysteine metabolism, however, the methionine supplement elevates blood homocysteine. Individuals with this very mild form of defect in homocysteine metabolism need to have their blood homocysteine levels measured a few hours after they have taken a methionine supplement to reveal their homocysteine defect.[36]

The homocysteine/methionine association also has important implications related to the risk from the toxic effects of homocysteine associated with a diet that is high in animal protein. Animal proteins, particularly egg protein, are very high in sulfur amino acids like methionine. Individuals who carry the mild form of defect in the metabolism of homocysteine, therefore, might have more risk of heart disease and dementia if they regularly consume a high-protein diet that is inadequate in vitamin B6, folate and vitamin B12.

The level of vitamins necessary to promote proper metabolism of homocysteine in individuals who carry these genetic uniquenesses is higher than the Recommended Dietary Allowances. Depending on the severity of the genetic uniqueness, a person might have to consume from 5 times to as much as 100 times the RDA levels of folate, vitamin B12 or vitamin B6 to lower his or her homocysteine levels.

It is worth noting that even Victor Herbert, M.D., J.D., an outspoken critic of vitamin supplementation, recently urged his medical and scientific colleagues to petition the Food and Drug Administration to supplement U.S. flour with higher-than-RDA levels of vitamin B12 and folate to protect against homocysteine-induced disease. He suggests the minimum safe daily oral dose of vitamin B12 should be 25 mcg per 100 grams of flour, which is four times the RDA for vitamin B12, along with 400 mcg of folate. He justifies this suggested supplementation of grains with high levels of folate and vitamin B12 by stating,

> The combined supplement will also prevent millions of Americans from getting vasculotoxic hyperhomocystemia, with its enormous cost in heart attack, stroke and other vasculotoxic morbidity and mortality, and billions more health-care dollars. We estimate that approximately 20 percent of all heart attacks, 40 percent of all thrombotic strokes, and 60 percent of all peripheral venous thromboses will be prevented by FDA implementation of our petition.[37]

This advocacy for nutrient supplementation of the food supply seems to be a remarkable change in position for Dr. Herbert, who for years has been a vociferous opponent of the nutritional supplementation or fortification of foods with micronutrients. Since Dr. Herbert is a recognized expert in vitamin B12 physiology and metabolism, his recent position indicates he now recognizes the benefits of nutritional supplementation for individuals at specific genetic risk.

In making his recommendations, Dr. Herbert also acknowledges the safety of these nutrients when given at that level. The risk to individuals who do not need them is insignificant relative to the extraordinary advantage for those who carry the genetic need for increased levels of vitamin B6, folate and vitamin B12.

John Hathcock, Ph.D., who was previously with the Food and Drug Administration as an expert in nutrient safety, recently wrote a comprehensive review paper on the safety and effectiveness of vitamin and mineral supplementation.[38] He indicated that the safety range for vitamin B12, vitamin B6 and folate, when given together, is very wide. It is well above the levels that are suggested for reducing the risk of the toxic effects of homocysteine.

Another important B-complex vitamin should be added to vitamin B12, folate and B6 in the Genetic Nutritioneering Program for individuals who want to reduce the risk of the toxic effects of homocysteine. This is the B-complex nutrient betaine. David Wilcken, M.D. and Bridget Wilcken, M.B., Ch.B. reported that some individuals with elevated homocysteine do not respond to administration of vitamin B12, folic acid and vitamin B6 alone. These individuals frequently respond to the addition of higher levels of betaine, however.[39]

The Wilckens found these individuals have a unique genetic need for supplemental betaine that is independent of vitamin B12, folate and vitamin B6. In their paper they reported that administering high doses of betaine to individuals whose elevated homocysteine condition was unresponsive to the traditional vitamin supplementation resulted not only in a reduction of homocysteine but also in a number of other positive influences on their health. They described one man whose prematurely gray hair returned to its natural color. In another case, a child's learning and behavior disorders improved dramatically and he was able for the first time to enter a normal school program. A man in his mid-20s, whose violence and behavior disorders had prevented him from holding a job, became much more tractable and was able to work for the first time in his life.

We are once again reminded that our bodies work not as a

collection of individual organs in isolation but as a collection of organ systems operating synergistically in a web-like manner. The role of homocysteine in the heart and brain illustrates the interconnectedness among organ systems. It points up the mistake we have traditionally made in medicine in isolating one system without examining its effect on others. Medical specialization has taught us more and more about the function of specific organs. Unfortunately, however, we have often failed to understand the interaction and synergy of the whole. The concept of genetic nutritioneering requires that we think in web-like patterns, in which interacting organ systems give rise to the function of the individual.

The revolution in understanding the relationship of homocysteine to a variety of age-related disorders originated with the discovery made by Dr. Kilmer McCully. The result has been the development of a genetic nutritioneering approach to manage homocysteinemia that uses a nutritional supplement described at the end of this chapter. The recommended dosages are based on contemporary published medical literature and represent the range of intake necessary to modify the phenotype in individuals with varying severity of genotype related to homocysteine production.[40,41]

Arginine and Heart Disease

With the increased understanding of the multiple genetic risk for heart disease and the realization that diet and nutrition can modify gene expression to result in a phenotype of low risk, new nutrients have come under scrutiny. One nutrient that is emerging in this regard is the amino acid L-arginine. When it is given in supplementary doses, arginine may help reduce the risk of heart disease.

Several years ago at the Wistar Institute in Philadelphia, Dr. David Kritchevsky found that blood cholesterol level and heart disease incidence increased in animals that had been given a diet that was low in the amino acid arginine and high in the amino acid lysine.[42] He suggested that dietary protein and the amino acids that are contained within it may contribute to heart disease in the same way as excessive intake of saturated fats. This information remained dormant in the medical literature for many years, but researchers recently found that L-arginine has an effect on the regulation of nitric oxide.[43] As a consequence of this discovery, medical investigators around the world are attempting to understand the role of L-arginine in immune defense, heart function, blood pressure control and brain chemistry.

Recently, medical investigators at the Hospital for Children in London, England, and the department of cardiology at the Prince Albert Hospital in Australia, examined the role of supplementary L-arginine in heart function in young adults with elevated blood cholesterol levels. They found that administration of 7 grams of arginine given three times a day had a positive effect on heart function and "may impact favorably on the atherogenic process" in these young adults.[44] Similarly, investigators at the medical school in Freiburg, Germany, found that L-arginine supplementation helped improve blood flow to the heart and other organs of the body in individuals with narrowing of the arteries as a consequence of elevated cholesterol and heart disease.[45]

L-arginine is just one tool of the genetic nutritioneering approach. Like many other nutrients, it has a much more complex role in the body than we formerly believed. It is more than a simple amino acid found in dietary protein. It has the ability to modify metabolic function and alter the way genes are expressed into their phenotype. This may explain why vegetable-based diets help some individuals reduce their risk of heart disease and other health-related problems. Vegetable proteins are commonly low in lysine and high in arginine. Lysine and arginine are two amino acids that play off against one another. Supplementation with L-lysine can increase blood cholesterol levels, while supplementation with

L-arginine reduces it and helps increase blood flow through the arteries.[46]

The frontier of medicine and research is moving rapidly to support a genetic nutritioneering approach. We now understand that an individual carries genetic markers for elevated homocysteine levels or inflammation that relates to increased risk of heart disease. He or she may be under oxidative stress that increases the risk of damage to the heart and arteries. These are examples of the advancing understanding of how genetics and nutrition work together to minimize the risk to a phenotype of age-related disease.

The headline of an article on a blood protein called apolipoprotein E (apoE) in a recent *Wall Street Journal* proclaimed, "A Gene Gives a Hint of How Long a Person Might Hope to Live."[47] ApoE, a protein that transports fat and cholesterol in the bloodstream, exists in three forms—apoE2, E3 and E4. Those who carry the genes for apoE2 seem to be able to eat a high-fat diet without risk of heart disease. Nor do they get Alzheimer's disease. Those who carry the genes for apoE4, however, have much higher risk for both heart disease and Alzheimer's disease. This information may seem to be the genetic luck of the draw, but evidence now indicates that if we know we carry the apoE4 genotype we can do something to reduce its expression as illness. ApoE is emerging as a classic example of the importance of applying the genetic nutritioneering concept.

The discovery that has rocked the medical community is that individuals who have the genetic characteristic for the apolipoprotein E4 have a much higher risk of both heart disease and the dementia of Alzheimer's.

How are the heart and the brain connected to a fat-carrying protein? What relationship does this have to the Genetic Nutritioning Program? Can a program be designed from the answers to these questions to help protect against both heart disease and Alzheimer's disease? The answers to these questions are the focus of the next chapter.

A PROGRAM TO MODIFY RISK FACTORS FOR HEART DISEASE

- Consume a diet that is low in saturated fats and partially hydrogenated oils by reducing your intake of meats, high-fat dairy products and processed foods.
- The primary sources of fats in your diet should be virgin olive and canola oils (monounsaturated).
- Eat fish two or three times a week.
- Eat soy foods two or three times each week.
- Make sure your diet includes ample amounts of unrefined or unprocessed vegetables, grains and fruits that are high in natural fiber.
- Treat chronic parasitic or bacterial infection.
- Engage in aerobic exercise or activity 20–30 minutes daily.
- Engage in stress management and relaxation therapy 20–30 minutes daily.
- Consume 5 daily portions of fresh fruits or vegetables, including members of the cabbage and broccoli family.

Genetic Nutritioneering Daily Support for the Cardiovascular System

Vitamin E, 400–800 IU

Vitamin C, 1,000–2,000 mg (except in high blood iron situations)

Mixed carotenoids, 10–30 mg

Selenium, 100–200 mcg

Zinc, 10–30 mg

Chromium, 100–300 mcg

Coenzyme Q10, 20–50 mg

L-arginine, 500–1,000 mg, 2 times daily

Magnesium, 400–800 mg
Omega 3 fish oils, 3–6 g

To manage homocysteine:

Vitamin B12, 25–1,000 mcg
Vitamin B6, 5–50 mg
Folic acid, 400–2,000 mcg
Betaine, 500–3,000 mg

For high blood iron levels:

Avoid iron-containing supplements and iron-fortified foods. Reduce your consumption of red meats. Increase your intake of manganese and calcium/magnesium by consuming low fat dairy products and dark green vegetables.

To reduce oxidative stress:

Do not smoke.
Reduce exposure to toxic metals (i.e. cadmium, lead, mercury).
If you have ApoE4 genotype, aggressively follow all suggestions on these pages.
If you have insulin resistance or high blood pressure, follow the recommendations given in Chapter 7.

1 | 0

REDUCING BRAIN AGING WITH NUTRITIONEERING

A RECENT ISSUE OF THE *Journal of the American Medical Association* included an article titled "Molecular Neurogenetics: The Genomc Is Settling the Issue."[1] The author stated in part:

> . . . The discipline of neurogenetics will rapidly and ultimately provide the greatest area of future development for the understanding of the major neurological diseases and their treatment. The era of molecular neurogenetics has arrived and has been highly beneficial by providing essential details of many inherited and noninherited neurological diseases. The progress in neurogenetics is gratifying and offers real hope for our patients.

Most individuals who have reached their middle years and have begun to notice signs that their bodies are aging are not concerned about something as complex as molecular neurogenetics. They worry about losing their memory and their ability to think clearly. According to the Canadian Study of Health and Aging, loss of cognitive function is the major concern of most individuals as they age. They have watched their parents lose their mental acuity even though they may not have been diagnosed with Alzheimer's or other neurological diseases.[2] Studies indicate that nearly 17 percent of people over 65 suffer from cognitive impairment with no signs of neurologic disease. This number is more than twice as high as the 8 percent who have all types of diagnosed dementia combined.[3]

What causes this decline in mental acuity with age? Can anything be done about it? Once again, genetic nutritioneering might provide the answers.

As people age, some genotypes seem to be associated with increased risk of dementia and loss of cognitive function and memory. The most common of these genotypes is the apolipoprotein E4 characteristic. Medical laboratories can now identify the apolipoprotein E genotype so individuals can know at an early age whether they carry the risk of dementia and heart disease related to this characteristic. It is one thing to know you carry a risk, and another to be able to do something to prevent the phenotype of premature loss of memory and cognitive function. The most exciting part of this story is that once we understand something about the predisposition to the loss of cognitive function, we can take steps to help prevent it.

As explained in Chapter 9, the three subtypes of the apolipoprotein E genotype include apoE2, apoE3 and apoE4. You got one gene message about your apoE type from your father and another from your mother, so your characteristics could be a combination of apoE2, E3 and E4. Individuals who carry at least one copy of the apoE4 gene are at increased risk for both dementia and heart disease. Those who received copies of the apoE4 from both their father and mother have a very significant increased risk for these conditions. On the other hand, individuals who received copies of the apoE2 gene from one or both parents have a very low risk of heart disease and dementia, which suggests this genotype may be protective.

Once again, however, your genotype is not your destiny. You

can modify the translation of your apoE genotype into phenotype by diet, lifestyle and environmental choices. Even if you carry the apoE4 characteristic you are not destined to express the phenotype of early-stage dementia and heart disease.

In a recent study at the Department of Internal Medicine at the University of Oulu Medical School in Finland, researchers evaluated the response of individuals who had the apoE2, E3 or E4 genotypes to high- and low-fat diets.[4] They found that when the subjects of the study consumed the high-fat diet, those who had the apoE4 characteristic had a much greater increase in blood cholesterol and other risk factors associated with heart disease than their counterparts with the apoE2 or E3 characteristic. When the individuals with the apoE4 characteristic consumed a low-fat diet, however, their cholesterol did not increase. This study suggests that dietary modification could be protective against heart disease and potential dementia in these apoE4 individuals.

Individuals with the apoE4 characteristic appear to be much more sensitive to fat, fiber and cholesterol in their diet than those who carry the apoE2 or E3 characteristics. The apoE4 genotype seems to be the most sensitive of the three to dietary variations.[5] To reduce the risk of expressing a genotype associated with increased risk of dementia or heart disease, these studies indicate, individuals who carry the apoE4 genotype may need to be much more careful about their dietary choices than those who carry either the apoE2 or E3 genotypes.[6]

The fact that apoE4 individuals have an increased risk of both dementia and heart disease is another reminder of the extraordinary web-like nature of human physiological function. The genes in various organs interact with one another to give rise to general patterns of disease risk or health.[7]

Individuals who carry this genetic apoE4 genotype characteristic are much more susceptible to inflammation than those individuals who carry apoE2 or E3 characteristics. Studies have indicated that if a person who carries the apoE4 genotype sustains a head injury, such as a concussion, he or she is more than twice as likely to sustain long-term damage than those who carry the apoE2 or E3 characteristics.[8] Similarly, boxers who sustain brain injury as a result of their sport are much more likely to have serious long-term damage if they carry the apoE4 characteristic.[9]

Studies have even found that older people who get into traffic accidents are more likely to have the apoE4 genotype than their peers who avoid traffic accidents.[10] The conclusion from this statistic is that many older-age people who carry the apoE4 characteristic are already suffering from loss of cognitive function, and their inability to make quick decisions while driving causes the accidents.

ApoE4 is also associated with increased Alzheimer's disease risk, and Alzheimer's patients who carry this genetic characteristic are much less responsive to drug therapy for their disease than Alzheimer's patients who carry apoE2 or E3 characteristics.[11,12] Autopsies have revealed that nearly 85 percent of diagnosed Alzheimer's disease patients who died carry the apoE4 characteristic. There is even a strong correlation between apoE4 and susceptibility to other neurological disorders, such as Creutzfeldt-Jakob disease.[13] This disorder, which is similar to Mad Cow disease, is described as a "spongiform encephalopathy" because examination of the brain reveals large, spongy holes that have been produced by a destructive inflammatory process. This inflammation of the brain appears to be much more prevalent in the apoE4 individual than in either the apoE2 or E3 individual. Any condition that could trigger inflammation might have more serious consequences for loss of brain function in the individual who carries the apoE4 characteristic.[14]

A recent study at the Molecular Neurobiology Laboratory, University of Manchester in England, may have explained the connection between the apoE4 characteristic and the risk of dementia in Alzheimer's disease.[15] DNA was extracted from samples of brain tissue from Alzheimer's disease patients and from similar samples from age-matched patients without Alzheimer's. Laboratory analysis revealed apoE gene type as well as the presence of agents that might initiate brain inflammation.

The researchers were surprised to find that carrying the apoE4 characteristic in the genes was not by itself a strong risk factor for Alzheimer's disease. ApoE4 became a concern only when the individual had a concomitant infection with herpes simplex, which created the brain inflammation associated with Alzheimer's. We associate the herpes simplex with cold sores and genital viral infections. The authors suggest that people who get cold sores and have the apoE4 characteristic may be much more at risk of damage to their nervous systems than if they carried apoE4 but not the herpes simplex virus.[15]

Herpes simplex is probably not the only agent that can initiate brain inflammation in the individual who carries the apoE4 characteristic. This research suggests that people who have the apoE4 genetic characteristic are much more susceptible to factors that induce inflammation, including viruses, toxic substances, allergic disorders, trauma and certain medications that may promote inflammation.

The research linking apoE4 and inflammation sheds light on the recent news that chronic arthritis sufferers who treated their arthritis with anti-inflammatory medications had much lower incidence of Alzheimer's disease.[16] Anti-inflammatory medications may help protect against Alzheimer's by blocking the inflammatory process associated with cellular destruction in the brain and other tissues. Individuals who carry the apoE4 genetic characteristic may be uniquely sensitive to inflammation. For them, anti-inflammatory therapy may be an important means of reducing their risk of loss of brain function and heart disease.[17]

In Chapter 8 we explained the role of inflammation in promoting heart disease. Individuals whose blood revealed elevated levels of inflammatory markers like C-reactive protein or serum amyloid A protein, which reflect gene expression of inflammation, had a much higher risk of heart disease than those who did not have these markers in their blood. Similarly, individuals who have elevated C-reactive protein in their blood also have increased risk of Alzheimer's disease.[18] This research has led to the recognition that chronic inflammation is associated with both heart disease and dementia, and individuals who carry the apoE4 genotype are at greatly increased risk for these problems.

Individuals who have inflammation associated with arthritis may reap an unexpected benefit from their disorder. The easily recognized pain and disability of arthritis are typically treated by anti-inflammatory, pain-reducing medications. The symptoms of Alzheimer's disease or other types of dementia, on the other hand, develop over years and are not easily recognized. Taking anti-inflammatory medications for arthritis pain, therefore, may coincidentally help protect against loss of brain function from chronic inflammation. This concept has been supported by numerous medical studies that indicate anti-inflammatory agents seem to protect against Alzheimer's disease.[19,20]

The trouble with using anti-inflammatory medications for many years is that adverse side effects may limit their use. As explained earlier, these side effects include increased risk of developing a leaky gut, kidney dysfunction and liver problems.[21] Although long-term use of anti-inflammatory medications may not be the answer, the dietary and lifestyle changes suggested in this book may be able to bring about the same reduction in inflammation.

FOOD SENSITIVITY AND LOSS OF BRAIN FUNCTION

Gluten sensitivity is an example of the role diet may play in increasing brain inflammation. Medical investigators in Scandinavia recently found a very high correlation between gluten-sensitive individuals who continue to eat wheat products and the early onset of dementia.[22] The researchers believe the dementia may result from a food allergy that activates the immune system and increases inflammatory response. In genetically susceptible individuals, that inflammation can result in loss of brain function.

Specific types of food allergy, when associated with genotypes such as apoE4, therefore, might enhance the body's inflammatory response and lead to accelerated loss of brain function over many years. A number of ongoing studies are trying to determine if a gluten-free diet will enable a gluten-sensitive person who carries the apoE4 genotype to avoid dementia.

Well before dementia sets in and an individual loses cognitive function, short-term memory and mental clarity, there is a long period of time during which he or she is simply confused or unable to think clearly. It is difficult for medicine to diagnose a mental disorder during this indeterminate time. Doctors may overlook the associations of food that produces an allergic reaction with increased risk of inflammation and the subtle loss of brain function.

Eliminating a food or food family to which a person is allergic may be an effective means of reducing inflammation, particularly in inflammation-prone individuals such as those with the apoE4 genotype. Doctors have long known that fasting brings about a significant reduction of pain, swelling and disability for those who suffer from rheumatoid arthritis.[23] This symptom reduction has been attributed to a lowered allergic response of the gut-associated lymphoid tissue (GALT) to specific food principles. The lowered GALT response reduces the blood level of alarm substances that create generalized inflammation in the body.

People cannot fast indefinitely, obviously, so fasting cannot be the treatment of choice for reducing food-related inflammation. Instead, eliminating reactive food proteins, based on the principles discussed in Chapter 5, and improving digestion and intestinal function, as described in Chapter 8, are a means of implementing the genetic nutritioneering approach in individuals who carry these genetic risks.

Chronic viral infections, certain food allergies, toxic reactions to environmental substances and adverse reactions to unfriendly bacteria that live in the intestinal tract may induce inflammation that, in the apoE4 individual, may greatly increase the risk of death of brain cells. Dementia results from the death of neurons in the brain, resulting in functional decline over years of damage. Neurologists have long believed that loss of brain cells and brain aging are inevitable aspects of normal aging, suggesting that everyone would suffer from dementia if he or she lived long enough. This belief was challenged recently, when scientists found that the death of brain cells is minimal in healthy aging and is not likely to account for age-related impairment in memory and cognitive function.[24] Genetic risk of brain inflammation combined with lifestyle, diet and environmental factors that increase exposure to inflammation-inducing substances cause the increased death of brain cells we associate with dementia.

BLOOD/BRAIN BARRIER: The barrier system separating the blood from the central nervous system.

As the inflammatory response of the body increases, the important blood/brain barrier (BBB) between the brain and the rest of the body loses its ability to defend the brain against substances in the blood. The brain becomes susceptible to toxins that can further increase inflammation and brain cell death.[25] Additional factors that increase inflammation and damage to the BBB and make the brain more susceptible to inflammation are the advanced glycosylation endproducts (AGE), described in Chapter 7. AGE proteins occur as a consequence of poor blood sugar control.[26] Loss of blood sugar control and insulin sensitivity is a principal feature of unhealthy aging, and we can now see the connection between this characteristic and the increased risk of brain and heart aging in individuals who carry the apoE4 genotype. AGE proteins induce inflammation in the brain and increase oxidative stress in brain cells, causing their early destruction.[27] Brain cells actually have receptor sites for the binding of AGEs, which induce brain toxicity and cause premature death of brain cells. These receptor sites are called receptors for advanced glycosylation endproducts, or RAGEs. Individuals who have poor control of blood sugar and insulin sensitivity may be at much higher risk of their brains becoming "en-RAGEd."[28]

For many years scientists have observed that individuals who are exposed to high levels of soluble aluminum through their water supply or medications like aluminum-containing antacids have an increased risk of developing Alzheimer's disease and other non-Alzheimer's dementias. Although the mechanism by which aluminum is associated with death to brain cells has been a mystery, recent research indicates that aluminum increases the formation of AGEs. Aluminum, therefore, might be a catalyst or promoter in the brain of the inflammatory process associated with Alzheimer's disease and the formation of "brain tangles."[29] Aluminum may be just one of many toxic substances that increase the risk of developing these brain tangles, which choke off brain cells and cause their premature death.[30]

BRAIN AGING AND MITOCHONDRIAL FUNCTION

It is clear that accelerated brain aging is a consequence of increased inflammatory processes in the brain. It is not so clear how inflammation of the brain actually causes premature death of brain cells and results in Alzheimer's or non-Alzheimer's dementia and other brain disorders. M. Flint Beal, M.D., a professor of neurology at Harvard Medical School, has been studying this relationship for many years. His research has uncovered a major link between the death of brain cells and the inflammatory process and oxidative stress. The evidence indicates the inflammatory process and agents that induce premature death of brain cells do so by uncoupling mitochondrial energy production in brain cells, causing them to undergo cellular suicide or apoptosis. Apoptosis describes the death of cells through a process by which they shrink and become dehydrated as their internal structure is damaged and choked off with proteins that produce tangles within the cells. One cause of apoptosis is the loss of proper mitochondrial energy production and release of oxidants from the mitochondria.[31]

The mechanism of destruction of brain cells is associated with a variety of neurological diseases, including not only Alzheimer's, but also Parkinson's disease and even amyotrophic lateral sclerosis (ALS or Lou Gehrig's disease). People with different genetic susceptibilities and various inflammatory mediators may experience different types and degrees of diseases of the brain, but they all may come from a similar mechanism.

Chemists have found that certain molds that grow on sugar cane produce a toxin called 3-nitro-propionic acid. When it is consumed as part of the moldy sugar cane, this substance is a mitochondrial poison that creates oxidative stress and causes suicide of brain cells.[32] In fact, it has been noted in the medical literature that some people who ate such fermented sugar developed severe brain injury. There are many other toxins that can be mitochondrial poisons. Some are derived from molds and fungi that may be present in the food supply, and others are environmental toxins and pollutants that come from occupational exposure.

This research makes it clear that oxidative stress plays a very important role in causing both Alzheimer's and Parkinson's disease. Individuals who cannot detoxify certain chemicals that are mitochondrial poisons have a much higher risk of Parkinson's disease than those who can effectively detoxify these chemicals. Exposure to environmental chemicals, poor detoxification capability, increased brain inflammation and oxidative stress all combine to give rise to a disorder such as Parkinson's disease, which many doctors still feel has no well-understood origin.[33-36]

Pharmaceutical companies are now actively pursuing ways of modifying the release of oxidants from the mitochondria of patients with various neurological disorders. Those at greatest risk to these problems could be those of specific genotypes, such as apoE4. Many medications may be developed in the years to come to treat these problems, once diagnosed, but with the knowledge available today we might be able to do something significant to prevent them.[37]

NUTRIENT PROTECTION AGAINST BRAIN INJURY

As a result of the emerging understanding of the links between brain inflammation, mitochondrial poisoning and oxidative stress, a number of medical investigators have begun to test the potential of antioxidants to defend against both Parkinson's disease and Alzheimer's disease. Stanley Fahn, M.D., a professor of medicine at the Department of Neurology, Columbia University College of Physicians and Surgeons in New York, found that vitamin E supplementation at 1000 mg per day seemed to help reduce the progression of Parkinson's disease.[38]

Another group of investigators at the Department of Neurology at Columbia University found that vitamin E helped in the treatment of patients with moderate impairment from Alzheimer's disease.[39] In this study, patients with diagnosed Alzheimer's disease received either 2,000 IU of vitamin E daily (which is more than 100 times the RDA) or a placebo. Compared to the placebo group, those who received the high-dose vitamin E experienced a significant delay in onset of more severe Alzheimer's disease.

Vitamin E is only one of a number of antioxidants that help defend the mitochondria against poisoning and oxidative stress. It is one component of a combination antioxidant therapy for individuals who have genetic risk of brain inflammation or who are exposed to brain toxins. This research provides hope that for individuals who carry the genetic apoE4 characteristic, the phenotype of dementia may not be inevitable. It also stresses the need for increased attention to reduction of inflammation, proper antioxidant nutrition with vitamin E, vitamin C and bioflavonoids, and reduced exposure to allergens or toxins that can induce mitochondrial poisoning or inflammation.

Another recent study found that vitamin C in its dehydroascorbate form was able to penetrate the blood/brain barrier and protect against oxidative stress in the brain.[40] This research once again emphasizes how the antioxidant nutrients vitamin C and vitamin E work together to defend against mitochondrial oxidative stress and the potential premature death of brain cells by apoptosis.

In foods, vitamin E exists as a mixture of substances. The most common supplemental form of vitamin E we consume is alpha-tocopherol. Research indicates, however, that the mixture of vitamin E as a natural source derived from soybean or palm oil, which contains alpha, beta, delta and epsilon tocopherol, along with tocotrienols, is the most potent inhibitor of mitochondrial oxidative stress.[41] For optimal benefit, therefore, you should supplement your diet with a range of antioxidants, and the vitamin E you consume should be a mixture from natural sources.

Vitamin E, vitamin C and bioflavonoids also work with two other antioxidants—coenzyme Q10 and lipoic acid. These two also help maintain proper mitochondrial function and reduce mitochondrial burnout.[42,43] Studies have shown that doses of coenzyme Q10 from 20 to 200 mg help control mitochondrial oxidative stress. Similarly, doses of 50 to 500 mg of lipoic acid, a natural antioxidant found within the mitochondria, have helped protect the brain, heart and liver against oxidative stress. Lester Packer, Ph.D., from the University of California at Berkeley, has suggested that lipoic acid may be one of the most important antioxidants that help defend the mitochondria against oxidative stress.[44]

In the list of beneficial nutrients for defending against inflammation and premature death of brain cells, vitamin B12, or cobalamin, may also be one of the most important. John Lindenbaum, M.D., a neurologist at the Columbia University College of Physicians and Surgeons, has for many years studied the role of vitamin B12 in protecting brain function in older individuals. In 1988 he reported that a variety of brain functional disorders in older-age individuals appear to be related to vitamin B12 deficiency. This was true despite the fact that these individuals did not have the classic signs of vitamin B12 deficiency, and their blood levels of vitamin B12 were within the range of normal.[45] He has found the best way to measure vitamin B12 insufficiency is to measure blood levels of the amino acid homocysteine and a chemical called methylmalonic acid. These two substances are good indicators of functional insufficiency of vitamin B12. The more elevated these substances are in the blood, the greater the functional vitamin B12 insufficiency and the more likely it is that the person's loss of brain function is related to vitamin B12 inadequacy.[46]

The more research that is done in this field, the more the realization grows that a great many older people are lacking in vitamin B12. Many medical investigators now concur that much of what we have considered dementia of old age is really a manifestation of vitamin B12 insufficiency.[47] They have also found a close correlation among low vitamin B12 status, increased methylmalonic acid in the blood and increased incidence of Alzheimer's dementia.[48]

Spouses of older individuals who have lost brain function as a consequence of low vitamin B12 status are also at risk of this problem, no doubt because they eat the same meals and share the same risk of B12 deficiency.[49] Even if the diet is adequate in vitamin B12, a person may not be absorbing adequate levels of the nutrient from food. Vitamin B12 is difficult to absorb. Its absorption depends upon the adequate secretion of stomach acid and a binding protein called intrinsic factor. Many people, as they age, lose the acid-secreting ability of their stomachs. In this case, or if they do not secrete sufficient intrinsic factor, they may not absorb vitamin B12 well and can develop a functional vitamin B12 deficiency.

Medications such as the acid-suppressing drug omeprazole,

which many older-age people take in the mistaken belief that they are producing too much acid, further suppress the absorption of vitamin B12.[50] This may be another contributor to the malabsorption of vitamin B12. Sometimes the only effective means of administering B12 in the elderly is by intramuscular injection.[51] Dr. Lindenbaum cautions physicians not to be misled when patients who seem to be losing cognitive function and brain power have normal blood levels of vitamin B12, because of the likelihood that they have elevated blood levels of homocysteine and methylmalonic acid, rendering their B12 blood levels insufficient. He recently evaluated the effect of intramuscular injection of a vitamin supplement containing 1,000 mcg of vitamin B12 (RDA 3–5 mcg), 1,100 mcg of folate (RDA 280 mcg) and 5 mg of vitamin B6 (RDA 1.8 mg) on blood levels of methylmalonic acid and homocysteine. The vitamin injections were administered eight times over a three-week period. He found that although these individuals had initially normal blood levels of vitamin B12, the injections significantly reduced both homocysteine and methylmalonic acid. Maximum effects of treatment were usually seen within 5 to 12 days. He also found the cognitive function of these older individuals improved significantly when they received the vitamin B12, folate and vitamin B6 injections.[52]

Many people insist they don't want to know if they carry a genetic risk for dementia. Using the information in this chapter, however, it is obvious that this knowledge does not sentence anyone to years of senility. On the contrary, knowing about genetic risk can be put to good use through the genetic nutritioneering approach. If you know you carry the apoE4 gene or the homocysteine characteristic, for example, you can alter your lifestyle, diet and environment to reduce inflammation, improve antioxidant defense systems and reduce homocysteine levels. Carrying the apoE4 genotype is merely an indicator of how to tailor the diet, lifestyle and environment to produce a phenotype that maintains a high level of brain function throughout life. The following chart indicates ways to reduce your risk of brain aging as well as heart disease regardless of your genetic inheritance.

Reducing the Risk of Brain Aging

- Eat a low saturated-fat diet
- Reduce chronic viral infections
- Reduce toxic mineral exposures (aluminum, lead, cadmium, mercury)
- Reduce toxic chemical exposure
- Improve detoxification function
- Reduce inflammation
- Reduce food allergies
- Improve digestion
- Ensure proper antioxidant nutrient protection—vitamin E, coenzyme Q10, lipoic acid, creatine, glutathione, carnitine, taurine, selenium
- Increase intake of vitamin B12, folic acid and betaine

The research I described in this chapter signals a new approach to the practice of medicine. Instead of waiting for a diagnosis of a neurological disorder like Alzheimer's or Parkinson's disease, it encourages the evaluation of genetic predisposition and the development of a tailored program to prevent the phenotype of dementia. In a recent discussion of the origin and treatment of Parkinson's disease, C.G. Clough, M.D., explained that 30 years or more before they can be diagnosed, individuals with a genetic risk of Parkinson's disease begin losing function in a specific portion of the brain called the dopaminergic neurons.[53] This prediagnosis period is the time when they can implement what Dr. Clough calls "neuroprotective therapy." The only way that therapy can be undertaken, however, is by determining whether they are at risk.

This is the basic concept underlying the genetic nutritioneering approach. By combining the best of modern medicine and the assessment of genetic risk factors and utilizing strategies to modify gene expression, the phenotype that is expressed can be that of an individual who is not at high risk of early-stage dementia or cardiovascular disease. The questions we ask—or fail to ask—at a younger age will provide the answers we live with later. Medicine is just beginning to ask these questions outside of the research laboratories, but those physicians who are practicing functional medicine, who are at the leading edge of their disciplines, are not only asking these questions but also assisting their patients with the answers.

Modification of genes by altering nutrition and the intake of specific nutrients extends to nearly all age-related diseases, including cancer. No area of molecular genetic investigation has received more attention than cancer. In the past few years we have begun to see tremendous breakthroughs in understanding the genetics of cancer and how the expression of certain cancer genes can be modified to prevent it. This extraordinary extension of the genetic nutritioneering approach is the focus of the next chapter.

A PROGRAM TO MODIFY RISK FACTORS FOR BRAIN AGING

- Make sure your diet is not too low in fat (i.e., less than 15 percent of the total calories).
- Treat chronic viral and parasitic infections.
- Consider taking a daily low-dose antiinflammatory such as ibuprofen.
- Eliminate foods to which you may be allergic or sensitive (such as wheat or dairy products).
- Improve your digestive function by applying the concepts described in Chapter 8.
- Reduce your exposure to chemicals and toxins and improve your detoxification function by eating more cruciferous

vegetables (i.e. broccoli, cauliflower, Brussels sprouts and cabbage).

- Do not smoke or use recreational drugs.
- Limit your use of medications and OTC drugs or exposure to anesthesia.
- Limit your intake of alcohol.

Genetic Nutritioneering Daily Support to Increase Mitochondrial Protection

Vitamin C, 1,000–2,000 mg (partially as dehydroascorbate)
Vitamin E, 400–1,000 IU
Coenzyme Q10, 20–200 mg
Lipoic acid, 50–500 mg
Creatine, 100–2,000 mg
Glutathione, 100–2,000 mg
L-Carnitine, 100–1,000 mg
Taurine, 100–500 mg
Selenium, 100–200 mcg
N-acetylcysteine, 100–1,000 mg
Zinc, 10–50 mg
Vitamin B12, 25–1,000 mcg
Vitamin B6, 5–25 mg
Folic acid, 400–1,000 mcg

If you have ApoE4 genotype, apply the concepts in this summary chart aggressively.

FIGHTING CANCER WITH NUTRITIONEERING

IN HIS RECENT BOOK, *Curing Cancer: Solving One of the Greatest Medical Mysteries of Our Time*, Pulitzer Prize–winning correspondent Michael Waldholz wrote:

> A cure for cancer, of course, does not yet exist. But for the first time in the century-long fight against the disease, scientists are producing the profound kind of insights that will lead to a cure. In just the past few years, researchers have uncovered genes that cause inherited forms of cancer of the breast and colon; and several dozen other cancer-causing genes have been identified or are on the verge of being revealed. The identification of these genes is giving researchers the first true picture of how cancer begins, and the same discoveries are already helping scientists find new ways to detect and prevent cancer, as well as assisting them in their efforts to invent new and powerful therapies.[1]

With the rapidly evolving insights into the genetic triggering of cancer, the door is now open for genetic nutritioneering to play a significant role in reducing the incidence of cancer and perhaps also to provide adjunctive therapy in its treatment. A recent *Science* magazine article pointed out:

> When it comes to cancer risk, not all men—or women or children for that matter—are created equal. New evidence suggests that small groups including women and the very young are more vulnerable to environmental insults such as exposure to cigarette smoke, hormones or toxic pollutants. Only about 5 percent of cancers are solely due to 'bad genes,' while 95 percent are due to an interaction between genes and environment, diet and lifestyle variables.[2]

Cancer is not inevitable. As Frederica Perera, M.D., of the Columbia University School of Public Health, stated in the article cited above, "Cancer is largely a preventable disease. To make greater strides in preventing cancer, we need public health strategies that reflect this knowledge." We need to make use of the latest information available about the way genes are modified by the environment. The evidence indicating that the interaction of genes with environmental exposures and diet is related to the expression of cancer comes from a number of discoveries, including the following:

1. One out of ten Caucasians carries a readily activated form of an enzyme that increases lung cancer risk in smokers.
2. Female smokers are up to three times as likely as males to develop lung cancer, despite similar smoking habits and intake.
3. About 50 percent of Caucasians lack a detoxifying enzyme called glutathione transferase M1, which increases their risk of lung and bladder cancer.
4. Forty percent of Caucasians, 35 percent of blacks and 14 percent of Asians deactivate carcinogens more slowly than others do. If these "slow acetylators" smoke, their risk of breast cancer or other cancers increases.

5. DNA repair enzymes, which help prevent cancer, may vary by a factor of from 180 to 300 times among individuals.
6. Black Americans have two to three times the risk of esophageal, liver, cervical and stomach cancer, and a 50 percent higher risk of mouth, throat, lung, prostate and pancreatic cancer compared with Caucasians.
7. Caucasian Americans have a greater risk of melanoma, leukemia, lymphoma and cancer of the endometrium, thyroid, ovary, testes and brain.

These facts reflect the rapidly increasing understanding of the relationship between genes and environment that can ultimately result in cancer. Specific genes whose modification of either structure or expression results in cancer have been identified only within the past decade. A few of these cancer genes are P21, P53, BRCA1, HBC1 and GSTM1. These genes help control the regulation of cellular growth, and alterations in their structure or function can greatly increase the risk of cancer.

Aristo Vojdani, Ph.D., M.T., from the Drew University School of Medicine and Science in California, recently described the various laboratory tests now available for evaluating genetic cancer risk. Sophisticated new molecular probes evaluate genetic uniqueness and make it possible to identify precancerous events taking place in the body at a stage early enough in the process so individuals can change their lifestyle, environment and diet to allow the natural cell regulatory systems to be reinstated.[3] Breast cancer susceptibility has been analyzed using the genetic marker BRCA1.[4] Prostate cancer risk has been identified by using the gene HPC1, and p21 and p53 gene products have been used as markers for risk of colon and other cancers.[5]

Sometimes alteration in these genes occurs at such a significant level that changes in environmental exposure, diet or lifestyle may not have a major impact on reducing the risk of cancer. Often, however, expression of these genetic characteristics can be significantly modified through application of concepts described in the genetic nutritioneering approach. These areas provide hope for a new focus on cancer prevention and adjunctive cancer treatment.

The identification of genes associated with increased cancer risk is as recent as the 1990s. In 1994 and 1995, for instance, scientists isolated a pair of genes implicated in breast cancer. When they are functioning normally, these "tumor suppressor" genes, known as BRCA1 and BRCA2, produce substances that regulate cell division. When these genes malfunction, however, the cells within specific organs can multiply unregulated, giving rise to breast cancer as well as tumors of the colon, brain, skin or lungs. Dr. Mary-Claire King, a director of the New York Breast Cancer Study, who revealed the existence of the breast cancer gene, recently asked, "Why is it some women with the [defective] gene get cancer early in life, why do some get recurrent cancers, and why do some escape? Is it the food they eat, when and whether they have children, their weight, their exposure to pesticides?"[6]

These are important questions. A woman would be disturbed to learn she carries a genetic characteristic that indicates she has an increased risk of breast cancer unless she also knew she could take action to minimize the expression of this genotype as breast cancer in the phenotype. Investigators from a number of scientific and medical disciplines are discovering it is not just the genes that influence risk of cancer. Much of the risk depends on the modification in expression of those genes through diet, lifestyle and environmental factors. Although we do not presently have the technology to modify our genes, we certainly can modify our diet, lifestyle and environmental exposures once we have been informed of our specific risks.

Medical journals, symposia and postgraduate education courses are now alerting physicians about the breakthroughs in this field and teaching them to counsel their patients on the proper use and interpretation of genetic screening tests. In place of the potentially extraordinary adverse psychological impact of learning they carry the genetic risk for cancer, patients are discovering they can take a number of specific actions to manipulate gene expression to prevent cancer or perhaps even treat it once it has been diagnosed.[7]

A major discovery concerning tumor suppressor genes resulted from the work of a research team at a company called Myriad Genetics, Inc. in Utah. This group found a gene that expressed a protein called p16 that acts as a natural "off-switch" preventing a variety of cancers. When the gene that makes p16 is damaged or is not working correctly, the cells can multiply uncontrollably, forming a cancerous tumor. This monumental discovery was the subject of a recent *Newsweek* cover story.[8]

An interesting aspect of this research discovery is that Dr. Sasha Kamb, who was a member of the research group that discovered the "mother of all tumor-suppressor genes," is the grandson of Linus Pauling, Ph.D. Dr. Pauling is considered the father of much of what we now understand about the structure and function of molecules in biological systems. As explained in Chapter 2, Dr. Pauling first used the term "molecular medicine" in a paper published in 1949 concerning the genetic defect that produces sickle cell anemia. Through Dr. Pauling's discoveries and those of his collaborators in the 1930s, '40s and '50s, molecular biology and molecular genetics were born, and molecular medicine started to come of age. Forty years later, Dr. Pauling's grandson is continuing the revolution in this field of understanding and paving the way for the application of molecular medicine in the prevention and treatment of disease.

FEMALE CANCERS AND HORMONES

Scientists now recognize that female cancers, including breast, ovarian and endometrial, may all relate, in part, to altered hormone patterns that create a cell-signaling message to the genes that express the potential for the unregulated cell growth we call cancer.[9] The

risk of hormone-induced cancer in women who carry the susceptibility genes may start as early as in the first few months of fetal
development. Increasing evidence indicates that a pregnant
woman's hormone patterns can, in fact, influence the development
of gene expression of the fetus, setting in motion the risk of breast
cancer in her daughters many years later.[10]

Research has long indicated breast cancer risk is increased in
women who have had no children, who had early onset of menstru-
ation, or who went through menopause at a later age. All of these
factors are associated with increased exposure to estrogen, suggesting that certain forms of estrogen might increase the expression of
genetic risk factors for breast cancer and other female cancers. We
are now finding that estrogen exposure may actually begin in the
womb, where the mother's estrogens bathe the fetus, altering gene
expression.[11] We also recognize that our environment now contains
increased levels of xenoestrogens such as dioxin, synthetic chemicals that resemble estrogen in their action. The combination of
increased exposure of the genes to estrogen and xenoestrogens in
women who are at risk for female cancers can greatly increase their
likelihood of developing cancer.

Evidence now indicates that estrogens produced during pregnancy impart an increase in cancer risk when the pregnancy occurs
later in a woman's life and may also increase the risk of her daughters'
developing breast cancer.[12] Multiple births expose a woman to more
estrogen over the course of her life and are also associated with
increased incidence of breast cancer.[13] Even the increased estrogen
production during pregnancy with twins suggests more breast cancer risk for both mother and daughters than in single-birth pregnancy.[14] Pregnancy and giving birth do not in themselves
automatically increase a woman's cancer risk. The evidence appears
to indicate that women who have one to four children have *decreased*
cancer risk, but having more than four children is an *increased* risk.
The greater exposure a woman has to estrogen throughout her life,
and the less effective her liver is at detoxifying estrogen, the greater
her risk of developing female hormone-related cancers.

The combination of exposure to environmental natural estrogens, increased genetic susceptibility, and reduced ability to detoxify estrogens through altered liver detoxification function add up to increased risk of a woman's developing breast cancer. As explained in Chapter 3, the liver is the major organ responsible for detoxifying foreign chemicals and natural substances like estrogen that are produced in the body. Differences in estrogen detoxification ability among women may account for their differences in susceptibility to estrogen and modification of breast cancer risk.[15]

A vigorous discussion is taking place in laboratories around the world regarding the effects of diet and nutrition in modifying detoxification function. Increasing evidence indicates that dietary modification with specific foods that contain phytonutrients that enhance gene expression of detoxification enzyme systems in the body can help improve the way a woman detoxifies both her own estrogens and xenoestrogens. Clearly, diet plays a role in hormone-related cancers. It can increase the risk of cancer-producing processes or it can help enhance detoxification enzyme systems that allow a woman to defend against potential gene-modulating substances like environmental chemicals or hormones. More than 30 years ago, Carlton Fredericks, Ph.D. discussed the important role of B vitamins and antioxidants like vitamin E in reducing the risk of hormone-related cancers like cancers of the breast and endometrium.[16] The mechanisms by which nutrition could modify gene expression and function were not understood in the 1960s, but Dr. Fredericks's observations now appear to be prescient given the advancing understanding of cancer genes and how their expression can be modified through improved nutrition.

The relationship between hormones and cancer also applies to prostate cancer in men. Statistics regarding breast cancer in women are mirrored by the statistics about prostate cancer in men, in both incidence and death rate. Within families, the incidence of sisters who get breast cancer and brothers who get prostate cancer is very similar. The breast and the prostate develop early in the fetus from similar types of tissue. In other words, they share a common heritage and a common genetic sensitivity. Just as exposure to high levels of maternal hormones in utero can increase breast cancer risk in females, elevated levels of certain pregnancy hormones can increase the risk of prostate cancer in males.[17] It is the total load of estrogen-like substances, both natural estrogens produced by the mother and xenoestrogens that interact with the genes of the fetus, that gives rise to the risk of prostate cancer. Testicular cancer has also been related to increased maternal exposure to estrogen-like substances, linking environment, genetic susceptibility, diet and lifestyle.[18]

The recent developments in the laboratories of molecular geneticists have caused pharmaceutical companies to race ahead in their research on new biological drugs to combat cancer. This pharmaceutical research is not attempting to find new ways to kill cancer cells, as traditional chemotherapeutic agents have done. It is trying to find natural biologically based substances that alter gene expression in cancer cells, arrest their growth and give the body's immune system an opportunity to kill them.

Genentech in South San Francisco, California, is developing one drug of this type for the treatment of breast cancer.[19] The drug, called Herceptin, has demonstrated significant benefit for patients with advanced forms of breast cancer. It slows tumor progression and shrinks tumors, including metastasized tumors that have spread from the breast to other organs. Herceptin is one of a class of bioengineered molecules called monoclonal antibodies which work by blocking the activity of the cancer-causing gene known as HER2.

Monoclonal antibodies have been studied for years with disappointing results. Recently, however, investigators have learned to make the drugs more compatible with the human body, thus preventing the immune system from attacking them. In this natural, biologically based therapy, the gene messages are turned off through a specific protein that masks a portion of the gene, causing the cell to return to normal.

Certain phytochemicals found in foods operate in a similar

manner to modify gene expression. A number of natural, food-derived antiestrogens help reduce the overstimulation of the genes by hormones. Certain cultures have consumed these food-derived, hormone-modulating nutrients for hundreds of years. This may explain why these cultures have a lower incidence of cancer than cultures in which these food substances are not consumed. Modification of hormone activities on genes could have significant benefit in preventing breast, endometrial and ovarian cancer in women and prostate cancer in men.[20]

A striking example of the relationship between dietary patterns and cancer incidence is the fact that the incidence of prostate cancer in American men is 30 to 50 times higher than in Asian men who eat a traditional Asian diet.[21] Reasons for this difference are not yet clear, but they may be related to the combination of diet and genetic susceptibilities. The prostate glands of some men produce higher levels of 5-dihydrotestosterone (DHT), a toxic derivative of testosterone which has the potential to produce cancer. The enzyme that converts testosterone into DHT is 5-alpha-reductase. Its production can be increased or decreased by modifying gene expression with specific dietary substances, the best known of which are genistein and daidzein, two isoflavones found in soy products. Because they eat more soy foods, Asian men and women consume more of these natural soy phytochemicals. Genistein and daidzein are hormone modulators that influence the production, activity and metabolism of various hormones.

DIETARY MODIFICATION OF HORMONE-RELATED CANCERS

The observation that isoflavones from soy and other foods can help to modify the risk of hormone-related cancers represents a breakthrough in understanding how to reduce risk of prostate cancer in men and breast cancer risk in women. Research by Herman Adlercreutz, M.D., Ph.D., from the University of Helsinki Medical

School,[22] and Kenneth Setchell, Ph.D., at the Cincinnati Children's Hospital,[23] revealed that the protective role of isoflavones is further amplified when a person's diet is rich in another family of phytochemicals called lignans. Foods that contain the highest level of lignans are flaxseed and flax meal and flour, although lignans are found in whole rye flour as well. Lignans work with isoflavones to modulate hormone activities and the gene response to them. Medical investigators from the Queen Elizabeth Medical Center in Perth, Australia, recently found that the combination of soy and flax in the diet increases levels of the cancer-fighting phytochemicals in the body. This may explain why women in Asia have much lower incidence of breast, ovarian and uterine cancer, and men in Asia have lower incidence of prostate cancer.[24]

Isoflavones and other phytochemicals found in soy products can increase the detoxification of potential cancer-producing chemicals, and they also help put the genes that may be associated with cancer production to sleep.[25,26]

Understanding of the relationship of dietary substances like isoflavones and lignans to cancer gene expression is still in its infancy. We cannot rush to the judgment that diet is the be-all and end-all for the prevention and potential treatment of cancer. We are, however, finding more evidence that much of what we considered the luck of the draw is really the result of genetic susceptibility, environmental exposures and altered dietary and lifestyle patterns. By examining our family histories, we can observe certain characteristics related to cancer incidence. Do you have a parent, grandparent, brother or sister who had a certain form of cancer? If so, what was the age of onset and did other members of your family experience similar forms of cancer? The answers to these questions are important in understanding genetic risk. Linking these answers to the lifestyle, diet and environment of those relatives provides early clues for designing your own genetic nutritioneering approach to prevent cancer.

Isoflavones, lignans and dietary fiber are just three of a myriad of nutrients now being evaluated for their impact on cancer gene expression and modification of risk. The theme emerging from these investigations is that we all have genes that, if they are improperly expressed, can give rise to the unregulated cell growth we call cancer. The structure of the genes of some individuals places them at seriously increased cancer risk. Most of us, however, have only minor risk from our genes. It is our inappropriate lifestyle, environmental exposure or dietary choices that increases the expression of the unlikely event we call cancer.

It is important to understand that cancer really is an unlikely event, because most of our cells undergo hundreds of perfectly normal divisions throughout our lifetime. It is an unlikely event when the genes of a specific cell at a moment in its cycle of division undergo damage or alteration in expression and cancer is initiated. Even then, however, all is not lost. Cells have a number of repair processes, including apoptosis, by which they can defend themselves against the expression of cancer even after a cell undergoes transformation. All of these defense systems have to fail before a malignancy can finally develop. Even when it does develop, the cancer cell is a very weak cell. Its metabolism is not nearly as vital as that of a normal cell. A healthy immune system can take advantage of this weakness, selectively killing the cancer cell and leaving the body's normal cells intact. A malignancy can develop into a diagnosed cancer only when all of these complex control processes break down. Diet and nutrition play an important role in supporting the defense against cancer at each of these levels and are fundamental tools in modifying genetic risk to cancer. Along with reducing exposure to environmental chemicals and xenoestrogens, genetic nutritioneering may be the main tool we have available today to prevent cancer.

MODIFYING ONCOGENE EXPRESSION

As stated earlier, every cell in the human body contains the same genetic information, although there is a great variation in the function and appearance of different cell types. Certain cells express only a part of the genetic message; the rest lie dormant and unexpressed. Cell-specific types of a gene expression pattern, which makes liver cells different from heart cells, for example, is established during early cell differentiation in the fetus. Scientists are just beginning to understand the mechanism by which differentiation and the masking of certain messages within genes occur. They have found that one principal way genes are blocked and prevented from being expressed is through a process called methylation.

METHYLATION: Addition of a methyl group (chemical group or radical CH_3) to a compound.

Methylation is the biological transfer of a methyl group (a carbon atom with three hydrogens attached to it), much like the passing of a baton from one runner to another in a relay race. The addition of a methyl group to a region of a gene alters its expression. Therefore, gene expression closely correlates with patterns of DNA methylation. Among our genes are tumor suppression genes and cell replication genes called oncogenes. The activity of both types of genes is controlled, in part, by methylation patterns. A reduction in the methylation of DNA increases the potential expression of the cancer production genes.[27] DNA methylation, therefore, is one of the most important processes that controls cancer regulatory genes for p21.[28] The cellular machinery that controls the production and transfer of methyl groups to the genes to regulate what part of the genome is expressed and what part is not is very sophisticated. An interruption in this closely controlled process can lead to increased slippage of the genetic message and raise the likelihood that expression of cancer-producing genes can be the outcome.

Medical investigators from the Norris Comprehensive Cancer Center at the University of Southern California School of Medicine investigated the importance of DNA methylation in the control of gene expression and cancer prevention. They found that reduced methylation of DNA increases susceptibility of the genes to cancer-producing chemicals and other factors that can encourage the production of a cancer cell.[29] As you read this book, investigators in laboratories and clinics around the world are working overtime to try to understand the complex mechanism by which the regulation of methylation occurs at the gene level. The payoff may be finding a principal key to regulating cancer gene expression.[30]

Methylation and the transfer of methyl groups are related to the same process by which homocysteine is metabolized. (We discussed this process in regard to heart disease in Chapter 9 and dementia in Chapter 10.) A central theme is emerging in regard to age-related diseases. It indicates that heart disease, dementia and cancer in genetically susceptible individuals are related, in part, to modifications in methylation. Vincent Wilson, M.D., from the Department of Pediatrics and Biochemistry at the University of Southern California School of Medicine, reported in 1983 that DNA methylation patterns decrease with cellular aging and that gene expression patterns may become more "sloppy" with increasing age.[31]

In 1997, Bruce Ames, M.D., and his colleagues at the University of California at Berkeley, Division of Biochemistry and Molecular Biology, reported that folic acid deficiency causes alteration in methylation and damage to DNA and chromosomes.[32] Folic acid is a principal nutrient in controlling the metabolism of homocysteine. Dr. Ames pointed out that a significant proportion of the U.S. population has low dietary folate levels and could be at risk for altered methylation patterns and chromosome breaks. Such breaks in altered gene expression could contribute, he pointed out, to the increased risk of cancer as well as to the age-associated loss of mental function and dementia. Folate does not work alone in the methyl transfer pathways in cells. It works in combination with other nutrients, including vitamin B6, vitamin B12 and betaine. Michael Fenech, Ph.D., from the Division of Human Nutrition at the Research Institute of Australia, recently reported that insufficiency of folate or vitamin B12 can increase DNA and chromosome damage in older men and may be an additional risk factor to modify gene expression and cancer.[33] The genes of animals placed on a diet insufficient in folate and vitamin B12 cannot properly regulate methylation patterns, and their cells die prematurely from the dehydration known as apoptosis or begin to proliferate rapidly, with increased incidence of cancer.[34] David Heber, M.D., Ph.D., from the University of California at Los Angeles Department of Medicine, recently reported that animals fed low folate-containing diets also have reduced detoxification ability and increased susceptibility to environmental carcinogens.[35]

As a whole, the discoveries by researchers around the world indicate that control of methylation patterns is critically important in regulating gene expression and controlling cellular growth. Insufficiencies of folate, vitamin B6, vitamin B12 and betaine may contribute to reduced ability to control methylation patterns, thus altering gene expression in susceptible gene regions and promoting the expression of oncogenes, or cancer-producing genes.

ONCOGENE: A gene capable under certain conditions of causing the initial and continuing conversion of normal cells into cancer cells.

ANTIOXIDANTS AND CANCER PREVENTION

Other researchers have examined the relationship between altered methylation patterns and oxidative stress, which can further interrupt proper gene expression and increase potential impact of cancer-producing genes. Animals fed a diet insufficient in folate, vitamin B12 and vitamin B6 experience increased oxidative stress from a compromised antioxidant defense system.[36] This discovery might help explain why diets low in vitamin C, vitamin E, carotenoids and flavonoids are associated with increased incidence of cancer in cultures worldwide. Alteration of gene expression from poor methylation may increase oxidative stress reactions, which increase the opportunity for the expression of cancer genes. Antioxidant supplementation or higher levels of antioxidants within the diet may help regulate these oxidative stress reactions and work with nutrients like folate, vitamin B12, vitamin B6 and betaine to reduce cancer risk.

A number of studies have indicated that antioxidant activities are reduced in tissues affected by cancer. This reduction probably results from increased oxidative stress in the tissue from altered gene expression and a shift toward cancer metabolism.[37] In addition to vitamin E, vitamin C and carotene, a number of other dietary antioxidants play a role in communicating with the genes to reduce cancer risk. One antioxidant nutrient that has recently been evaluated is resveratrol, a phytochemical found in grapes. Investigators from the University of Illinois College of Pharmacy in Chicago have found this substance may be a powerful chemopreventive agent. It enhances detoxification of carcinogenic chemicals, lowers inflammation and discourages the promotion of cancer genes.[38]

The regulation of methylation patterns and oxidant stress reactions in cells may be fundamental tools in the modification of gene expression related to cancer initiation and promotion. In 1956, Otto Warburg, M.D., Ph.D. wrote a landmark article titled "On the Origin of Cancer Cells." He explained that cancer cells have a very different physiology from normal cells. Although a normal cell utilizes oxygen efficiently to produce energy through mitochondrial function, the cancer cell has "poisoned mitochondria" and generates its energy by a different mechanism, called lactate fermentation.[39] Based upon his extensive studies with cancerous and normal cells, Dr. Warburg believed that alteration of the way cells use oxygen caused by mitochondrial poisoning could play a significant role in cancer formation. He suggested the modified gene expression that resulted in cancer cell physiology was, in part, a consequence of the inability of the mitochondria to utilize oxygen and produce metabolic energy. As a cell became oxygen starved, it shifted its gene expression to develop a cancer personality.

Throughout the past 40 years the understanding of this process has grown. In 1965, Nobel Prize winner Dr. Albert Szent-Gyorgyi described the cancer research that enabled him to discover substances produced by healthy cells that communicated chemically with other cells, creating proper mitochondrial energy production and the use of oxygen. In cancer cells, he found, different substances were produced which served as mitochondrial toxins and shifted the cell into a precancerous state.[40] Toxins that come from the environment, from altered intestinal bacteria or through altered cellular function could communicate with the genes to block the messages for gene expression and shift the cells into the metabolism that both Warburg and Szent-Gyorgyi identified as the oxygen-deprived metabolism found in cancer cells.

Warburg and Szent-Gyorgyi opened the door for research into the role of oxidants in the cancer process. They believed that the key to cancer prevention would be uncovered by better understanding of this important area of discovery.

In an article in the prestigious *New England Journal of Medicine* in 1986, Drs. John Bailar and Elaine Smith from the Harvard School of Public Health advocated a shift in cancer research emphasis from treatment to prevention.[41] They reached this conclusion following an analysis that indicated very little progress in the treatment of cancer after a major investment in its research. In a follow-up paper in 1997, Dr. Bailar stated his conclusion that the new treatments for cancer have been largely disappointing and called once more for more emphasis on prevention.[42]

Fortunately, during those same years from 1986 to 1997, significant progress has been made in understanding the mechanisms of cancer prevention. Much of this progress has come as a result of improved understanding of the way certain nutrients, particularly antioxidant nutrients, influence gene expression and activity related to cancer prevention.

Research on the role of specific antioxidant nutrients in cancer prevention has taken an interesting path. It ranges from a study showing that Brussels sprouts increase the genetic expression of the enzymes in the intestinal tract responsible for detoxification of cancer-producing chemicals[43] to one demonstrating the cancer-preventing role of specific phytonutrients in green tea and citrus.[44,45]

Research interest in the potential effect of nutritional supplementation on cancer prevention reached a new level in 1993. Dr. William Blot from the International Epidemiology Institute reported that people in a certain province of China who took a multivitamin/mineral supplement had significantly reduced cancer mortality compared to their peers who took a placebo pill containing no nutrients.[46] The nutrients believed to have the most potent cancer-protective effect were the antioxidants—vitamin E, vitamin C, carotene and the mineral selenium.

A number of studies have evaluated the role of vitamin E in preventing various cancers. The initial understanding of the role of vitamin E and other antioxidants in cancer prevention came from animal studies. Vitamin E was found to be very important in helping to prevent carcinogen-induced breast cancer in animals, for example. The evaluation of breast cancer patterns in humans has suggested that women who consume diets higher in vitamin E and other antioxidants have lower incidence of breast cancer.[47]

Researchers have found that vitamin E, along with other antioxidants, helps send the genes a message that normalizes cell division and aids in combatting cancer.[48] This may help explain the observation that prevention of a number of cancers—including breast, prostate and lung cancers—seems to be associated with intake of vitamins E, C and A above the Recommended Dietary Allowance levels.[49]

Research has even indicated that vitamin E supplementation may help reduce the side-effects and improve the results of certain types of chemotherapy, including the drugs 5-fluorouracil and doxorubicin.[50]

The effects of vitamin E and beta carotene supplementation on lung cancer risk in smokers was evaluated in a very large trial funded by the National Institutes of Health a few years ago. The results have led to some confusion. Daily supplementation with 50 mg of vitamin E resulted in a lower incidence of cancer, but daily supplementation with 20 mg of beta carotene had no positive effect and may have actually slightly increased the cancer incidence.[51] The lack of benefit from carotene supplementation was confirmed in another study at the Fred Hutchinson Cancer Research Center in Seattle, Washington. This study indicated that vitamin E appears to be more important as an antioxidant in cancer prevention.[52]

The most remarkable recent study of the role of antioxidant nutrients on cancer prevention evaluated the effect of 200 mcg of daily supplementation with the antioxidant mineral selenium. This trial found that selenium supplementation resulted in a nearly 50 percent reduction in overall cancer incidence.[53] The mechanism by which selenium provides this protection against cancer is not fully understood, but the suggestion is that it participates in normalizing the signals to the genes for cell growth and differentiation through its antioxidant influence.[54]

Recently, Stanislaw Burzynski, M.D., Ph.D., a former professor of medicine at Baylor Medical School and president of the Burzynski Research Institute in Houston, Texas, followed up on the observations of Warburg and Szent-Gyorgyi. He found two types of substances produced in cells that help regulate gene expression and cellular division. These are the proteins produced from specific regions of the genes (called ras), such as p21 and p53, which help regulate gene expression. Second, he validated Szent-Gyorgyi's observation that small molecules that are not proteins produced by cells regulate cell division. He describes these small molecules as "antineoplastons," because they help protect against neoplasia, or cancer.

Burzynski's research led to the conclusion that cancer is a consequence of alterations in the production of both protein substances that communicate with genes (e.g., p21), and small molecules called antineoplastons. As individuals grow older, the production of antineoplastons by the cells decreases, increasing the risk of expression of cancer genes. Burzynski has isolated these substances from the urine of healthy individuals with antineoplastic activity, and in clinical trials he has been able to readminister them to individuals with terminal cancer. His results, which have been very encouraging, are the focus of a book, *The Burzynski Breakthrough*.[55]

ANTINEOPLASTONS: Substances produced by the body that turn off the cancer message in the genes (small molecules such as phenylacetate).

The frontiers of investigation are expanding. Scientists are discovering how genes express either normal regulation of cell function or the abnormal function that is called cancer. The research that is explaining how this process relates to diet, environment and lifestyle is providing options for assessing the risk of cancer and acting to modify that risk before cancer develops. The tools that are available in the form of diet and nutritional supplements to prevent the altered gene expression we associate with cancer are increasing day by day as more research is published.

A diet that is low in total fat and high in fiber and vegetables, unrefined grains, fruits and legumes is a prudent first choice in cancer prevention. Going beyond diet to examine family history for evidence of prostate and breast cancer is the next step. Indications of increased genetic risk of cancer could lead one to increase dietary levels of isoflavones from soy and lignans from flax. Next, one might examine the sufficiency in the diet of vitamin B12, folate, vitamin B6 and betaine to support proper methylation patterns. (As explained in Chapters 9 and 10, elevated levels of homocysteine in the blood indicate poor control of methylation.) Finally, antioxidants, regulation of mitochondrial function and reduction of oxidative stress may also play an important role in communicating to the genes and reducing the possibility of expressing cancer genes.

The genetic nutritioneering approach toward the prevention of cancer begins with a knowledge of your genetic inheritance. Then you can modulate the expression of these characteristics by selecting foods that contain nutrients that help promote cellular differentiation and control of cell signaling. We now know that not only do certain genes encode for a higher risk of cancer, but they also may encode for reduced ability to defend against potential cancer-producing substances. These genetic uniquenesses are contained within the detoxification enzyme genes. We previously discussed the influence that poor acetylator status might have on smoking-induced breast cancer in women. It would be very wise for individuals who carry this unique genotype to stop smoking and follow a diet that is rich in nutrients that help support the detoxification function.[56]

High-fat diets also increase the risk of cancer. A recent report from the Karolinska Institute in Stockholm indicated that monounsaturated fat, the kind found in olive and canola oil, can cut a woman's risk of breast cancer nearly in half. This report was based on a study of more than 61,000 Swedish women between the ages of 40 and 70 who were checked from 1987 to 1990. Asking the women what they ate and then checking a cancer registry to determine who among them later developed breast cancer, the researchers found that monounsaturated fat in the diet appeared to reduce the risk of breast cancer by 45 percent.[57]

Evidence that dietary fat alters the cancer process causes us once again to ask how this dietary variable could influence gene expression or gene modulation. Several years ago, Dr. Ewan Cameron, Richard Marcuson and I published a study in which we evaluated the influence of various dietary fats on breast cancer in mice. We were surprised to learn that by increasing fish oils and flaxseed oil in the diets of the mice, we were able to lower the incidence of breast cancer produced by exposure to a known carcinogen by more than 70 percent.[58]

Evidence is now accumulating that modification of the amount and type of dietary fat can also play a significant role in reducing the relative risk of cancer expression. It is prudent to avoid diets that are high in partially hydrogenated vegetable oils, saturated animal fats and warm-weather vegetable oils (including corn, safflower and sunflower seed oil) and to replace these fats with monounsaturated olive and canola oil, flaxseed oil and omega-3 fish oils.[59]

One recent report found that women who regularly consume over-the-counter analgesics, such as acetaminophen-containing products, have a lower risk of ovarian cancer.[60] This reduction in cancer incidence was also observed in women who regularly consumed aspirin, but no such association was seen with women who consumed ibuprofen. Acetaminophen and aspirin share common detoxification pathways, so regular consumption of these substances might serve to upregulate the expression of certain genes that are involved with detoxification, including not only drugs but also other environmental carcinogens.

Rather than take analgesics as a preventive measure, the best way for a woman to lower her risk of developing ovarian cancer is to improve her body's detoxification pathways naturally. She can do so by eating cruciferous vegetables (cabbage, Brussels sprouts, broccoli, cauliflower) and taking supplemental doses of N-acetylcysteine, zinc, copper, molybdenum, iron, selenium and B vitamins.

And, as Dr. Frederica Perera recently stated, "Acting in concert with individual susceptibility, environmental factors such as smoking, diet and pollutants play a role in most human cancer."[61] We therefore should not diminish the importance of a clean environment, as free of toxic substances as possible, as an objective for the prevention of cancer.

Dr. Eric Fearon recently wrote, "Though hereditary cancer syndromes are rare, their study has provided powerful insights into more common forms of cancer. . . . Further investigation of inherited mutations that affect susceptibility to cancer will aid efforts to effectively prevent, detect and treat the disease."[62]

A comprehensive application of the genetic nutritioneering approach would be to move toward improving the quality of the environment, thereby reducing the exposure to environmental carcinogens while also providing adequate nutritional support for the individual to detoxify toxic substances before they influence gene expression or function. Prevention of cancer is going to depend upon our learning more about genetic susceptibilities while improving environmental quality and enhancing the regulation of genes engaged in carcinogen detoxification and cellular regulation. Diets that are low in vitamin B12, folate, vitamin B6 and other nutrients required for the support of the detoxification process, or diets that are unable to support the needs for proper genetic expression, will result in increased risk of cancer gene expression.[63]

Beyond prevention of cancer there is the exciting field of adjunctive nutritional support for cancer management. A number of studies now indicate that nutrients may be useful for modulating the body's immune defense processes and increasing the likelihood of remission from cancer after therapy. One study that recently looked at vitamin E's role in enhancing the benefit of 5-fluorouracil treatment of colorectal cancer indicates we still have much to learn about the way nutrients influence both the prevention and treatment of cancer.[64]

As we move to the year 2000, we are witnessing the emergence of a new proactive approach toward cancer prevention and treatment. As Dr. Mary-Claire King recently stated, "We all believe that these gene hunts are going to change the direction of cancer research forever. That's why we do what we do as scientists. Ultimately, our goal is to cure these diseases. What's so great is that these days, we have the technology at hand and a pretty clear idea of how to go about trying. Do I think all this someday will lead to a cure? You bet I do."[65]

By implementing genetic nutritioneering strategy described in this chapter, you can take a giant step toward using the results of this extraordinary new research to your benefit.

A PROGRAM TO MODIFY CANCER RISK FACTORS

- No smoking.
- Reduce consumption of smoked cured meats, high saturated fat foods, fried foods and highly processed foods.
- Increase the intake of cruciferous vegetables, green tea, soy products and fiber-rich foods.
- Emphasize legumes, carotenoid-rich vegetables (i.e. carrots, yams, winter squash).
- Include lignin-rich flaxseed or whole rye flour.
- Increase the consumption of cancer-fighting foods such as red grapes, garlic, and spices such as curcumin (i.e., turmeric) and ginger.
- Avoid hydrogenated and partially hydrogenated fats. Emphasize virgin olive oil and canola oil.
- Avoid rancid oil products, which are bitter to the taste.
- Eat fatty types of fish (e.g., salmon) two or more times per week.

Genetic Nutritioneering Daily Support to Increase Protection Against Cancer

Vitamin B12, 25–1,000 mcg
Folic acid, 400–1,000 mcg
Vitamin B6, 5–20 mg
Betaine, 100–1,000 mg

HOW TO TRANSFORM YOUR GENETIC DESTINY

THROUGH THE FIRST ELEVEN CHAPTERS of this book, we have explained how your genetic inheritance can be expressed in different ways. Many of the concepts presented were discovered within the last 10 years, and ours is the first generation that can use this information to improve the expression and functional outcome of our genes. After reading this book you should no longer believe that your genetic inheritance is set in stone and nothing you can do will change it.

The Human Genome Project has uncovered thousands of variations among human genetic inheritance factors from individual to individual. This genetic polymorphism helps explain the amazing diversity of function that exists within the human population. Our metabolic differences are far greater than the differences in the color of our skin, hair or eyes, or differences in stature or physical appearance. Even more remarkable is the fact that our genetic inheritance factors can be expressed in a number of different ways, depending upon how we treat our genes. Scientists call this the difference between our *genotype* and our *phenotype*.

Your genotype was determined when you were conceived and

you received your 23 pairs of chromosomes from your parents. However, you can influence your phenotype, or the ways your genes are expressed, by the way you treat your genes. Granted, the expression of some genetic inheritance factors cannot easily be modified by diet, lifestyle or environmental exposures. These are your *constitutional* genetic factors. It is your *inducible* genetic factors over which you have some control, and scientists are finding that many more genetic characteristics than anyone previously thought are, in fact, inducible. These inducible characteristics are the focus of the Genetic Nutritioneering Program.

The foundations of genetic nutritioneering are based in a variety of scientific and medical disciplines including genetics, molecular biology, nutrition, immunology, endocrinology, neurology, cardiology and gerontology. By distilling the contributions of these disciplines, we arrive at the following basic points:

1. Your genes are unique and not identical to anyone else's even if you are an identical twin.
2. All the genetic messages you need to remake yourself are present in every cell of your body.
3. At any one time some genes are being expressed and others are not.
4. Genetic messages may be partially expressed.
5. You can modify the expression of many genes through diet, nutrients, exercise, lifestyle and environment.
6. The genetic nutritioneering approach employs nutrients, diet and lifestyle to improve genetic expression, resulting in healthy aging.

It is one thing to understand the basic principles of the genetic nutritioneering approach. The real challenge is in knowing how to apply them to make a difference in your health and function. Over the past seven years, the Institute for Functional Medicine* has

---

* The Institute for Functional Medicine web page is *http://www.fxmed.org.*

supported research, symposia, seminars and meetings among health professionals and researchers to determine better ways to apply the vast and growing body of knowledge to improve health outcomes. These discussions have resulted in a simplified Genetic Nutritioneering Program, which can be broken down into two components: "What You Need to Know" and "What to Do about It."

WHAT YOU NEED TO KNOW

To design your own Genetic Nutritioneering Program, ask yourself some specific questions about your genetic uniqueness. The following categories of information will help you understand your genetic blueprint and how it is being expressed as your phenotype:

1. Family health history
2. Personal health history
3. Biomarkers of function
4. Dietary habits and responses
5. Use of over-the-counter and prescription medications
6. Specific medical laboratory tests for defining function (optional)

1. Family health history

Ask the following questions about the health histories of your parents, grandparents, uncles, aunts, brothers, sisters and children.

- Is there a prevalence of cancer in the family, and, if so, what types of cancer?
- Is there a family history of heart disease or stroke?
- Diabetes?
- Arthritis?
- Dementia?

- Osteoporosis?
- Obesity?
- Allergies?
- Alcoholism?

Genetic research has revealed all of these conditions have a link to genetic predisposition. In a recent book, *The Variation in the Human Genome*, Kenneth Weiss, Ph.D., from the Department of Anthropology at Pennsylvania State University, wrote, "Genetic characteristics that have a strong effect on the risk of disease are usually rare. For most genetic characteristics, their effect on disease risk is modest. From a health perspective, however, the genetic characteristics with strong risk to disease are the ones that are much more easily understood and can be easily evaluated through family history."[1]

Understanding something of the disease patterns in your family history will help you understand your potential genetic rough spots and where you need to concentrate your efforts to improve genetic expression.

2. Personal health history

- Do you have a history of chronic pain or fatigue?
- Are you susceptible to every cold or flu that comes along?
- Do you have a craving for sugar?
- Do you have allergies or chronic infections such as recurring sinus infections?

The answers to all of these questions reflect how your genes are being expressed into your phenotype and how well matched your genes are with your diet and lifestyle choices. Understanding something about your family health history and your own personal health history helps you understand your predisposition to disease. If you find your parents and grandparents were healthier than you are, you should suspect that you may be making some poor choices about your diet and lifestyle and other factors that modify genetic expression.

3. Biomarkers of function

These are measurable symptoms of biological aging that can be halted or reversed, once they have been identified, using the Genetic Nutritioneering Program.

- Is your vision deteriorating?
- Is your hearing deteriorating?
- Is your reaction time less than it once was?
- Can you stand on one leg with your eyes closed and your arms outstretched?
- Is your strength decreasing dramatically?
- Are you easily winded with mild exercise?
- Are you having problems digesting foods that you previously tolerated well?
- Are you becoming more sensitive to alcohol, perfumes or air pollution?
- Are you increasingly stiff when you get up in the morning?
- Do you have chronic pain and/or inflammation?
- Do you get shaky if you don't eat regularly?
- Are you having problems managing your weight?
- Do you have more allergies than you formerly did?
- Do you have problems remembering details?

4. Dietary habits and responses

- What do you normally eat?
- Do you live principally from hand to mouth, surviving on convenience, snack and highly processed foods?
- Is your diet limited, so that most of your calories come from just a few foods?

How does your body respond to the foods you eat?

- Do you get a runny nose every time you eat peanuts?
- Do dairy products cause intestinal discomfort and diarrhea?
- Does wheat give you stomach pain or a headache?
- Does coffee wind you up?
- Does alcohol depress you?
- Does shellfish give you hives?
- Do you get sore joints and muscles after eating fish, meat or shellfish?
- Are you sensitive to foods that contain monosodium glutamate (MSG)?
- Do you get a headache when you eat cheese or drink red wine?
- Do you get muscle cramping after you eat at a salad bar where the lettuce is treated with sulfites?

The answers to all of these questions indicate how you respond to your individual dietary choices.

What are your "comfort foods?"

- Sweet foods? A sweet tooth may indicate you have trouble normalizing your blood sugar. If so, be sure to eat at regular times, have adequate protein at each meal, and choose only carbohydrates that are unrefined and low in sugar.
- Salty foods? A craving for salty foods may indicate you are under great stress and your adrenal glands may be working overtime.
- Foods high in carbohydrate? A craving for starchy carbohydrate-rich foods may mean your brain needs more of the mood-elevating hormone serotonin, which is stimulated when you eat higher-carbohydrate foods.
- Protein-rich foods? If you crave protein, your body may be telling you it is "carbohydrate sensitive" and you need to

derive more of your calories from protein-rich foods for optimal metabolism.
- High-fat foods? A craving for fat may indicate a problem with regulation of your thyroid gland, the master gland that controls your metabolic rate.

Each predisposition says something about your genetic uniqueness. In each case, if you ask the right questions about your diet and your responses to it, you may discover some unique aspects of your genotype and the way it is being expressed as your phenotype. You can use these discoveries to help you to design a diet to improve genetic expression and rebalance your metabolism.

The next area to explore is your response to specific components of your diet.

- Does your blood pressure go up when you eat salty foods? If so, you are no doubt salt-sensitive, and controlling salt in your diet is important.
- Does your blood cholesterol level rise significantly after you have been eating dietary cholesterol from egg yolks or high-saturated-fat foods? If so, dietary management of cholesterol and saturated fat from animal products will help lower your risk of heart disease.
- Do you frequently have muscle cramps, including those that come on in your sleep at night? If so, you may not be getting adequate calcium or magnesium in your diet, and you should eat more calcium-rich, low-fat dairy products, green leafy vegetables and whole grains that are high in magnesium.
- If you are a woman, do you have difficulty with menstrual periods or with the transition into menopause?
- If you are a man, is your prostate gland inflamed or enlarged? Answering yes to either of the last two questions may indicate your hormones are out of balance. The expression of the genetic characteristics related to hormone pro-

duction and metabolism may be improved if you consume more soy products and dietary fiber rich in lignans from flaxseed and rye flour.

- Do you frequently have skipped heartbeats or extra heartbeats that normalize when you eat more potassium- and magnesium-rich vegetables and fruits? If so, your heart function may be improved if you regularly drink fruit and vegetable juices to provide more of these critical nutrients.

- Have you tried to follow a vegetarian diet but found you are anemic? If so, you may not be well suited for a vegetarian diet and should eat more iron- and vitamin B12-rich lean animal protein.

- Do you have a history of eczema or sandpaper-like skin on the backs of your arms or on your legs? If so, you need to augment your diet with nutrients like vitamin A, essential fatty acids and magnesium.

- Does your hair lack luster? If so, you should increase the unsaturated vegetable oil content of your diet and eat more leafy green vegetables and whole grains that are rich in magnesium and other essential minerals.

- Are your lips frequently chapped, or do you have cracks at the corners of your mouth, or enlarged pores on your nose and face? If so, you might benefit from eating more vitamin B-rich foods, including lean muscle meats, whole grains and wheat germ, or taking a multivitamin/multi-mineral supplement.

These are all examples of individual responses that help you understand aspects of your genotype and how it is being expressed in your phenotype.

5. Medications

The most common medications people use are over-the-counter products like aspirin, acetaminophen, ibuprofen, antacids, laxatives and sleeping pills. Regular consumption of these medications indicates your body is not in optimal balance. Depending on medications to reduce unpleasant symptoms of pain, insomnia, or an acid stomach indicates your phenotype is not reflecting the optimal expression of your genes.

The same can be said of prescription medications like antidepressants, acid-blocking drugs or antiinflammatories which you may have used to modify your function over a long period of time. Although these medications may be effective in managing health problems in the short term, they can be very damaging to long-term health and function. In a sense, they mask the symptoms your body has produced to alert you to the fact that your genes are not being expressed correctly.

When your body sends such a message, you can respond by doing something about it or you can suppress the message, thinking symptom relief means the problem is solved. The underlying problem can still progress, however, resulting in even more serious health problems down the road. For example, long-term consumption of acetaminophen can result in potential injury to the kidneys, and long-term consumption of ibuprofen and other pain medications can result in damage to the intestinal tract.

Even blood pressure–lowering medications, which may be very useful in managing a potentially dangerous short-term episode of high blood pressure, can in the long term produce adverse side effects such as male impotence. As an alternative to blood pressure medication, a person could implement a Genetic Nutritioneering Program. The program would involve decreasing salt, alcohol and saturated fat in the diet and increasing polyunsaturated oils, magnesium- and calcium-rich foods, potassium- and magnesium-rich whole grains, fruits and vegetables. It would also mean maintaining an appropriate weight and implementing a regular exercise/activity program. This is a better long-term program than blood pressure medication for individuals who suffer from mild hypertension.

Similarly, individuals who regularly rely on laxatives may be better off increasing their water intake, consuming more dietary fiber and exercising regularly. The increased fiber communicates the appropriate message to the genes for long-term healthy digestive function rather than overriding this message with laxatives.

6. Laboratory tests

The final, optional category of information is medical laboratory testing to evaluate genetic uniqueness and function. Tests for genetic characteristics like ApoE 4, homocysteine, insulin sensitivity, digestive function, detoxification ability and oxidative stress can help you understand more about your unique genotype and how your diet and lifestyle can modify the expression of these genetic characteristics for optimal function. An increasing number of doctors are becoming better informed about using these tests with their patients.

Tests to evaluate some aspects of function are quite simple. They might include strength, flexibility and cardiovascular endurance tests. You can also easily have your body composition measured to determine your percentage of body fat. All of these tests are biomarkers of vitality and can help you understand how your genes are being expressed as functional characteristics. Trained exercise counselors or physiologists at good health clubs or health promotion clinics can measure strength, flexibility, cardiovascular endurance and body composition.

In their book *Biomarkers: The Ten Keys to Prolonging Vitality*,[2] William Evans, Ph.D. and Irwin Rosenberg, M.D., professors of nutrition and medicine at Tufts University, wrote, "Disease-free aging is partly within your control." And it may start by understanding more about your biomarkers of aging. Individuals who have poor strength, flexibility or cardiovascular function and increased levels of body fat have a much higher risk of unhealthy aging than those who have better function in these areas. Each of these characteristics, which many people assume are simply the consequence of bad genes, is modifiable by practicing the right program. Improved diet, reduced alcohol consumption and regular activity, including both endurance and strength-building activities, can make tremendous differences in improving these biomarkers of aging.

Modifiable Factors of Unhealthy Aging

1. Poor strength
2. Reduced flexibility
3. Poor aerobic ability
4. Inappropriately high level of body fat
5. Poor control of insulin and blood sugar
6. Increased inflammation
7. Increased risk of heart disease
8. Accelerated brain aging
9. Increased risk of cancer

In a new book titled *Inducible Gene Expression: Environmental Stresses and Nutrients*, Dr. Stefan Oehler, from the Institute of Genetics at the University of Cambridge, describes how important nutrition and environmental factors are in modifying gene expression and altering our phenotype.[3] Dr. Carolyn Berdanier, from the Department of Foods and Nutrition at the University of Georgia, described the same theme in her book, *Nutrients and Gene Expression*. She discusses the increasing understanding within medicine of the importance of specific nutrients in modifying function throughout the aging process as a consequence of their ability to communicate with the genes.[4]

Both authors concur that diet and nutrients can modify an individual's risk of developing diabetes, heart disease, dementia or cancer. The way to improve the association between diet and gene expression to decrease risk in each of these areas can be summarized in the following way:

1. Improved control of insulin and blood sugar. Reduce the levels of saturated fat and sugar in the diet, increase consumption of lean protein, whole grains and dietary fiber. If you are overweight, reduce body fat by modest calorie reduction and exercise. Increase your intake of vitamin E, chromium, vanadium, magnesium and fish oils.

2. Reduced inflammation and chronic pain. Implement a low-allergy diet, limiting dairy products and wheat. Supplement your diet with *Lactobacillus acidophilus* and *Bifidobacteria bifidus*, found in certain strains of yogurt or as a food supplement. Supplement with the amino acid L-glutamine. If you are not allergic to soy, increase your consumption of soy products. Eat more legumes, rice, flax and rye. Consider taking nutritional supplements of niacinamide, glucosamine sulfate and the Indian herb Boswellia.

3. Reduced risk of heart disease. Consume a diet low in saturated fat and high in dietary fiber and whole-grain carbohydrate. Eliminate possible chronic infection from protozoa or viruses. Increase intake of fish and fish oils, vitamin E, selenium, magnesium, vitamin B6, folic acid and vitamin B12. Vitamin C and coenzyme Q10 and the amino acid L-arginine may also help reduce risk.

4. Reduced brain aging. Reduce inflammation and infection (as indicated in #2, above). Avoid allergy- or hypersensitivity-producing foods to lower inflammatory response. Eat more vegetables that help improve detoxification, including cruciferous vegetables (broccoli, Brussels sprouts, cabbage, cauliflower) and soy products. Consider supplementation with vitamin E, lipoic acid, vitamin C, coenzyme Q10, N-acetylcysteine, zinc and copper.

5. Reduced cancer risk. Increase the consumption of substances that improve detoxification of potential cancer-producing chemicals, including soy, green tea, cruciferous vegetables, dietary fiber, and spices like curcumin and garlic. Eat more fruits like grapes and grape juice and more fish, fish oils and flaxseed oil. Consider supplementation with vitamin B12, folate and vitamin B6.

If you want to find more information about specific foods and meal plans, a 20-day diet plan that incorporates many of these suggestions is described in my recent book, *The 20-Day Rejuvenation Diet Program*.[5]

PUTTING IT ALL TOGETHER

In her book *Does It Run in the Family?* Doris Teichler Zallen states,

> Scientific research is now giving us powerful insights into our genes, making it possible to reveal our previously unknown and unimagined genetic secrets. If we are to derive real and enduring benefit from these scientific victories, we must be alert to the problems that this knowledge may create. And we must be prepared to confront problems with caring, creativity and courage."[6]

Medical scientists have learned throughout years of observation and research that almost anything can go wrong with our bodies, and the likelihood that problems will develop increases as we get older. Some of us make it to age 80 or 90 in good shape, while others have major problems at 40 or 50. By reading this book you have learned that the aging process can be modified to promote healthy aging if you take into account your genetic uniqueness and modify the expression of your genes through appropriate diet and lifestyle choices. In a recent book, *Why We Age: What Science Is Discovering About the Body's Journey Through Life,* Steven Austad, Ph.D. expressed the optimistic view that the genome revolution will allow us to access information within our genes that helps promote health and reduce the risk of disease while enhancing our functional vitality throughout the life process.[7] The door is open to a new field of gerontology based on promoting healthy aging.

There is reason for optimism about our ability to live a long, healthy life. John Rowe, M.D., president of the Mount Sinai Medical Center, recently stated, "Preventive gerontology now aims not just to retard disease but to prevent functional decline. Health and functional status in late life are increasingly seen as under our own control. The stage is set for major community-based intervention studies designed to enhance the likelihood of older persons not only to avoid disease and disability but to truly age successfully."[8]

We seem to be recrafting the eugenics philosophy of the early 20th century. Charles Darwin's cousin Sir Francis Galston defined eugenics as the science of improving heredity. American eugenicists sponsored a diverse range of activities, including statistically sophisticated analyses of disease inheritance and "better baby" contests modeled on rural livestock shows. Unfortunately, they also advocated the forced sterilization of criminals and the retarded, selective ethnic restriction on immigration and euthanasia for those deemed unfit to live because of their view that getting rid of bad genes would improve society.[9]

The Genetic Nutritioneering Program is the polar opposite of this eugenics philosophy. Instead of getting rid of bad genes, we advocate working to improve the function of the genes you possess. The rich diversity of genetic characteristics is what gives the human species its stability and plasticity, its ability to survive changing environments. In no way would we want to limit this extraordinary diversity, but we do want to optimize the expression of those characteristics in our genes to achieve the highest level of function and health. By maximizing the genetic potential we presently have through improved gene expression, we can better address the many problems that confront our society. According to researchers from the Stanford University School of Medicine, "Defining the role of each gene in these genomes will be a formidable task, and understanding how the genome functions as a whole in the complex natural history of a living organism presents an even greater challenge." The more we learn about gene expression the more we recognize that the function of the organism, as expressed as its phenotype, can be modified as a consequence of altered nutrition and environmental exposures.[10]

Each of us possesses a wide range of possible functions, depending upon how we treat our genes through our lifestyle, diet, nutrition and environmental selections. Even nutritious foods that benefit most of us may produce adverse effects for some individuals because of their genetic predisposition. For example, some young children's sensitivity to proteins in cow's milk can create an adverse reaction with their immune system and contribute to the genetic expression of diabetes.[11,12] Restricting these children's exposure to cow's milk protein early in life can help reduce immune-related problems that could otherwise plague them throughout their lives.

A recent report in the *Journal of the American Medical Association* provided another example of how nutrients can modify the genetic risk of disease. Individuals who took antioxidant vitamin supplements before a high-fat meal had improved heart and blood vessel function compared to others who did not take vitamins C and E before the high fat meal.[13] Not all individuals have the same response to supplementation with antioxidants. But for those with specific genetic characteristics, the expression of function after consuming high-fat meals can be greatly modified by taking antioxidants. The participants in this study consumed a supplement containing 1,000 mg of vitamin C and 800 IU of vitamin E. This single study, conducted at the Department of Cardiology, University of Maryland School of Medicine, does not prove that antioxidants prevent heart disease. It is simply one more piece of information that indicates genetic predisposition can be modified through specific diet, nutrient and lifestyle modifications. Health and vitality throughout the aging process are not locked in the genes; they are capable of being modified.

Sandra Steingraber, Ph.D. described the interaction of genes and environment in promoting health and disease in her book *Living Downstream*.[14]

> The human body is an endless construction site, where demolition and renovation occur simultaneously and continuously. Different tissues carry on this work at different rates; the lining of the stomach is entirely overhauled every few days, while a complete restoration of the bones and internal scaffolding requires years. All tissues replace themselves throughout this orderly process. . . . Damaged and aged cells slated for removal undergo a programmed form of death known as apoptosis. All this activity is coordinated through an elaborate system of communication that cell biologists are just beginning to understand. . . . We know also that the chemical signals from neighboring cells can alter the pace of this process, and we know that marching orders sometimes arrive from distant headquarters.

These messages from distant headquarters can come from foods you eat, nutrients you consume, stress and activity patterns or environmental exposures. Understanding your genetic background and how your genes are expressed through the diet and lifestyle selections you make creates a proactive approach toward healthy aging rather than a reactive approach in which you wait for disease to develop and then see your doctor to have something done about it. In her book, *Market Driven Health Care*, Regina Herzlinger, from the Harvard School of Business, wrote, "Doctor, wake up and smell the decaf lite cappuccino. Well-informed, mastery seeking Americans are no longer going to put doctors or anyone else up on a pedestal. Rather, the patients will make the doctor their partner in the health-care process."[15]

In the health care of the future, patients and health practitioners will be partners working together to understand how the patient's genes can best be expressed into full function and healthy aging. Let your diet and lifestyle speak gently but firmly to your genes throughout your aging process to promote optimal expression of healthy aging. You can put genetic messages to sleep that steal the quantity and quality of your life and awaken and express messages of health and vitality within your genetic structure. Your family inheritance has given you your potential. You can express this potential fully by making the appropriate decisions about what you eat and how you live. Throughout your life the most profound influences on your health, vitality and function are not the doctors that you visited or the drugs, surgery or other therapies you have undertaken. The most profound influences are the cumulative effects of the decisions you make about your diet and lifestyle on the expression of your genes. The genetic nutritioneering approach provides the framework from which you can construct your future health.

REFERENCES

CHAPTER ONE

1. Sacks O. *The Island of the Colorblind and Cycad Island.* Alfred A. Knopf. New York, 1997.
2. Ibid.
3. Herrnstein R, Murray C. *The Bell Curve: Intelligence and Class Structure in American Life.* Free Press. New York, 1994.
4. Wilmut I, Schnieke AE, McWhir J, Kind AJ, Campbell KHS. "Viable Offspring Derived from Fetal and Adult Mammalian Cells," *Nature.* Vol. 385, pp. 810–813, 1997.
5. Wyke A. *21st-Century Miracle Medicine.* Plenum Trade. New York, 1997.
6. Deutsch D. *The Fabric of Reality.* The Penguin Press. London, England, 1997.
7. Zallen DT. *Does It Run in the Family?* University Press. New Jersey, 1997.
8. Bishop JE, Waldholz M. *Genome.* Simon & Schuster. New York, 1990.
9. Pauling L, Itano H. "Sickle Cell Anemia, a Molecular Disease," *Science.* Vol. 110, pp. 543–647, 1949.

10. Williams R. *Biochemical Individuality*. 2nd Edition. Keats Publishing, Inc. New Canaan, Conn., 1998.

CHAPTER TWO

1. Steingraber S. *Living Downstream: An Ecologist Looks at Cancer and the Environment*. Addison-Wesley Publishing Company, Inc. Reading, Mass., 1997.
2. Watson JD, Crick FH. "Molecular Structure of Nucleic Acids," *Nature*. Vol. 171, no. 4356, pp. 737–738, 1953.
3. Sikorski R, Peters R. "Internet Resources for Medical Genetics," *Journal of the American Medical Association*. Vol. 278, pp. 1212–13, 1997.
4. Nowak R. "Mining Treasures from 'Junk DNA,' " *Science*. Vol. 263, pp. 608–10, 1994.
5. Lin HJ. "Smokers and Breast Cancer. 'Chemical Individuality' and Cancer Predispositon," *Journal of the American Medical Association*. Vol. 276, pp. 1511–12, 1996.
6. Pyeritz RE. "Family History and Genetic Risk Factors. Forward to the Future," *Journal of the American Medical Association*. Vol. 278, pp. 1284–85, 1997.
7. Collins FS. "Preparing Health Professionals for the Genetic Revolution," *Journal of the American Medical Association*. Vol. 278, pp. 1285–86, 1997.
8. Williams R. *Biochemical Individuality*. 2nd Edition. Keats Publishing, Inc. New Canaan, Conn., 1988.
9. Williams R, Beerstecher E. "The Concept of Genetotrophic Disease," *Lancet*. Vol. 1, pp. 287–89, 1950.
10. Davis DR, Williams RJ. "Potentially Useful Criteria for Judging Nutritional Adequacy," *American Journal of Clinical Nutrition*. Vol. 29, pp. 710–15, 1976.
11. Pauling L, Itano HA. "Sickle Cell Anemia, a Molecular Disease," *Science*. Vol. 110, pp. 543–47, 1949.
12. Ezzell C. "Awakened Gene Aids Inherited Anemias," *Science News*. Vol. 143, p. 52, 1993.

Chapter Three

1. Sapolsky RM. *Why Zebras Don't Get Ulcers*. W.H. Freeman & Co. New York, N.Y., 1994.
2. Burt V, Whelton P, Roccella E, et al. "Prevalence of Hypertension in the US Adult Population: Results From the Third National Health and Nutrition Examination Survey," *Hypertension*. Vol. 25, pp. 305–313, 1995.
3. Sullivan J. "Salt-Sensitivity: Definition, Conception, Methodology, and Long-Term Issues," *Hypertension*. Vol. 17 (suppl.), pp. 173–74, 1991.
4. Dreon D, Fernstrom H, Miller B, Krauss R. "Low-Density Lipoprotein Subclass Patterns and Lipoprotein Response to a Reduced Fat Diet in Men," *FASEB*. Vol. 8, pp. 121–26, 1994.
5. Miller G, Groziak S. "Diet and Gene Interactions," *Journal of the American College of Nutrition*. Vol. 16, pp. 293–295, 1997.
6. Motulsky AG. "The 1985 Nobel Prize in Physiology or Medicine," *Science*. Vol. 231, p. 126, 1986.
7. Qureshi AA, Qureshi N, Wright JJK, et al. "Lowering of Serum Cholesterol in Hypercholesterolemic Humans by Tocotrienols (Palmvitee)," *American Journal of Clinical Nutrition*. Vol. 53, pp. 1021S-26S, 1991.
8. Ascherio A, Hennekens C, Willett WC, et al. "Prospective Study of Nutritional Factors, Blood Pressure, and Hypertension among US Women," *Hypertension*. Vol. 27, pp. 1065–72, 1996.
9. "Dietary Fat, Hypertension, and Stroke." In: *Fats and Oils in Human Nutrition – Report of a Joint Expert Consultation*. United Nations and World Health Organization, Rome, Italy, pp. 95–98, 1994.
10. Franz MJ. "Protein: Metabolism and Effect on Blood Glucose Levels," *Diabetes Education*. Vol. 23, pp. 643–46, 1997.
11. Block G, Patterson B, Subar A. "Fruit, Vegetables, and Cancer Prevention: A Review of the Epidemiological Evidence," *Journal of Nutrition and Cancer*. Vol. 18, pp. 1–29, 1992.
12. Block G. "Dietary Guidelines and the Results of Food Consumption Surveys," *American Journal of Clinical Nutrition*. Vol. 53, pp. 56–57S, 1991.

13. Ameer B, Weintraub RA. "Drug Interactions With Grapefruit Juice," *Clinical Pharmacokinetics.* Vol. 33, pp. 103–21, 1997.

14. Milner JA. "Garlic: Its Anticarcinogenic and Antitumorigenic Properties," *Nutrition Reviews.* Vol. 54, pp. 82–86.

15. Sreejayan R. "Nitric Oxide Scavenging by Curcuminoids," *Journal of Pharmaceutical Pharmacology.* Vol. 49, pp. 105–07, 1997.

16. Joe B, Rao UJ, Likesh BR. "Presence of an Acidic Glycoprotein in the Serum of Arthritic Rats: Modulation by Capsaicin and Curcumin." *Molecular Cell Biochemistry.* Vol. 169, pp. 125–34, 1997.

17. Xu YX, Pindolia KR, Janakiraman N, et al. "Curcumin, a Compound with Anti-Inflammatory and Anti-Oxidant Properties, Down-Regulates Chemokine Expression in Bone Marrow Stromal Cells," *Experimental Hematology.* Vol. 25, pp. 413–22, 1997.

18. Chan MM, Ho CT, Huang HI. "Effects of Three Dietary Phytochemicals from Tea, Rosemary and Turmeric on Inflammation-Induced Nitrite Production," *Cancer Letters.* Vol. 96, pp. 23–29, 1995.

19. Sato M, Miyazaki T, Kambe F, et al. "Quercetin, a Bioflavonoid, Inhibits the Induction of Interleukin 8 and Monocyte Chemoattractant Protein-1 Expression by Tumor Necrosis Factor-*a* in Cultured Human Synovial Cells," *Journal of Rheumatology.* Vol. 24, pp. 1680–84, 1997.

20. Keli SO, Hertog GL, Feskens EJ, Kromhout D. "Dietary Flavonoids, Antioxidant Vitamins, and Incidence of Stroke," *Archives of Internal Medicine.* Vol. 154, pp. 637–42, 1996.

21. Ruch RJ, Cheng S, Klaunig JE. "Prevention of Cytotoxicity and Inhibition of Intercellular Communication by Antioxidant Catechins Isolated from Chinese Green Tea," *Carcinogenesis.* Vol. 10, pp. 1003–08, 1989.

22. Formica JV, Regelson W. "Review of the Biology of Quercetin and Related Bioflavonoids," *Food & Chemical Toxicology.* Vol. 33, pp. 1061–80, 1995.

CHAPTER FOUR

1. Yang MG, Kobayashi A, Mickelsen O. "Bibliography of Cycad Research," *Federation Proceedings.* Vol. 31, pp. 1543–46, 1972.

2. Zhang ZX, Anderson DW, Mantel N, Roman GC. "Motor Neuron Disease in Guam: Geographic and Familial Occurrence, 1956–85," *Acta Neurologica Scandinavica.* Vol. 94, no. 1, pp. 51–59, 1996.

3. Ginsburg H, Atamna H, Shalmiev G, Kanaani J, Krugliak. "Resistance of Glucose-6–phosphate Dehydrogenase Deficiency to Malaria: Effects of Fava Bean Hydroxypyrimidine Glucosides on *Plasmodium falciparum* Growth in Culture and on the Phagocytosis of Infected Cells," *Parasitology.* Vol. 113, pp. 7–18, 1996.

4. Gottschall E. *Breaking the Vicious Cycle: Intestinal Health Through Diet.* Kirkton Press. Kirkton, Ontario, Canada, 1994.

5. Yunginger JW. "Lethal Food Allergy in Children," *New England Journal of Medicine.* Vol. 327, pp. 421–22, 1992.

6. Schiodt FV, Rochling RA, Casey DL, Lee WM. "Acetaminophen Toxicity in an Urban County Hospital," *New England Journal of Medicine* Vol. 337, pp. 1112–17, 1997.

7. Ambrosone CB, Freudenheim JL, Graham S, et al. "Cigarette Smoking, N-Acetyltransferase 2 Genetic Polymorphisms, and Breast Cancer Risk," *Journal of the American Medical Association.* Vol. 276, no. 18, pp. 1494–1501, 1996.

8. Ryberg D, Skaug V, Hewer A, et al. "Genotypes of Glutathione Transferase M1 and P1 and Their Significance for Lung DNA Adduct Levels and Cancer Risk," *Carcinogenesis.* Vol. 18, no. 7, pp. 1285–89, 1997.

9. Hemminki K, Dickey C, Karlsson S, et al. "Aromatic DNA Adducts in Foundry Workers in Relation to Exposure, Life Style and CYP1A1 and Glutathione Transferase M1 Genotype," *Carcinogenesis.* Vol. 18, No. 2, pp. 345–50, 1997.

10. Sinha R, Caporaso N. "Heterocyclic Amines, Cytochrome P4501A2, and N-Acetyltransferase: Issues Involved in Incorporating Putative Genetic Susceptibility Markers into Epidemiological Studies," *Annals of Epidemiology.* Vol. 7, no. 5, pp. 350–56, 1997.

11. Williams AC, Steventon GB, Sturman S, Waring RH. "Hereditary Variation of Liver Enzymes Involved with Detoxification and Neurodegenerative Disease," *Journal of Inherited Metabolic Disorders.* Vol. 14, no. 4, pp. 431–35, 1991.

12. Bandmann O, Vaughan J, Holmans P, et al. "Association of Slow

Acetylator Genotype for N-Acetyltransferase 2 with Familial Parkinson's Disease," *Lancet.* Vol. 350, pp. 1136–39, 1997.

13. Masimirembwa CM, Beke M, Hasler JA, et al. "Low CYP1A2 Activity of Rural Shona Children of Zimbabwe," *Clinical Pharmacology and Therapeutics.* Vol. 57, pp. 25–31, 1995.

14. Jover R, Carnicer F, Sanchez-Paya J, Climent E, Sirvent M, Marco JL. "Salivary Caffeine Clearance Predicts Survival in Patients with Liver Cirrhosis," *American Journal of Gastroenterology.* Vol. 92, no.10, pp. 1905–08, 1997.

15. Brown RR, Miller JA, Miller EC. "Dietary Factors Enhancing Demethylation In Vitro," *Journal of Biological Chemistry.* Vol. 209, pp. 211–22, 1954.

16. Patel DK, Ogunbona A, Notarianni LJ, Bennett PN. "Depletion of Plasma Glycine and Effect of Glycine by Mouth on Salicylate Metabolism during Aspirin Overdose," *Human & Experimental Toxicology.* Vol. 9, pp. 389–95, 1990.

17. Quick AJ. "The Conjugation of Benzoic Acid in Man," *Journal of Biological Chemistry.* Vol. 92, pp. 65–85, 1931.

18. Nijhoff WA, Grubben JA, Nagengast FM, et al. "Effects of Consumption of Brussels Sprouts on Intestinal and Lymphocytic Glutathione S-transferases in Humans," *Carcinogenesis.* Vol. 16, no. 9, pp. 2125–28, 1995.

19. Le Marchand L, Franke AA, Custer L, et al. "Lifestyle and Nutritional Correlates of Cytochrome CYP1A2 Activity: Inverse Associations with Plasma Lutein and Alpha-Tocopherol," *Pharmacogenetics.* Vol. 7, pp. 11–19, 1997.

20. Appelt LC, Reicks MM. "Soy Feeding Induces Phase II Enzymes in Rat Tissues," *Nutrition and Cancer.* Vol. 28, no. 3, pp. 270–75, 1997.

21. Ibid.

22. Messina M, Messina V, Setchell K. *The Simple Soybean and Your Health.* Avery Publishing Group. Garden City Park, N.Y., 1994.

23. Canivenc-Lavier MC, Vernevaut MF, Totis M, Siess MH, Magdalou J, Suschetet M. "Comparative Effects of Flavonoids and Model Inducers on Drug-Metabolizing Enzymes in Rat Liver," *Toxicology.* Vol. 114, no. 1, pp. 19–27, 1996.

CHAPTER FIVE

1. Final Report of the Task Force on Genetic Testing. Editors: NA Holtzman, M.D., and MS Watson, Ph.D. "Promoting Safe and Effective Genetic Tests in the United States." Sept. 1997.

2. Landsteiner K. *The Specificity of Serological Reactions.* Dover Publications, Inc. New York, 1962.

3. Jansky J. "Haematologische Studien bei Psychotikern," *Jahresb. F. Neurol. U. Psychiat.* Vol. 11, p. 1092, 1907.

4. Alexander W. "An Inquiry Into the Distribution of the Blood Groups in Patients Suffering From 'Malignant Disease,' " *The British Journal of Experimental Pathology.* Vol. 2, pp. 66–69, 1921.

5. Buchanan JA. "The Relationship of Blood Groups to Disease," *British Journal of Experimental Pathology.* Vol. 2, pp. 247–253, 1921.

6. Roberts JA. "Blood Groups and Susceptibility to Disease: A Review," *British Journal Prev Society Medicine.* Vol. 11, pp. 107–25, 1957.

7. Camps FE, Dodd BE, Lincoln PJ. "Frequencies of Secretors and Nonsecretors of ABH Group Substances among 1,000 Alcoholic Patients," *British Medical Journal.* Vol. 4, pp. 457–59, 1969.

8. Allan TM, Dawson AA. "ABO Blood Groups and Ischaemic Heart Disease in Men," *British Heart Journal.* Vol. 30, pp. 377–82, 1968.

9. Hein HO, Sorensen H, Suadicani P, Gyntelberg F. "Alcohol Consumption, Lewis Phenotypes, and Risk of Ischaemic Heart Disease," *Lancet.* Vol. 341, pp. 377–82, 1968.

10. D'Adamo P. *Eat Right for Your Type.* G.P. Putnam & Sons. New York, 1997.

11. Nachbar MS, Oppenheim JD, Thomas JO. "Isolation and Characterization of a Lectin from the Tomato (Lycopersicon Esculentum)," *Journal of Biological Chemistry.* Vol. 255, pp. 2056–61, 1980.

12. Nachbar MS, Oppenheim JD. "Lectins in the United States Diet: A Survey of Lectins in Commonly Consumed Foods and a Review of the Literature," *American Journal of Clinical Nutrition,* Vol. 33, pp. 2338–45, 1980.

13. Freed DL. "Lectins," *British Medical Journal.* Vol. 290, pp. 584–85, 1985.

14. Chang DM. "Immunoregulatory Effects of a Synthetic Monosaccharide," *Immunopharmacology and Immunotoxicology*, Vol. 17, pp. 437–50, 1995.
15. Marshall B, McCallum RW, Guerrant RL (Ed.). *Helicobacter Pylori in Peptic Ulceration and Gastritis.* Blackwell Science Inc. Malden, Mass., 1991.
16. Simon PM, Goode PL, Mobasseri A, Zopf D. "Inhibition of *Helicobacter Pylori* Binding to Gastrointestinal Epithelial Cells by Sialic Acid-Containing Oligosaccharides," *Infection and Immunity.* Vol. 65, pp. 750–57, 1997.

CHAPTER SIX

1. Fries J, Crapo LM. *Vitality and Aging.* W.H. Freeman & Company. San Francisco, 1981.
2. Evans W, Rosenberg I. *Biomarkers: The 10 Keys to Prolonged Vitality.* Simon and Schuster, p. 38, New York, 1991.
3. Rowe JW. "The New Gerontology," *Science.* Vol. 278, p. 367, 1997.
4. Ibid.
5. Peto R, Doll R. "There is No Such Thing as Aging. Old Age Is Associated with Disease, but Does Not Cause It," *British Medical Journal.* Vol. 315, p. 115, 1997.
6. Finch C. "Genetics of Aging," *Science.* Vol. 278, p. 407, 1997.
7. Van Weel C, Michels J. "Dying, Not Old Age, to Blame for Costs of Health Care," *Lancet.* Vol. 350, p. 1159, 1997.
8. Mulley GP. "Myths of Ageing," *Lancet.* Vol. 350, p. 1160, 1997.
9. Gordon M. "Is the Best Yet to Be?" *Lancet.* Vol. 350, p. 1166–67, 1997.
10. "Testosterone—Super Hormone Therapy: Can It Keep Men Young?" *Newsweek.* September 16, 1996, pp. 69–75.
11. Lamberts SW, van den Beld AW, van der Lely AJ. "The Endocrinology of Aging," *Science.* Vol. 278, pp. 419–24, 1997.
12. Henderson VW, Watt L, Buckwalter JG. "Cognitive Skills Associated with Estrogen Replacement in Women with Alzheimer's Disease," *Psychoneuroendocrinology.* Vol. 21, p. 421–30, 1996.
13. Morley JE, Kaiser F, Raum WJ, et al. "Potentially Predictive and

Manipulable Blood Serum Correlates of Aging in the Healthy Human Male: Progressive Decreases in Bioavailable Testosterone, Dehydro-epiandrosterone Sulfate, and the Ratio of Insulin-Like Growth Factor 1 to Growth Hormone," *Proceedings of the National Academy of Sciences.* Vol. 94, pp. 7537–42, 1997.

14. Mariotti S, Sansoni P, Barbesino G, et al. "Thyroid and Other Organ-Specific Autoantibodies in Healthy Centenarians," *Lancet.* Vol. 339, pp. 1506–08, 1992.

15. Orr WC, Sohal RS. "Extension of Life-Span by Overexpression of Superoxide Dismutase and Catalase in *Drosophila melanogaster,*" *Science.* Vol. 263, pp. 1128–30, 1994.

16. Harman D. "Aging: A Theory Based on Free Radical and Radiation Chemistry," *Journal of Gerontology.* Vol. 11, pp. 298–300, 1956.

17. Harman D. "The Aging Process," *Proceedings of the National Academy of Science.* Vol. 78, pp. 7124–28, 1981.

18. Orr WC, Sohal RS. Op.cit.

19. Fackelmann KA. "Two New Wrinkles for Cigarette Smokers," *Science News.* Vol. 139, p. 309, 1991.

20. Wallace D. "Mitochondrial DNA in Aging and Disease," *Scientific American.* Vol. 277, pp. 40–47, 1997.

21. Margulis L. "A Review. Genetic and Evolutionary Consequences of Symbiosis," *Experimental Parasitology.* Vol. 39, pp. 277–349, 1976.

22. "Rare Muscular Disease Forces LeMond to Retire," *USA Today/Int'l Edition.* December 5, 1994, p. 1B.

23. Johns DR. "Seminars in Medicine of the Beth Israel Hospital, Boston: Mitochondrial DNA and Disease," *New England Journal of Medicine.* Vol. 333, pp. 638–44, 1995.

24. Cohen LP. "Innovative DNA Test Is an ID Whose Time Has Come for the FBI," *The Wall Street Journal.* Friday, Dec.19, 1997, p. A.1.

25. Richter C, Park JW, Ames B. "Normal Oxidative Damage to Mito-chondrial and Nuclear DNA Is Extensive," *Proceedings of the National Academy of Sciences.* Vol. 85, pp. 6465–67, 1988.

26. Suzuki YJ, Forman HJ, Sevanian A. "Oxidants as Stimulators of Signal Transduction," *Free Radical Biology and Medicine.* Vol. 22, pp. 269–85, 1997.

27. Palmer HJ, Paulson KE. "Reactive Oxygen Species and Antioxidants

in Signal Transduction and Gene Expression," *Nutrition Reviews.* Vol. 55, pp. 353–61, 1997.

28. Christen S, Woodall AA, Ames BN, et al. "*y*-Tocopherol Traps Mutagenic Electrophiles Such as NOx and Complements *a*-Tocopherol: Physiological Implications," *Proceedings of the National Academy of Sciences.* Vol. 94, pp. 3217–22, 1997.

29. Schneider. E, Vining EM, Hadley EC, Farnham SA. "Recommended Dietary Allowances and the Health of the Elderly," *New England Journal of Medicine.* Vol. 314, pp. 157–60, 1986.

CHAPTER SEVEN

1. Kimura KD, Tissenbaum HA, Liu Y, Ruvkun G. "DAF-2, an Insulin Receptor-Like Gene That Regulates Longevity and Diapause in *Caenorhabditis elegans*," *Science.* Vol. 277, p. 946, 1997.

2. Roush W. "Worm Longevity Gene Cloned," *Science.* Vol. 277, pp. 897–98, 1997.

3. Ibid.

4. Ibid.

5. "Lifetime Benefits and Costs of Intensive Therapy as Practiced in the Diabetes Control and Complications Trial," *Journal of the American Medical Association.* Vol. 276, pp. 1409–15, 1996.

6. Gold PE. "Role of Glucose in Regulating the Brain and Cognition," *American Journal of Clinical Nutrition.* Vol. 61 [suppl.], pp. 987–95S, 1995.

7. Leibson CL, Rocca WA, Hanson VA, et al. "Risk of Dementia among Persons with Diabetes Mellitus: A Population-Based Cohort Study," *American Journal of Epidemiology.* Vol. 145, pp. 301–08, 1997.

8. Messier C, Gagnon M. "Glucose Regulation and Cognitive Functions: Relation to Alzheimer's Disease and Diabetes," *Behavioral Brain Research.* Vol. 75, pp. 1–11, 1996.

9. Medeiros LC, Liu YW, Park S, Chang PH, Smith AM. "Insulin, But Not Estrogen, Correlated with Indexes of Desaturase Function in Obese Women," *Hormone and Metabolism Research.* Vol. 27, pp. 235–38, 1995.

10. Winslow R. "Insulin's Value for Many Diabetics Is Questioned," *Wall Street Journal*. Wednesday, November 26, 1997, B10.

11. Reaven G. "Pathophysiology of Insulin Resistance in Human Disease," *Physiological Reviews*. Vol. 75, pp. 473–86, 1995.

12. Despres JP, Lemieux S, Lamarche B, et al. "The Insulin Resistance-Dyslipidemic Syndrome: Contribution of Visceral Obesity and Therapeutic Implications," *International Journal of Obesity*. Vol. 19, S76–86, 1995.

13. "The Hot New Diet Pill," *Time*. P. 61, Sept. 23, 1996.

14. Jensen MD. "Lipolysis: Contribution from Regional Fat," *Annual Review of Nutrition*. Vol. 17, pp. 127–39, 1997.

15. Considine RV, Sinha MK, Heiman ML, et al. "Serum Immunoreactive-Leptin Concentrations in Normal-Weight and Obese Humans," *New England Journal of Medicine*. Vol. 334, pp. 292–95, 1996.

16. Wolever TM. "The Glycemic Index: Flogging a Dead Horse?" *Diabetes Care*. Vol. 20, pp. 452–56, 1997.

17. Schiltz B. *The Unique Role of Carbohydrate Metabolism in the Regulation of Glycemic Index*. Bothell, Wash. Bastyr University; 1997. Master's Thesis.

18. Brown I. "Complex Carbohydrates and Resistant Starch," *Nutrition Reviews*. Vol. 54, pp. S115–19, 1996.

19. Girard J, Gerre P, Foufelle F. "Mechanisms by Which Carbohydrates Regulate Expression of Genes for Glycolytic and Lipogenic Enzymes," *Annual Review of Nutrition*. Vol. 17, pp. 325–52, 1997.

20. Towle HC, Kaytor KN, Shih HM. "Regulation of the Expression of Lipogenic Enzyme Genes by Carbohydrate," *Annual Review of Nutrition*. Vol. 17, pp. 405–33, 1997.

21. Perseghin G, Price TB, Petersen KF, et al. "Increased Glucose Transport-Phosphorylation and Muscle Glycogen Synthesis after Exercise Training in Insulin-Resistant Subjects," *New England Journal of Medicine*. Vol. 355, pp. 1357–62, 1996.

22. Sears B. *The Zone: A Dietary Road Map*. Harper Collins Publishers. New York, 1995.

23. Spiller GA, Jensen CD, Pattison TS, et al. "Effect of Protein Dose on Serum Glucose and Insulin Response to Sugars," *American Journal of Clinical Nutrition*. Vol. 46, pp. 474–80, 1987.

24. Giugliano D, Ceriello A, Paolisso G. "Diabetes Mellitus, Hypertension, and Cardiovascular Disease: Which Role for Oxidative Stress?" *Metabolism.* Vol. 44, pp. 363–68, 1995.

25. Rattan SI. "Synthesis, Modifications, and Turnover of Proteins during Aging," *Experimental Gerontology.* Vol. 31, pp. 33–47, 1996.

26. Rattan SI, Derventzi A, Clark BF. "Protein Synthesis, Posttranslational Modifications, and Aging," *Annals of New York Academy of Sciences.* Vol. 663, pp. 48–62, 1992.

27. Miyata T, Hori O, Zhang JH, et al. "The Receptor for Advanced Glycation End Products (RAGE) Is a Central Mediator of the Interaction of AGE-*B2* Microglobulin with Human Mononuclear Phagocytes via an Oxidant-Sensitive Pathway," *Journal of Clinical Investigation.* Vol. 98, pp. 1088–94, 1996.

28. Radda GK, Odoom J, Kemp G, et al. "Assessment of Mitochondrial Function and Control in Normal and Diseased States," *Biochemica et Biophysica Acta.* Vol. 1271, pp. 15–19, 1995.

29. Iehara N, Takeoka H, Yamada Y, et al. "Advanced Glycation End Products Modulate Transcriptional Regulation in Mesangial Cells," *Kidney International.* Vol. 50, pp. 1166–72, 1996.

30. Wolff SP, Bascal ZA, Hunt JV. " 'Autoxidative Glycosylation': Free Radicals and Glycation Theory," *Progress in Clinical Biology Research.* Vol. 304, pp. 259–75, 1989.

31. Gerbityz KD, Gempel K, Brdiczka D. "Mitochondria and Diabetes. Genetic, Biochemical, and Clinical Implications of the Cellular Energy Circuit," *Diabetes.* Vol. 45, pp. 113–26, 1996.

32. Aoki Y, Yazaki K, Shirotori K, et al. "Stiffening of Connective Tissue in Elderly Diabetic Patients: Relevance to Diabetic Nephropathy and Oxidative Stress," *Diabetalogica.* Vol. 36, pp. 79–83, 1993.

33. Dyer DG, Dunn JA, Thorpe SR, et al. "Accumulation of Maillard Reaction Products in Skin Collagen in Diabetes and Aging," *Journal of Clinical Investigation.* Vol. 91, pp. 2463–69, 1993.

34. Ballou SP, Lozanski GB, Hodder S, et al. "Quantitative and Qualitative Alterations of Acute-phase Proteins in Healthy Elderly Persons," *Age and Aging.* Vol. 25, pp. 224–30, 1996.

35. Miyata T, Hori O, Zhang JH, et al. Op. cit.

36. Schmidt AM, Weidman E, Lalla E, et al. "Advanced Glycation End-

products (AGEs) Induce Oxidant Stress in the Gingiva: A Potential Mechanism Underlying Accelerated Periodontal Disease Associated with Diabetes," *Journal of Periodontal Research*. Vol. 31, pp. 508–15, 1996.

37. Stehouwer CD, Schaper NC. "The Pathogenesis of Vascular Complications of Diabetes Mellitus: One Voice or Many?" *European Journal of Clinical Investigation*. Vol. 26, pp. 535–43, 1996.

38. Bilato C, Crow MT. "Atherosclerosis and the Vascular Biology of Aging," *Aging, Clinical and Experimental Research*. Vol. 8, pp. 221–34, 1996.

39. Westerhuis LW, Venekamp JR. "Serum Lipoprotein-A Levels and Glyco-Metabolic Control in Insulin and Non-Insulin Dependent Diabetes Mellitus," *Clinical Biochemistry*. Vol. 29, pp. 255–59, 1996.

40. Anderson RA, Polansky MM, Bryden NA, Roginsky EE, Mertz W, Ginsmann W. "Chromium Supplementation of Human Subjects: Effects on Glucose, Insulin, and Lipid Variables," *Metabolism*. Vol. 32, pp. 894–99, 1983.

41. Goldfine AB, Simonson DC, Folli F, Patti ME, Kahn CR. "Metabolic Effects of Sodium Metavanadate in Humans with Insulin-Dependent and Noninsulin-Dependent Diabetes Mellitus *in Vivo* and *in Vitro* Studies," *Journal of Clinical Endocrinology and Metabolism*. Vol. 80, pp. 3311–20, 1995.

42. Ibid.

43. Armstrong AM, Chestnutt JE, Gormley MJ, Young IS. "The Effect of Dietary Treatment on Lipid Peroxidation and Antioxidant Status in Newly Diagnosed Noninsulin Dependent Diabetes," *Free Radical Biology and Medicine*. Vol. 21, pp. 719–26, 1996.

44. Takahashi Y, Takayama S, Itou T, Owada K, Omori Y. "Effect of Glycemic Control on Vitamin B12 Metabolism in Diabetes Mellitus," *Diabetes Research and Clinical Practice*. Vol. 25, pp. 13–17, 1994.

45. Dines KC, Cameron NE, Cotter MA. "Comparison of the Effects of Evening Primrose Oil and Triglycerides Containing *y*-Linolenic Acid on Nerve Conduction and Blood Flow in Diabetic Rats," *Journal of Pharmacology and Experimental Therapeutics*. Vol. 273, pp. 49–55, 1995.

46. Lubec B, Hayn M, Kitzmuller I, Vierhapper H, Lubec G. "L-Arginine

Reduces Lipid Peroxidation in Patients with Diabetes Mellitus," *Free Radical Biology & Medicine.* Vol. 22, pp. 355–57, 1997.

CHAPTER EIGHT

1. Marston W. "Gut Reactions," *Newsweek.* November 17, 1997, pp. 95, 99.
2. Galland L. *The Four Pillars of Healing.* Random House. New York, 1997.
3. Bjarnason I. "The Leaky Gut of Alcoholism: Possible Route of Entry for Toxic Compounds," *Lancet.* Vol. 8370, pp. 179–82, 1984.
4. Dalton RH. "The Limit of Human Life and How to Live Long," *Journal of the American Medical Association.* Vol. 20, pp. 599–600, 1893.
5. Roggero E, Zuca E, Cavalli F. "Gastric Mucosa-Associated Lymphoid Tissue Lymphomas: More Than a Fascinating Model," *Journal of the National Cancer Institute.* Vol. 89, pp. 1328–30, 1997.
6. Alican I, Kubes P. "A Critical Role for Nitric Oxide in Intestinal Barrier Function and Dysfunction," *American Journal of Physiology.* Vol. 270, pp. G225–37, 1996.
7. Clancy RM, Abramson SB. "Nitric Oxide: A Novel Mediator of Inflammation," *Proceedings of the Society of Experimental Biology and Medicine.* Vol. 210, pp. 93–101, 1995.
8. Hartung T, Sauer A, Hermann C, Brockhaus F, Wendel A. "Overactivation of the Immune System by Translocated Bacteria and Bacterial Products," *Scandinavian Journal of Gastroenterology.* Vol. 32, [suppl. 222], pp. 98–99, 1997.
9. Bernhardt H, Knoke M. "Mycological Aspects of Gastrointestinal Microflora," *Scandinavian Journal of Gastroenterology.* Vol. 32, [suppl. 222], pp. 102–06, 1997.
10. Riddington DW, Venkatesh B, Boivin CM, et al. "Intestinal Permeability, Gastric Intramucosal pH, and Systemic Endotoxemia in Patients Undergoing Cardiopulmonary Bypass," *Journal of the American Medical Association.* Vol. 275, pp. 1007–12, 1996.
11. D'Eufemia P, Celli M, Finocchiaro R, et al. "Abnormal Intestinal Permeability in Children with Autism," *Acta Pediatrics.* Vol. 85, pp. 1076–79, 1996.

12. Uil JJ, van Elburg RM, van Overbeek FM, et al. "Clinical Implications of the Sugar Absorption Test: Intestinal Permeability Test to Assess Mucosal Barrier Function," *Scandinavian Journal of Gastroenterology.* Vol. 32, [suppl. 223], pp. 70–78, 1997.

13. Lichtman SN, Wang J, Sartor RB, et al. "Reactivation of Arthritis Induced by Small Bowel Bacterial Overgrowth in Rats: Role of Cytokines, Bacteria, and Bacterial Polymers," *Infection and Immunity.* Vol. 63, pp. 2295–2301, 1995.

14. Moulton PJ. "Inflammatory Joint Disease: The Role of Cytokines, Cyclooxygenases and Reactive Oxygen Species," *British Journal of Biomedical Science.* Vol. 53, pp. 317–24, 1996.

15. Renoux M, Hilliquin P, Galoppin L, Florentin J, Menkes CJ. "Cellular Activation Products in Osteoarthritis Synovial Fluid," *International Journal of Pharmacology Research.* Vol. 15, pp. 135–38, 1995.

16. Mielants H, De Vos M, Goemaere S, et al. "Intestinal Mucosal Permeability in Inflammatory Rheumatic Diseases. II. Role of Disease," *Journal of Rheumatology.* Vol. 18, pp. 394–400, 1991.

17. Mielants H, Veys EM, Cuvelier C, De Vos M. "Ilecolonoscopic Findings in Seronegative Spondyloarthropathies," *British Journal of Rheumatology,* Vol. 27, [suppl.], pp. 95–105, 1988.

18. Moreland LW, Scott, Baumgartner, et al. "Treatment of Rheumatoid Arthritis with a Recombinant Human Tumor Necrosis Factor Receptor (p75)-Fc Fusion Protein," *New England Journal of Medicine.* Vol. 337; pp. 141–47, 1997.

19. Firestein GS, Zvaifler NJ. "Anticytokine Therapy in Rheumatoid Arthritis," *New England Journal of Medicine.* Vol. 337, pp. 195–97, 1997.

20. Needleman P, Isakson PC. "Selective Inhibition of Cyclooxygenase 2," *Science & Medicine.* Vol. 5, no. 1, pp. 26–35, 1998.

21. Zimmermann J. "Biotech Firms Target Immune Cascade Pathway to Treat Inflammatory Disorders," *Genetic Engineering News.* Vol. 17, no. 19, p. 24, 1997.

22. Elmer GW, Surawicz CM, McFarland LV. "A Neglected Modality for the Treatment and Prevention of Selected Intestinal and Vaginal Infections," *Journal of the American Medical Association.* Vol. 275, pp. 870–76, 1996.

23. Kleesen B, Sykura B, Zunft HJ, Blaut M. "Effects of Inulin and Lactose on Fecal Microflora, Microbial Activity, and Bowel Habit in Elderly Constipated Persons," *American Journal of Clinical Nutrition.* Vol. 65, pp. 1397–1402, 1997.

24. Bouhnik Y, Flourie B, D'Agay-Abensour, L, et al. "Administration of Transgalacto-Oligosaccharides Increases Fecal Bifidobacteria and Modifies Colonic Fermentation Metabolism in Healthy Humans," *Journal of Nutrition.* Vol. 127, pp. 444–48, 1997.

25. Wilmore D, Lacey JM, Soultanakis RP, et al. "Factors Predicting a Successful Outcome after Pharmacologic Bowel Compensation," *Annals of Surgery.* Vol. 226, pp. 292–93, 1997.

26. Shabert J. *The Ultimate Nutrient, Glutamine.* Avery Publishing Group. Garden City Park, N.Y., 1995.

27. Van der Hulst RR, van Kreel BK, von Meyenfeld MF, Brummer RJ, Arends Weutz NE, Soeters PB. "Glutamine and the Preservation of Gut Integrity," *Lancet.* Vol. 341, pp. 1363–65, 1993.

28. Smith RJ. "Glutamine-Supplemented Nutrition," *Journal of Parenteral and Enteral Nutrition.* Vol. 21, pp. 183–84, 1997.

29. Chandra R. "Nutrition and the Immune System: An Introduction," *American Journal of Clinical Nutrition.* Vol. 66, pp. 478–84S, 1997.

30. Jeng KC, Yang CS, Siu WY, et al. "Supplementation with Vitamins C and E Enhances Cytokine Production by Peripheral Blood Mononuclear Cells in Healthy Adults," *American Journal of Clinical Nutrition.* Vol. 64, pp. 960–65, 1996.

31. Christen S, Woodall AA, Shigenaga MK, et al. "y-Tocopherol Traps Mutagenic Electrophiles such as No_x and Complements a-tocopherol: Physiological Implications," *Proceedings of the National Academy of Sciences.* Vol. 94, pp. 3217–22, 1997.

32. Kaufman W. "Niacinamide Therapy for Joint Mobility," *Connecticut State Medical Journal.* Vol. 17, pp. 584–89, 1953.

33. Jonas WB, Rapoza CP, Blair WF. "The Effect of Niacinamide on Osteoarthritis: A Pilot Study," *Inflammation Research.* Vol. 45, pp. 330–34, 1996.

34. Safayhi H, Mack T, Ammon HP. "Protection by Boswellic Acids against Galactosamine/Endotoxin-Induced Hepatitis in Mice," *Biochemical Pharmacology.* Vol. 41, pp. 1536–37, 1991.

35. Safayhi H, Sailer ER, Ammon HP. "Mechanism of 5–Lipoxygenase Inhibition by Acetyl-11–keto-*B*-Boswellic Acid," *Molecular Pharmacology*. Vol. 47, pp. 1212–16, 1995.
36. Safayhi H, Mack T, Sabieraj J, et al. "Boswellic Acids: Novel, Specific, Nonredox Inhibitors of 5–Lipoxygenase," *Journal of Pharmacology and Experimental Therapeutics*. Vol. 261, pp. 1143–46, 1992.

CHAPTER NINE

1. Cook R. *Chromosome Six*. G.P Putnam's Sons. New York, 1997.
2. Wesslen L, Pahlson C, Lindquist O, et al. "An Increase in Sudden Unexpected Cardiac Deaths among Young Swedish Orienteers During 1979–1992," *European Heart Journal*. Vol. 17, pp. 902–10, 1996.
3. Muhlestein JB, Hammond EH, Carlquist JF, et al. "Increased Incidence of *Chlamydia* Species within the Coronary Arteries of Patients with Symptomatic Atherosclerotic Versus Other Forms of Cardiovascular Disease," *Journal of the American College of Cardiology*. Vol. 27, pp. 1555–61, 1996.
4. Patel P, Mendall MA, Carrington D, et al. "Association of *Helicobacter pylori* and *Chlamydia pneumoniae* Infections with Coronary Heart Disease and Cardiovascular Risk Factors," *British Medical Journal*. Vol. 311, pp. 11–14, 1995.
5. Mendall MA, Patel P, Ballam L, Strachan D, Northfield TC. "C-Reactive Protein and Its Relation to Cardiovascular Risk Factors: A Population Based Cross Sectional Study," *British Medical Journal*. Vol. 312, pp. 1061–65, 1996.
6. Ridker PM, Cushman M, Stampfer MJ, Tracy RP, Hennekens CH. "Inflammation, Aspirin, and the Risk of Cardiovascular Disease in Apparently Healthy Men," *New England Journal of Medicine*. Vol. 336, pp. 973–79, 1997.
7. Maseri A. "Inflammation, Atherosclerosis and Ischemic Events— Exploring the Hidden Side of the Moon," *New England Journal of Medicine*. Vol. 336, pp. 1014–15, 1997.
8. Murray WM. "Inflammation, Aspirin, and the Risk of Cardiovascular Disease," *New England Journal of Medicine*. Vol. 337, pp. 422–24, 1997.

9. Haverkate F, Thompson SG, Pyke SD, Gallimore JR, Pepys MB. "Production of C-reactive Protein and Risk of Coronary Events in Stable and Unstable Angina," *Lancet.* Vol. 349, pp. 462–66, 1997.

10. Connor WE, Connor SL. "Should a Low-Fat, High-Carbohydrate Diet Be Recommended for Everyone?" *New England Journal of Medicine.* Vol. 337, pp. 562–67, 1997.

11. Harris WS, Connor WE, McMurry MP. "The Comparative Reductions of the Plasma Lipids and Lipoproteins by Dietary Polyunsaturated Fats: Salmon Oil Versus Vegetable Oils," *Metabolism.* Vol. 32, pp. 179–84, 1983.

12. Katan MB, Grundy SM, Willett WC. "Beyond Low-Fat Diets," *New England Journal of Medicine.* Vol. 337, pp. 563–66, 1997.

13. Weverling-Rijnsburger AW, Blauw GJ, Lagaay AM, Knook DL, Meinders AE, Westendorp RG. "Total Cholesterol and Risk of Mortality in the Oldest Old," *Lancet.* Vol. 350, pp. 1119–23, 1997.

14. Joseph JA, Villalobos-Molinas R, Denisova NA, Erat S, Strain J. "Cholesterol: A Two-Edged Sword in Brain Aging," *Free Radical Biology & Medicine.* Vol. 22, pp. 455–62, 1997.

15. Superko HR. "The Atherogenic Lipoprotein Profile," *Science & Medicine.* Vol. 4, No. 5, pp. 36–45, 1997.

16. Taylor CB, Peng SK, Lee KT. "Spontaneously Occurring Angiotoxic Derivatives of Cholesterol," *American Journal of Clinical Nutrition.* Vol. 32, pp. 40–57, 1979.

17. Peng S, Taylor CB. "Cytotoxicity of Oxidation Derivatives of Cholesterol on Cultured Aortic Smooth Muscle Cells and Their Effects on Cholesterol Biosynthesis," *American Journal of Clinical Nutrition.* Vol. 32, pp. 1033–42, 1979.

18. Benditt E. "The Origin of Atherosclerosis," *Scientific American.* Vol. 236, pp. 74–85, 1977.

19. Diaz MN, Frei B, Vita JA, Keanet JF. "Antioxidants and Atherosclerotic Heart Disease," *New England Journal of Medicine.* Vol. 337, pp. 408–09, 1997.

20. McCully K. *The Homocysteine Revolution: Medicine for the New Millenium.* Keats Publishing, Inc. New Canaan, Conn., 1997.

21. Shute E. *The Vitamin E Story: The Medical Memoirs of Evan Shute.* Welch Publishing Company. Burlington, Ontario, Canada, 1985.

22. Stacey M. "The Fall and Rise of Kilmer McCully," *New York Times Magazine.* Pp. 25–29, Aug. 10, 1997.

23. Kluger J. "Beyond Cholesterol," *Time.* P. 48, Aug. 4, 1997.

24. Nygard O, Nordrehaug JE, Refsum H, et al. "Plasma Homocysteine Levels and Mortality in Patients with Coronary Artery Disease," *New England Journal of Medicine.* Vol. 337, pp. 230–36, 1997.

25. McCully KS. "Chemical Pathology of Homocysteine. III. Cellular Function and Aging," *Annals of Clinical and Laboratory Science.* Vol. 24, pp. 134–52, 1994.

26. McCully KS. "Importance of Homocysteine-Induced Abnormalities of Proteoglycan Structure in Arteriosclerosis," *American Journal of Pathology.* Vol. 59, pp. 181–93, 1970.

27. Egerton W, Silberberg J, Crooks R, et al. "Serial Measures of Plasma Homocyst(e)ine after Acute Myocardial Infarction," *American Journal of Cardiology,* Vol. 77, pp. 759–61, 1996.

28. Graham IM, Daly LE, Refsum HM, et al. "Plasma Homocysteine as a Risk Factor for Vascular Disease," *Journal of the American Medical Association.* Vol. 277, pp. 1775–81, 1997.

29. Fredman P, Wallin A, Blennow K, et al. "Sulfatide as a Biochemical Marker in Cerebrospinal Fluid of Patients with Vascular Dementia," *Acta Neurologica Scandinavica.* Vol. 85, pp. 103–06, 1992.

30. Verhoef P, Kok FJ, Druyssen DA, et al. "Plasma Total Homocysteine, B Vitamins, and Risk of Coronary Atherosclerosis," *Arteriosclerosis, Thrombosis, and Vascular Biology.* Vol. 17, pp. 989–95, 1997.

31. Malinow MR, Nieto FJ, Kruger WD, et al. "The Effects of Folic Acid Supplementation on Plasma Total Homocysteine are Modulated by Multivitamin Use and Methylenetetrahydrofolate Reductase Genotypes," *Arteriosclerosis, Thrombosis, and Vascular Biology.* Vol. 17, pp. 1157–62, 1997.

32. Schwartz SM, Siscovick DS, Malinow R, et al. "Myocardial Infarction in Young Women in Relation to Plasma Total Homocysteine, Folate, and a Common Variant in the Methylenetetrahydrofolate Reductase Gene," *Circulation.* Vol. 96, pp. 412–17, 1997.

33. Hegele RA, Tully C, Young TK, Connelly PW. "V677 Mutation of Methylenetetrahydrofolate Reductase and Cardiovascular Disease in Canadian Inuit," *Lancet.* Vol. 349, pp. 1221–22, 1997.

34. Molloy AM, Daly S, Mills JL, et al. "Thermolabile Variant of 5,10–Methylenetetrahydrofolate Reductase Associated with Low Red-Cell Folates: Implications for Folate Intake Recommendations," *Lancet.* Vol. 349, pp. 1591–93, 1997.

35. Verhoef P, Stampfer MJ, Buring JE, et al. "Homocysteine Metabolism and Risk of Myocardial Infarction: Relation with Vitamins B6, B12, and Folate," *American Journal of Epidemiology.* Vol. 143, pp. 845–49, 1996.

36. Munshi MN, Stone A, Fink L, Fonseca V. "Hyperhomocysteinemia Following a Methionine Load in Patients with Non-Insulin-Dependent Diabetes Mellitus and Macrovascular Disease," *Metabolism.* Vol. 45, pp. 133–35, 1996.

37. Herbert V, Bigaouette J. "Call for Endorsement of a Petition to the Food and Drug Administration to Always Add Vitamin B-12 to Any Folate Fortification or Supplement," *American Journal of Clinical Nutrition.* Vol. 65, pp. 572–73, 1997.

38. Hathcock JN. "Vitamins and Minerals: Efficacy and Safety," *American Journal of Clinical Nutrition.* Vol. 66, pp. 427–37, 1997.

39. Wilcken DE, Wilcken B, Dudman NP, Tyrrell PA. "Homocystinuria – The Effects of Betaine in the Treatment of Patients Not Responsive to Pyridoxine," *New England Journal of Medicine.* Vol. 309, pp. 448–53, 1983.

40. Ronge E, Kjellman B. "Long Term Treatment with Betaine in Methylenetetrahydrofolate Reductase Deficiency," *Archives of Disease in Childhood.* Vol. 74, pp. 239–41, 1996.

41. Wilcken DE, Dudman NP, Tyrrell PA. "Homocystinuria Due to Cystathionine B-Synthase Deficiency—The Effects of Betaine Treatment in Pyridoxine-Responsive Patients," *Metabolism.* Vol. 34, pp. 1115–21, 1985.

42. Kritchevsky D, Tepper S, Klurfeld D. "Cholesterol and Dietary Protein. Dietary Protein and Atherosclerosis," *Journal of the American Oil Chemists Society.* Vol. 64, pp. 1167–71, 1987.

43. Nagase S. Takemura K, Ueda A, et al. "A Novel Nonenzymatic Pathway for the Generation of Nitric Oxide by the Reaction of Hydrogen Peroxide and D- or L-Arginine." *Biochemical and Biophysical Research Communications.* Vol. 233, pp. 150–53, 1997.

44. Clarkson P, Adams MR, Powe AJ, et al. "Oral L-Arginine Improves Endothelium-Dependent Dilation in Hypercholesterolemic Young Adults," *Journal of Clinical Investigation.* Vol. 97, pp. 1989–94, 1996.

45. Drexler H, Zeiher AM, Meinzer K, Just H. "Correction of Endothelial Dysfunction in Coronary Microcirculation of Hypercholesterolaemic Patients by L-Arginine," *Lancet.* Vol. 338, pp. 1546–50, 1991.

46. Chowienczyk P, Ritter J. "Arginine: No More Than a Simple Amino Acid?" *Lancet.* Vol. 350, pp. 901–02, 1997.

47. Bishop JE. "A Gene Gives a Hint of How Long a Person Might Hope to Live," *The Wall Street Journal.* Oct.19, 1995, p. A1, A6.

CHAPTER TEN

1. Rosenberg RN. "Molecular Neurogenetics: The Genome Is Settling the Issue," *Journal of the American Medical Association.* Vol. 278, pp. 1282–83, 1997.

2. Graham JE, Rockwood K, Beattie BL, et al. "Prevalence and Severity of Cognitive Impairment with and without Dementia in an Elderly Population, *Lancet.* Vol. 349, pp. 1793–96, 1997.

3. Ibid.

4. Rantala M, Savolainen MJ, Kervinen K, Kesaniemi YA. "Apolipoprotein E Phenotype and Diet-Induced Alteration in Blood Pressure," *American Journal of Clinical Nutrition.* Vol. 65, pp. 543–50, 1997.

5. Lehtimaki T, Frankberg-Lakkala H, Solakivi T, et al. "The Effect of Short-Term Fasting, Apolipoprotein E Gene Polymorphism, and Sex on Plasma Lipids," *American Journal of Clinical Nutrition.* Vol. 66, pp. 599–605, 1997.

6. Wolever TM, Hegele RA, Connelly PW, et al. "Long-Term Effect of Soluble-Fiber Foods on Postprandial Fat Metabolism in Dyslipidemic Subjects with ApoE3 and ApoE4 Genotypes," *American Journal of Clinical Nutrition.* Vol. 66, pp. 584–90, 1997.

7. Hofman A, Ott A, Breteler MM, et al. "Atherosclerosis, Apolipoprotein E, and Prevalence of Dementia and Alzheimer's Disease in the Rotterdam Study," *Lancet.* Vol. 349, pp. 151–54, 1997.

8. Teasdale GM, Nicoll JA, Murray G, Fiddes M. "Association of Apolipoprotein E Polymorphism with Outcome After Head Injury," *Lancet.* Vol. 350, pp. 1069–71, 1997.

9. Jordan BD, Relkin NR, Ravdin LD, et al. "Apolipoprotein E4 Associated with Chronic Traumatic Brain Injury in Boxing," *Journal of the American Medical Association.* Vol. 278, pp. 136–40, 1997.

10. Johansson K, Bogdanovic N, Kalimo H, et al. "Alzheimer's Disease and Apolipoprotein E S4 Allele in Older Drivers Who Died in Automobile Accidents," *Lancet.* Vol. 349, p. 1143, 1997.

11. Richard F, Helbecque N, Neuman E, et al. "APOE Genotyping and Response to Drug Treatment in Alzheimer's Disease," *Lancet.* Vol. 349, p. 539, 1997.

12. Poirier J, Delisle MC, Quirion R, et al. "Apolipoprotein E4 Allele as a Predictor of Cholinergic Deficits and Treatment Outcome in Alzheimer Disease," *Proceedings of the National Academy of Sciences USA,* Vol. 92, pp. 12260–64, 1995.

13. Amouyel P, Vidal O, Launay JM, Laplanche JL. "The Apolipoprotein E Alleles as Major Susceptibility Factors for Creutzfeldt-Jakob Disease," *Lancet.* Vol. 344, pp. 1315–18, 1994.

14. McGeer PL, Walker DG, Pitas RE, et al. "Apolipoprotein E4 (ApoE4) But Not ApoE3 or ApoE2 Potentiates *B*-Amyloid Protein Activation of Complement In Vitro," *Brain Research.* Vol. 749, pp. 135–38, 1997.

15. Fitzhaki RF, Lin WR, Shang D, et al. "Herpes Simplex Virus Type 1 in Brain and Risk of Alzheimer's Disease," *Lancet. Vol.* 349, pp. 241–44, 1997.

16. MacKenzie IR. "Antiinflammatory Drugs in the Treatment of Alzheimer's Disease," *Journal of Rheumatology.* Vol. 23, pp. 806–08, 1996.

17. Breitner JC. "Inflammatory Processes and Antiinflammatory Drugs in Alzheimer's Disease: A Current Appraisal," *Neurobiology of Aging.* Vol. 17, pp. 789–94, 1996.

18. Duong T, Nikolaeva M, Acton PJ. "C-Reactive Protein-Like Immunoreactivity in the Neurofibrillary Tangles of Alzheimer's Disease," *Brain Research.* Vol. 749, pp. 152–56, 1997.

19. McGeer PL, Schulzer M, McGeer EG. "Arthritis and Anti-

Inflammatory Agents as Possible Protective Factors for Alzheimer's Disease: A Review of 17 Epidemiologic Studies," *Neurology.* Vol. 47, pp. 425–32, 1996.

20. Breitner JC. "The Role of Anti-Inflammatory Drugs in the Prevention and Treatment of Alzheimer's Disease," *Annual Review of Medicine.* Vol. 47, pp. 401–11, 1996.

21. Lucca U, Tettamanti M, Forloni G, Spagnoli A. "Nonsteroidal Anti-inflammatory Drug Use in Alzheimer's Disease," *Biological Psychiatry.* Vol. 36, pp. 854–56, 1994.

22. Hadjivassiliou M, Gibson A, Davies-Jones GA, et al. "Does Cryptic Gluten Sensitivity Play a Part in Neurological Illness?" *Lancet.* Vol. 347, pp. 369–71, 1996.

23. Skoldstam L, Magnusson KE. "Fasting, Intestinal Permeability, and Rheumatoid Arthritis," *Rheumatic Disease Clinics of North America.* Vol. 17, pp. 363–71, 1991.

24. Morrison JH, Hof PR. "Life and Death of Neurons in the Aging Brain," *Science.* Vol. 278, pp. 412–19, 1997.

25. Perry VH, Anthony DC, Bolton SJ, Grown HC. "The Blood-Brain Barrier and the Inflammatory Response," *Molecular Medicine Today.* Vol. 4, pp. 335–40, 1997.

26. Yan SD, Zhu H, Fu J, et al. "Amyloid-*B* Peptide—Receptor for Advanced Glycation Endproduct Interaction Elicits Neuronal Expression of Macrophage-Colony Stimulating Factor: A Proinflammatory Pathway in Alzheimer Disease," *Proceedings of the National Academy of Science USA.* Vol. 94, pp. 5296–5301, 1997.

27. Yan SD, Yan SF, Chen X, et al. "Non-Enzymatically Glycated Tau in Alzheimer's Disease Induces Neuronal Oxidant Stress Resulting in Cytokine Gene Expression and Release of Amyloid B-Peptide," *Nature Medicine.* Vol. 1, pp. 693–96, 1995.

28. Yan SD, Chen X, Fu J, et al. "RAGE and Amyloid-B Peptide Neurotoxicity in Alzheimer's Disease," *Nature Medicine.* Vol. 382, pp. 685–91, 1996.

29. Exley C, Schley L, Murray S, et al. "Aluminum, B-Amyloid and Non-Enzymatic Glycosylation," *Federation of Experimental Biology Letters.* Vol. 364, pp. 182–84, 1995.

30. Armstrong RA, Winsper SJ, Blair JA. "Aluminum and Alzheimer's

Disease: Review of Possible Pathogenic Mechanisms," *Dementia*. Vol. 7, pp. 1–9, 1996.

31. Beal MF. "Aging, Energy, and Oxidative Stress in Neurodegenerative Disease," *Annals of Neurology*. Vol. 38, pp. 357–66, 1995.

32. Ibid.

33. Schapira AH. "Oxidative Stress and Mitochondrial Dysfunction in Neurodegeneration," *Current Opinion in Neurology*. Vol. 9, pp. 260–64, 1996.

34. Benzi G, Moretti A. "Are Reactive Oxygen Species Involved in Alzheimer's Disease?" *Neurobiology of Aging*. Vol. 16, pp. 661–74, 1995.

35. Bandmann O, Vaughan J, Holmans P, et al. "Association of Slow Acetylator Genotype for N-Acetyltransferase 2 with Familial Parkinson's Disease," *Lancet*. Vol. 350, pp. 1136–39, 1997.

36. "More Evidence for a Mitochondrial DNA Defect in Parkinson's Disease," *Parkinson's Update*. Vol. 73, pp. 460–61, 1996.

37. Liszewski, K. "Alzheimer's: Pursuing New Strategies and Approaches for Diagnosis and Treatment," *Genetic Engineering News*. Vol. 17, p. 13, 1997.

38. Fahn S. "A Pilot Trial of High-Dose Alpha-Tocopherol and Ascorbate in Early Parkinson's Disease," *Annals of Neurology*. Vol. 32, pp. S128–32, 1992.

39. Sano M, Ernesto C, Thomas RG, et al. "A Controlled Trial of Selegiline, Alpha-Tocopherol, or Both as Treatment for Alzheimer's Disease," *New England Journal of Medicine*. Vol. 336, pp. 1216–22, 1997.

40. Agus DB, Gambhir SS, Pardridge WM, et al. Vitamin C Crosses the Blood-Brain Barrier in the Oxidized Form Through the Glucose Transporters," *Journal of Clinical Investigation*. Vol. 100, pp. 2842–48, 1997.

41. Kamat JP, Davasagayam TP. "Tocotrienols from Palm Oil as Potent Inhibitors of Lipid Peroxidation and Protein Oxidation in Rat Brain Mitochondria," *Neuroscience Letters*. Vol. 195, pp. 179–82, 1995.

42. Lenaz G, Battino M, Castelluccio C, et al. " Studies on the Role of Ubiquinone in the Control of the Mitochondrial Respiratory Chain," *Free Radical Research Communications*. Vol. 8, pp. 317–27, 1990.

43. Sen CK, Roy S, Han D, Packer L. "Regulation of Cellular Thiols in

Human Lymphocytes by a-Lipoic Acid: A Flow Cytometric Analysis," *Free Radical Biology and Medicine.* Vol. 22, pp. 1241–57, 1997.

44. Packer L, Witt E, Jurgen H, et al. "Antioxidant Properties and Clinical Implications of Alpha Lipoic Acid." In *Biothiols in Health and Disease.* Packer L, Cadenas E, Eds. Marcel Dekker, Inc. New York, N.Y., 1995.

45. Lindenbaum J, Healton EB, Savage DG, et al. "Neuropsychiatric Disorders Caused by Cobalamin Deficiency in the Absence of Anemia or Macrocytosis," *New England Journal of Medicine.* Vol. 318, pp. 1720–28, 1988.

46. Stabler SP, Allen RH, Savage DG, Lindenbaum J. "Clinical Spectrum and Diagnosis of Cobalamin Deficiency," *Blood.* Vol. 76, pp. 871–81, 1990.

47. Pennypacker LC, Allen RH, Lindenbaum J, et al. "High Prevalence of Cobalamin Deficiency in Elderly Outpatients," *Journal of the American Geriatric Society.* Vol. 40, pp. 1197–1204, 1992.

48. Kristensen MO, Gulmann NC, Christensen JE, et al. "Serum Cobalamin and Methylmalonic Acid in Alzheimer Dementia," *Acta Neurologica Scandinavica.* Vol. 87, pp. 475–81, 1993.

49. Carmel R, Cairo K, Bondareff W, et al. "Spouses of Demented Patients with Low Cobalamin Levels: A New Risk Group for Cobalamin Deficiency," *European Journal of Hematology.* Vol. 57, pp. 62–67, 1996.

50. Saltzman JR, Kemp JA, Golner BB, et al. "Effect of Hypochlorhydria Due to Omeprazole Treatment or Atrophic Gastritis on Protein-Bound Vitamin B12 Absorption," *Journal of the American College of Nutrition.* Vol. 13, pp. 584–91, 1994.

51. Mitsuyama Y, Kogoh H. "Serum and Cerebrospinal Fluid Vitamin B12 Levels in Demented Patients with CH3–B12 Treatment—Preliminary Study," *Japanese Journal of Psychiatry and Neurology.* Vol. 42, pp. 65–71, 1988.

52. Naurath HJ, Joosten E, Riezler R, et al. "Effects of Vitamin B12, Folate, and Vitamin B6 Supplements in Elderly People with Normal Serum Vitamin Concentrations," *Lancet.* Vol. 356, pp. 85–89, 1995.

53. Clough CG. "Parkinson's Disease: Management," *Lancet.* Vol. 337, pp. 1324–27, 1991.

CHAPTER ELEVEN

1. Waldholz M. *Curing Cancer,* Simon & Schuster. New York, N.Y., pp. 13–14, 1997.
2. Perera FP. "Environment and Cancer: Who Are Susceptible?" *Science.* Vol. 278, pp. 1068–73, 1997.
3. Vojdani A, Ghoneum M, Choppa P. "Minimizing Cancer Risk Using Molecular Techniques: A Review. *Toxicology and Industrial Health,* Vol. 13, pp. 589–624, 1997.
4. Roberts L. "Zeroing in on a Breast Cancer Susceptibility," *Science.* Vol. 259, pp. 622–25, 1993.
5. Giardiello FM. "Genetic Testing in Hereditary Colorectal Cancer." *Journal of the American Medical Association.* Vol. 278, pp. 1278–80, 1997.
6. Waldholz M. "A Cancer Survivor's Genetic Time Bomb." *Wall Street Journal,* p. B9, Nov. 10, 1997.
7. Murphy P, Bray W. "How Cancer Gene Testing Can Benefit Patients," *Molecular Medicine Today.* Vol. 3, pp. 147–52, 1997.
8. Begley S. "The Cancer Killer," *Newsweek.* Vol. 128, pp. 42–48, 1996.
9. Chuaqui RF, Zhuang Z, Merino MJ. "Molecular Genetic Events in the Development and Progression of Ovarian Cancer in Humans." *Molecular Medicine Today.* Vol. 3, pp. 207–13, 1997.
10. Ekbom A, Hsieh CC, Lipworth L, et al. "Intrauterine Environment and Breast Cancer Risk in Women: A Population-Based Study." *Journal of the National Cancer Institute,* Vol. 89, pp. 71–76, 1997.
11. Adami HO, Persson I, Ekbom A, et al. "The Aetiology and Pathogenesis of Human Breast Cancer." *Mutation Research.* Vol. 333, pp. 29–35, 1995.
12. Hsieh CC, Pavia M, Lambe M, et al. "Dual Effect of Parity on Breast Cancer Risk." *European Journal of Cancer,* Vol. 30A, pp. 969–73, 1994.
13. Hsieh CC, Goldman M, Pavia M, et al. "Breast Cancer Risk in Mothers of Multiple Births." *International Journal of Cancer,* Vol. 54, pp. 81–84, 1993.

14. Hsieh CC, Lan SJ, Ekbom A, et al. "Twin Membership and Breast Cancer Risk." *American Journal of Epidemiology*, Vol. 136, pp. 1321–26, 1992.

15. Coker AL, Crane MM, Sticca RP, Sepkovic DW. "Re: Ethnic Differences in Estrogen Metabolism in Healthy Women." *Journal of the National Cancer Institute*, Vol. 89, pp. 89–90, 1997.

16. Fredericks C. *Breast Cancer: A Nutritional Approach.* Grossett & Dunlap. New York, Oct. 1977.

17. Ekbom A, Hsieh CC, Lipworth L, et al. "Perinatal Characteristics in Relation to Incidence of and Mortality from Prostate Cancer." *British Medical Journal*, Vol. 313, pp. 337–41, 1996.

18. Akre O, Ekbom A, Hsieh CC, et al. "Testicular Nonseminoma and Seminoma in Relation to Perinatal Characteristics." *Journal of the National Cancer Institute*, Vol. 88, pp. 883–89, 1996.

19. King RT. "Genentech Sees Promising Data on Cancer Drug." *Wall Street Journal*, December 22, 1997, p. B4.

20. Tonetti DA, Jordan VC. "Targeted Anti-Estrogens to Treat and Prevent Diseases in Women." *Molecular Medicine Today*, Vol. 3, pp. 218–23, 1996.

21. Hsing AW. "Hormones and Prostate Cancer: Where Do We Go from Here?" *Journal of the National Cancer Institute*, Vol. 88, pp. 1093–94, 1996.

22. Adlercreutz H. "Phytoestrogens: Epidemiology and a Possible Role in Cancer Protection," *Environmental Health Perspectives.* Vol. 103, pp. 103–12, 1995.

23. Barnes S, Peterson G, Grubbs C, Setchell K. "Potential Role of Dietary Isoflavones in the Prevention of Cancer." *Advances in Experimental Medicine and Biology*, Vol. 354, pp. 135–47, 1994.

24. Ingram D, Sanders K, Kolybaba M, Lopez D. "Case-Control Study of Phyto-Oestrogens and Breast Cancer." *Lancet*, Vol. 350, pp. 990–94, 1997.

25. Constantinou AI, Mehta RG, Vaughan A. "Inhibition of N-Methyl-N-Nitrosourea-Induced Mammary Tumors in Rats by the Soyubean Isoflavones." *Anticancer Research*, Vol. 16, pp. 3293–98, 1996.

26. Tamkins T. "Phytoestrogen Lowers Breast Cancer Risk." *Lancet.* Vol. 350, pp. 971–72 and 990–94, 1997.

27. Laird PW. "Oncogenic Mechanisms Mediated by DNA Methylation." *Molecular Medicine Today,* Vol. 3, pp. 223–29, 1997.

28. Chuang LS, Ian HI, Koh TW, Ng HH, Xu G, Li BF. "Human DNA-(Cytosine-5) Methyltransferase-PCNA Complex as a Target for p21[WAF1]. *Science,* Vol. 277, pp. 1996–99, 1997.

29. Zingg JM, Jones PS. "Genetic and Epigenetic Aspects of DNA Methylation on Genome Expression, Evolution, Mutation, and Carcinogenesis." *Carcinogenesis,* Vol. 18, pp. 869–82, 1997.

30. Baylin SB. "Tying It All Together: Epigenetics, Genetics, Cell Cycle, and Cancer." *Science,* Vol. 277, pp. 1948–49, 1997.

31. Wilson VL. "DNA Methylation Decreases in Aging But Not in Immortal Cells." *Science,* Vol. 220, pp. 1055–57, 1983.

32. Blount BC, Mack MM, Wehr CM, et al. "Folate Deficiency Causes Uracil Misincorporation into Human DNA and Chromosome Breakage: Implications for Cancer and Neuronal Damage." *Proceedings of the National Academy of Sciences, USA,* Vol. 94, pp. 3290–95, 1997.

33. Fenech MF, Dreosti IE, Rinaldi JR. "Folate, Vitamin B12, Homocysteine Status and Chromosome Damage Rate in Lymphocytes of Older Men." *Carcinogenesis,* Vol. 18, pp. 1329–36, 1997.

34. James SJ, Miller BJ, Basnakian G, et al. "Apoptosis and Proliferation under Conditions of Deoxynucleotide Pool Imbalance in Liver of Folate/Methyl Deficient Rats." *Carcinogenesis,* Vol. 18, pp. 287–93, 1997.

35. Zhang J, Henning SM, Heber D, et al. "NADPH-Cytochrome P-450 Reductase, Cytochrome P-450 2C11 and P-450 1A1, and the Aryl Hydrocarbon Receptor in Livers of Rats Fed Methyl-Folate-Deficient Diets." *Nutrition and Cancer,* Vol. 28, pp. 160–64, 1997.

36. Henning SM, Swendseid ME, Ivandic BT, Liao F. "Vitamins C, E, and A, and Heme Oxygenase in Rats Fed Methyl/Folate-Deficient Diets." *Free Radical Biology & Medicine,* Vol. 23, pp. 936–42, 1997.

37. Punnonen K, Ahotupa M, Asaishi K, Hyoty M, Kudo R, Punnonen R. "Antioxidant Enzyme Activities and Oxidative Stress in Human Breast Cancer," *Journal of Cancer Research and Clinical Oncology.* Vol. 120, pp. 374–77, 1994.

38. Jang M, Cai L, Udeani GO, et al. "Cancer Chemopreventive Activity

of Resveratrol, a Natural Product Derived from Grapes." *Science.* Vol. 275, pp. 218–20, 1997.

39. Warburg O. "On the Origin of Cancer Cells." *Science.* Vol. 123, pp. 309–14, 1956.

40. Szent-Gyorgyi A. "Cell Division and Cancer." *Science.* Vol. 149, pp. 34–37, 1965.

41. Bailar JC III, Smith EM. "Progress Against Cancer?" *New England Journal of Medicine.* Vol. 314, pp. 1226–32, 1986.

42. Bailar JC III, Gornik HL. "Cancer Undefeated," *New England Journal of Medicine.* Vol. 336, pp. 1569–74, 1997.

43. Nijhoff WA, Peters WHM. "Effects of Consumption of Brussels Sprouts on Intestinal and Lymphocytic Glutathione S-Transferases in Humans," *Carcinogenesis.* Vol. 16, pp. 2125–28, 1995.

44. Tanaka T, Ohigashi H. "Chemoprevention of Carcinogen Induced Oral Cancer by Citrus Auraptene in Rats," *Carcinogenesis.* Vol. 19, pp. 425–31, 1998.

45. Khafif A, Sacks PG. "Quatitation of Chemopreventive Synergism between Epigallocatechin-3-Gallate and Curcumin in Normal, Premalignant and Malignant Human Oral Epithelial Cells," *Carcinogenesis.* Vol. 19, pp. 419–24, 1998.

46. Blot WJ, Lin JY, Taylor PR. "Nutrition Intervention Trials in Linxian, China: Supplementation with Specific Vitamin/Mineral Combinations, Cancer Incidence, and Disease-Specific Mortality in the General Population," *Journal of the National Cancer Institute.* Vol. 85, pp. 1483–92, 1993.

47. Kimmick GG, Bell A, Bostick RM. "Vitamin E and Breast Cancer," *Nutrition and Cancer.* Vol. 27, pp. 109–17, 1997.

48. Liehr JG. "Androgen Induced Redox Changes in Prostate Cancer Cells: What Are the Causes and Effects?" *Journal of the National Cancer Institute.* Vol. 89, pp. 40–48, 1997.

49. Olson KB, Pienta KJ. "Vitamins A and E: Further Clues for Prostate Cancer Prevention," *Journal of the National Cancer Institute.* Vol. 90, pp. 414–15, 1998.

50. Kastan MB. "To Oxidize or Not to Oxidize?" *Nature Medicine.* pp. 1192–93, 1997.

51. "The Effect of Vitamin E and Beta Carotene on the Incidence of Lung

Cancer and Other Cancers in Male Smokers," *New England Journal of Medicine*. Vol. 330, pp. 1029–35, 1994.

52. Omenn GS, Goodman GE, Hammar S. "Effects of a Combination of Beta Carotene and Vitamin A on Lung Cancer and Cardiovascular Disease," *New England Journal of Medicine*. Vol. 334, pp. 1150–55, 1996.

53. Clark LC, Sanders BB. "Effects of Selenium Supplementation for Cancer Prevention in Patients with Carcinoma of the Skin," *Journal of the American Medical Association*. Vol. 276, pp. 1957–63, 1996.

54. Colditz GA, "Selenium and Cancer Prevention," *Journal of the American Medical Association*. Vol. 276, pp. 1984–85, 1996.

55. Elias T. *The Burzynski Breakthrough*. W. Quay Hays Publishing Company, Santa Monica, Calif., 1997.

56. Hunter DJ, Hankinson SE, Hough H, et al. "A Prospective Study of *NAT2* Acetylation Genotype, Cigarette Smoking, and Risk of Breast Cancer," *Carcinogenesis*. Vol. 18, no. 11, pp. 2127–32, 1997.

57. Wolk A, Bergstrom R, Hunter D, et al. "A Prospective Study of the Association of Monounsaturated Fat with Other Types of Fat with Risk of Breast Cancer. *Archives of Internal Medicine*. Archives of Internal Medicine, Vol. 158, no. 1, pp. 41–45, 1998.

58. Cameron E, Bland JS, Marcuson R. "Divergent Effects of Omega-6 and Omega-3 Fatty Acids on Mammary Tumor Development in C3H Mice Treated with DMBA," *Nutrition Research*. Vol. 9, pp. 283–93, 1989.

59. Raclot T, Groscolas R, Langin D, Ferré P. "Site-Specific Regulation of Gene Expression by n-3 Polyunsaturated Fatty Acids in Rat White Adipose Tissues," *Journal of Lipid Research*. Vol. 38, p. 1963, 1997.

60. Cramer DW, Harlow BL, Titus-Ernstoff L, et al. "Over-the-Counter Analgesics and Risk of Ovarian Cancer," *The Lancet*. Vol. 351, pp. 104–07, Jan. 10, 1998.

61. Perera FP. "Environment and Cancer: Who Are Susceptible?" *Science*. Vol. 278, pp. 1068–73, Nov. 1997.

62. Fearon ER. "Human Cancer Syndromes: Clues to the Origin and Nature of Cancer," *Science*. Vol. 278, pp. 1043–50, Nov. 7, 1997.

63. Pogribny IP, Muskhelishvili L, Miller, BJ, James SJ. "Presence and

Consequence of Uracil in Preneoplastic DNA from Folate/Methyl-Deficient Rats," *Carcinogenesis*. Vol. 18, No. 11, pp. 2071–76, 1997.

64. Chinery R, Brockman JA, Peeler, MO, et al. "Antioxidants Enhance the Cytotoxicity of Chemotherapeutic Agents in Colorectal Cancer: A p53–Independent Induction of p21$^{WAF1/CIP1}$via C/EBPß," *Nature Medicine*. Vol. 3, No. 11, pp. 1233–41, Nov. 1997.

65. Waldholz M. *Curing Cancer*. Simon & Schuster. New York, N.Y., p. 286, 1997.

CHAPTER TWELVE

1. Weiss K. *The Variation in the Human Genome*. John Wiley & Sons. New York, p. 3, 1996.

2. Evans W, Rosenberg I. *Biomarkers: The Ten Keys to Prolonging Vitality*. Simon and Schuster. New York, p. 33, 1991.

3. Ochler S. *Inducible Gene Expression: Environmental Stresses and Nutrients*. P.A. Baeuerle, editor. Birkhauser. Boston, Mass., 1995.

4. Berdanier C. *Nutrients and Gene Expression*. CRC Press. New York, 1996.

5. Bland J, Benum S. *The 20–Day Rejuvenation Diet Program*. Keats Publishing, Inc. New Canaan, Conn., 1996.

6. Zallen DT. *Does It Run in the Family?* Rutgers University Press. New Brunswick, N.J., p. 176, 1997.

7. Austad S. *Why We Age: What Science Is Discovering About the Body's Journey Throughout Life*. John Wiley & Sons. New York, 1997.

8. Rowe J. "The New Gerontology," *Science*. Vol. 278, p. 367, 1997.

9. Pernick MS. "Eugenics and Public Health in American History," *American Journal of Public Health*. Vol. 87, pp. 1767–72, 1997.

10. DeRisi JL, Iyer VR, Brown P. "Exploring the Metabolic and Genetic Control of Gene Expression on a Genomic Scale," *Science*. Vol. 278, pp. 680–85, 1997.

11. Savilahti E, Saukkonen TT, Virtala ET, Tuomilehto J, Akerblom HK. "Increased Levels of Cow's Milk and *B*-lactoglobulin Antibodies in Young Children With Newly Diagnosed IDDM," *Diabetes Care*. Vol. 16, p. 984, 1993.

12. Akerblom HK, Savilahti E, Saukkonen TT, et al. "The Case for Elim-

ination of Cow's Milk in Early Infancy in the Prevention of Type 1 Diabetes: The Finnish Experience," *Diabetes and Metabolism.* Vol. 28, pp. 269–78, 1993.

13. Plotnick GD, Corretti MC, Vogel RA. "Effect of Antioxidant Vitamins on the Transient Impairment of Endothelium-Dependent Brachial Artery Vasoactivity Following a Single High-Fat Meal," *Journal of the American Medical Association.* Vol. 278, pp. 1682–86, 1997.

14. Steingraber S. *Living Downstream.* Addison Wesley Publishing Co. New York, p. 239, 1997.

15. Herzlinger R. *Market Driven Health Care.* Addison Wesley Publishing Co. New York, p. 26, 1997.

RESOURCES

Great Smokies Diagnostic Laboratory
63 Zillicoa Street
Asheville, NC 28801-1974
(704) 253-9621 or (800) 522-4762

ESA, Inc. & ESA International, Inc.
22 Alpha Road
Chelmsford, MA 01824-4171
(508) 250-7000

Immunosciences Lab, Inc.
8730 Wilshire Blvd., #305
Beverly Hills, CA 90211
(310) 657-1077 or (800) 950-4686

Institute for Functional Medicine
5800 Soundview Drive
P.O. Box 1729
Gig Harbor, WA 98335
www.fxmed.org

American Academy of Environmental Medicine
4510 West 89th Street, #110
Prairie Village, KS 66207
(913) 642-6062

American College for the Advancement of Medicine
23121 Verdugo Drive, #204
Laguna Hills, CA 92653
(714) 583-7666

INDEX